INTERNATIONAL
MONETARY COOPERATION

1945–7

Brian Tew

Midland Bank Professor of Money and
Banking in the University of Nottingham

HUTCHINSON UNIVERSITY LIBRARY
LONDON

HUTCHINSON & CO (*Publishers*) LTD
178–202 Great Portland Street, London W1

London Melbourne Sydney
Auckland Johannesburg Cape Town
and agencies throughout the world

First published 1952
Second edition 1954
Third edition 1956
Fourth edition 1958
Fifth (revised) edition 1960
Sixth edition 1962
Seventh (revised) edition 1963
Eighth (revised) edition 1965
Ninth (revised) edition 1967
Tenth (revised) edition 1970

This book has been set in Times type, printed in Great Britain
on smooth wove paper by Anchor Press, and
bound by Wm. Brendon, both of Tiptree, Essex

ISBN 0 09 105040 5 (cased)
0 09 105041 3 (paper)

INTERNATIONAL
MONETARY COOPERATION
1945–70

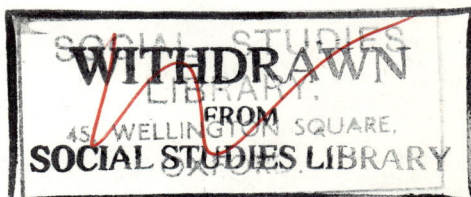

Economics

Editor
SIR ROY HARROD
F B A
Hon. Student of Christ Church, Oxford,
and Hon. Fellow of Nuffield College

CONTENTS

PART II

THE MACHINERY OF INTERNATIONAL
MONETARY COOPERATION

PART III

THE COURSE OF EVENTS SINCE
THE WAR

Contents

TABLES

KEY TO ABBREVIATIONS USED

BIS   Bank for International Settlements
CRU   Composite Reserve Unit
ECA   Economic Cooperation Administration
ECE   Economic Commission for Europe
EEC   European Economic Community
EMA   European Monetary Agreement
EPU   European Payments Union
GAB   General Arrangements to Borrow
GATT   General Agreement on Tariffs and Trade
IEPA   Intra-European Payments Agreement
IMF   International Monetary Fund
ITO   International Trade Organisation
OECD   Organisation for Economic Cooperation and Development
OEEC   Organisation for European Economic Cooperation
OSA   Outer Sterling Area
SDRs   Special Drawing Rights (in the IMF)
W.P.3   Working Party No. 3 (of the OECD)
One billion = 1,000 millions

PREFACE

This book treats the theory and practice of international monetary cooperation, with special reference to the problems which have arisen since the last war, and the institutions which have been developed to meet them. Part I is mainly analytical, Part II mainly institutional, and Part III mainly historical.

The term 'monetary' in the title of this book is intended in its narrow sense of 'pertaining to the settlement of accounts': no attempt has been made to describe or explain international capital movements not intended primarily for this purpose.

No prior technical knowledge is expected of the reader, but an elementary knowledge of the relevant parts of economic theory will be found helpful. A suitable introduction to the subject would be Sir Roy Harrod's *International Economics* or my own *Wealth and Income*.[1]

The first edition of *International Monetary Cooperation* went to press in February 1952 but the extensive amendments in subsequent editions have kept it up to date. In particular the present edition incorporates substantial amendment and additions in Parts II and III, so as to take the story up to July 1970.

I wish to record my great indebtedness to the officials, especially those in international institutions, who have been to so much trouble to assist my researches. I must, however, stress that I alone am responsible for any errors of fact and that the conclusions I have drawn commit no one else.

Nottingham, *July 1970*   BRIAN TEW

[1] See the reading list, pp. 271–2.

Part I

First principles

I

INTER-COUNTY PAYMENTS

I am an inhabitant of a country, the United Kingdom, and as such I cannot but be aware that I and my fellow countrymen are collectively concerned—and, to judge by the pronouncements of statesmen and financial journalists, very deeply concerned—with certain problems of international payments, problems arising for example when we make and receive payments for the goods and services we buy from and sell to other countries or when we borrow and lend abroad. In the first place, we from time to time become anxious lest we should collectively suffer the embarrassment of running short of the means of settling our accounts with the rest of the world as a whole or with certain so-called 'hard-currency' countries in particular. This problem may be described as one of *external liquidity*. Then our anxiety is increased when we contemplate the difficulties involved in removing the causes of such an embarrassment. This second source of anxiety is, in technical terms, a matter of correcting an *external disequilibrium*. (A disequilibrium may be either a surplus or a deficit, but deficits are more important as a source of anxiety.) Lastly, we are aware that our internal level of business activity and employment is influenced by the inward and outward flows of payments which arise from our exports and imports of goods and services: in other words we are aware of the problem of the *employment effects* of such payments. Consequently, if we are suffering a depression, or if we fear one in the future, we are inclined to favour policies which promote exports and discourage imports. Since our imports are someone else's exports, and vice versa, such an inclination may be somewhat loosely described as a resolve not to import other countries' unemployment, amounting in some cases to a desire to export our own unemployment.

I am also an inhabitant of a sub-division of the United Kingdom, the county of Nottingham. I and my fellow inhabitants of this county, to whom for convenience I shall apply the label 'Nottspeople', frequently make payments to, and receive payments from, the inhabitants of the rest of the world, so that Nottinghamshire, no less than the United Kingdom, has somehow or other to settle her accounts with the rest of the world, to suffer changes in circumstances which may lead to external disequilibria, and to suffer also unemployment which may have been imported and could possibly be exported. Yet no one seems to consider these matters as worthy of attention, let alone as cause for anxiety. No industrious statisticians attempt to calculate the size or composition of Nottinghamshire's receipts and payments, no morbid economists draw depressing conclusions from the trend of Nottinghamshire's exports, no anxious statesman designates Lincolnshire or Yorkshire a hard-currency area. How are we to account for such a state of indifference?

The problem of external liquidity

So far as external liquidity is concerned, the most obvious circumstance which distinguishes payments into and out of Nottinghamshire from payments into and out of the United Kingdom is that Nottinghamshire does not have a distinctive currency of her own but instead has a single currency in common with all other British counties, and this currency (sterling) can be transferred without restriction from one county to another. This arrangement has two important features. First, Nottinghamshire has a completely effective means of multilateral settlement with other counties: receipts obtained from any one county can be used for making payments to any other county. Second, Nottspeople always have the means of external settlement if they have the means of settling with each other, since the two media are identical.

The problem of external disequilibrium

The worst that could happen, if Nottspeople persistently spent more in the rest of Britain than the inhabitants of the rest of Britain spent in Nottinghamshire, would be that Nottspeople would eventually run out of money; their holdings of notes and bank deposits would be depleted and ultimately exhausted. In practice such a depletion of cash has never occurred on a scale sufficient to attract attention to the problem, but if a considerable depletion did occur the consequences would be serious, since if Nottspeople ran out of cash they would have nothing to spend and in consequence there would be local depression and unemployment. Such an outcome would represent an extreme manifestation of uncorrected external disequilibrium.

It may perhaps be thought that business depressions which Nottinghamshire has suffered in the past may have been due to a shortage of cash, which the inhabitants of Nottinghamshire stupidly failed to notice at the time. However, such a diagnosis of past depressions overlooks two important facts:

First, if Nottspeople are on balance paying out cash, other counties must be receiving it. Hence a depletion of cash holdings in Nottinghamshire, due to an excess of external payments over receipts, would not account for a *general* depression affecting the whole of Britain, and past depressions have in practice almost always affected all counties, though admittedly with unequal severity.

Second, even purely local depressions may well not be attributable to a shortage of cash. Nobody need spend his money if he does not want to, and there are many reasons why spending might fall off in a particular county, apart from a shortage of cash. There is for instance no evidence that the decline in expenditure in the 'Depressed Areas' of the 1930s was attributable to a shortage of cash in these areas.

It will shortly be argued that there are corrective forces which would come into play long before Nottspeople's aggregate cash holdings became so depleted as to cause an increase in unemployment, but first it must be made clear that even a mild local depression is itself an appreciable corrective to any cash outflow from the county. For unemployed workers and impoverished businessmen are poor customers, and in particular are poor customers for goods produced over the county boundary, so that any diminution in the prosperity of Nottinghamshire, compared with that of other counties, would produce a rapid contraction in Nottinghamshire's imports from, and payments to, other counties. Here then is a powerful corrective to any outflow of money, but it is a very unsatisfactory remedy, since it involves a local depression. Happily, however, with reasonable luck, the nasty medicine need never be taken, except perhaps in small doses, for other forces are at work to correct the shortage of cash.

In the first place, Nottspeople own a large amount of securities which may or may not have originated in the county but which can be sold at any time on the stock exchanges. If the purchaser of the securities is not a Nottsperson—as is likely if Nottspeople are getting short of money—the sale of any of these securities represents a transfer of cash to Nottinghamshire from the rest of the country. In much the same way, Nottspeople may remedy a shortage of money by borrowing from Nottinghamshire branches of the nationwide joint stock banks. Many Nottspeople are sufficiently credit-worthy to qualify for overdrafts at their bank, and an overdraft granted represents so much more money at the disposal of Nottspeople. Moreover, Nottinghamshire businesses in need of money may issue new securities, whether debentures or shares, and sell them to the British public at large, including that part of the British public which lives outside Nottinghamshire, and Nottinghamshire local authorities may likewise borrow from the British public at large.

The ability of Nottspeople to borrow or sell securities—whether old ones or new ones—over the county boundary, is facilitated by two factors: first, the existence of a common currency—sterling—throughout Britain is a great help, for all loans and securities are promises of money in the future, and investors commonly prefer promises of the type of money with which they are familiar; and second, neither Nottinghamshire nor any other British county imposes restrictions on capital transactions (whether in loans or securities) between one county and another or on the payment of interest or dividends over a county boundary.

These two factors, taken together, ensure that when Nottinghamshire has an export surplus (an excess of exports of goods and services to other counties over imports from other counties) Nottinghamshire investors use much of the resulting inflow of cash for buying sterling securities, and that both these accumulated securities and also newly issued ones can be readily sold outside Nottinghamshire, if ever the tide of trade should turn. There can be little doubt that the free flow of borrowing and lending between one county and another, particularly in the form of movements of securities, is a great benefit to the British people as a whole and to each single county. Counties with export surpluses of goods will almost inevitably contain people with money to invest; counties with import surpluses will almost inevitably contain people wishing to borrow or to sell their securities. What could be better than that the two parties should get together and undertake transactions which are to their own personal advantage and which, from a national point of view, perform the valuable service of promoting the even distribution of money throughout the country?

If, therefore, we wish to understand why Nottinghamshire can so readily find the means of settling her accounts with other counties, and of doing so on a multilateral basis, and can in addition so readily correct disequilibria between her receipts from, and payments to, other counties, we should bear in mind these aspects of the county's economic health: first, a common currency and banking system with the rest of Britain and second, the absence of restrictions on capital transactions.

The problem of the transmission of business depressions

Thus far, then, Nottinghamshire's indifference to problems of inter-county payments seems to be justified on the ground that the problems so far considered are much less serious for Nottinghamshire than for the United Kingdom, but when we pass to our last problem, that of the employment effects of such payments, this particular ground for indifference is entirely absent. For Nottinghamshire is a completely open economy. Without tariffs, quotas, exchange controls, or any restrictions on transactions with other counties, Nottinghamshire has no means of resisting the import of unemployment or of favouring the export of unemployment. Nottspeople are aware that this is so, but accept the situation as it is, on account of the political and social solidarity which they feel towards other British people. Because of this solidarity, Nottspeople would regard it as illegitimate to attempt to export their depressions to neighbouring counties; moreover they regard a depression in another part of Britain as a disease which needs to be cured, not simply isolated. If each British county were a sovereign state, things would probably be otherwise. Nottspeople might then think it permissible to adopt 'beggar-my-neighbour' remedies for unemployment, and even if they fell short of that degree of irresponsibility they might well take the line that unemployment in Lancashire and Yorkshire was solely the private affair of Lancspeople and Yorkspeople and that, if the people directly concerned failed to cure their own malady, it was proper that Nottspeople should safeguard their own interests by insulating themselves from the source of infection, for example by imposing new tariffs.

Conclusion

The example of Nottinghamshire is instructive for two reasons. First, it serves to show why specifically inter-*national* payments present special problems which require separate study, and second, it represents a small-scale model whose efficiency of working would be regarded by many economists as an appropriate measuring rod for judging the efficiency of international monetary arrangements.

It is the aim of the next four chapters to explain in general terms the specifically international problems which arise when we transfer our attention from Nottinghamshire to an independent country such as the United Kingdom. One characteristic of independent countries in practice is that each has its own currency, so that great importance attaches to the terms and conditions on which one currency may be exchanged for another. This question is treated in Chapter 2. When an economy has a separate currency, this currency will normally be in widespread use for making payments within the economy, but it is most unlikely to enjoy un-limited acceptability as a means of payment outside the economy. Hence for such an economy there arises the question of the avail-ability of means of settling with other economies—the question of international liquidity, which is the subject of Chapter 3. Next, in Chapter 4, on 'The Adjustment Process', we consider the remedies which are available to a country whose means of international settlement are becoming unduly depleted—i.e. the remedies for a persistent international disequilibrium. Finally, there remains the question of how the tendency for business depressions to spread from one economy to another is regarded by the governments of the economies concerned when each economy is a sovereign state and not merely a minor political sub-division like Nottingham-shire. This question will be considered in Chapter 5.

2

EXCHANGE RATES

Though it is impossible to point to a good present-day example of an international monetary system comparable with the inter-county monetary system described in the previous chapter, we can nevertheless find a reasonably good historical example if we go back to the gold currency standard of the nineteenth century. It may therefore be useful to state briefly the basic principles on which this standard operated, even though space does not permit reference to many important complications and imperfections which overlay these basic principles in practice.[1]

In order that there may be no confusion between our statement of the basic principles of the standard and the standard as it actually existed, let us imagine a purely hypothetical case and assume the British counties each to have a separate gold currency and all to adhere to the rules of the gold currency standard. Each county, then, has an internal currency comprising its own distinctive gold coins—the 'Nottscrown', the 'Cornish sovereign', and so on—the manufacture of which is exclusively in the hands of the county's official mint. However, each county's mint, though a monopolist, is prepared to mint coins (for a small commission) for anyone supplying the necessary gold. In addition holders of coins are quite free to melt them down into bars, so

[1] One of the complications which we shall ignore is that Britain and other countries adhering to the gold currency standard usually had a second type of internal currency in the form of paper money, i.e. of bank-notes and bank deposits. More-over, as we shall see in Chapter 13, English paper money (sterling) acted in effect as an alternative to gold for making international payments, so that the so-called gold standard was in practice a gold-cum-sterling standard.

that both coins and bar gold are readily convertible into one another. Thus to the extent that gold can be freely transported from one county to another—a necessary condition for the efficient working of the system—inter-county payments can always be made in gold, which is at the same time the normal means of making payments within each county. Admittedly, inter-county payments in gold are a little more troublesome than internal payments, because they involve the cost of melting down and re-minting and also of transporting the gold for a longer distance, but apart from this complication there would be in effect a single currency in use throughout the whole of Britain, just as in real life: this common currency would however in our imaginary example be gold, whereas in real life it is a paper currency, sterling.

But let us now consider the consequences of the expense involved in re-minting andl ong-distance transport whenever payments are made from one county to another by actually sending gold. Let us suppose, for example, that though the Nottscrown has the same gold content as the Hantscrown, a Nottsperson needing to pay 100 Hantscrowns to a creditor in Hampshire would have to melt down 105 Nottscrowns in order to provide the necessary margin for expenses, and that for similar reasons 100 Hantscrowns melted down and sent to Nottingham, would yield, net of expenses, only 95 Nottscrowns. In these circumstances Nottspeople and Hantspeople would be pleased to find an alternative way of making payments to each other, and happily an alternative way is available, namely that of exchanging coins. If, for example, Mr A in Nottingham needs to pay Mr B in Southampton, while Mr C in Southampton needs to pay Mr D in Nottingham, the costs of melting, re-minting and transport could be avoided if Mr A puts his Nottscrowns at Mr C's disposal in Nottingham, in exchange for Mr C's putting Hantscrowns at Mr A's disposal in Southampton, thereby enabling Mr C to pay Mr D in Nottscrowns and Mr A to pay Mr B in Hantscrowns. Such a procedure would, however, give rise to a phenomenon which is *not* found in real life in the British internal monetary system, the phenomenon of an exchange rate between the currencies in use in different parts of the country, for Mr A must have bought Hantscrowns with Nottscrowns by exchanging so many Hantscrowns per 100 Nottscrowns. It should however be noted that under the gold currency standard the exchange rate between any two currencies is closely determined by the relative gold contents of the two types of coin. Thus in our example, where the two coins (the Nottscrown and the Hantscrown) are supposed to have the same gold content, the exchange rate between the two will never differ greatly from 100 Hantscrowns = 100 Nottscrowns. More precisely, on the assumption we have made, the exchange rate will always lie between 100 Hantscrowns = 95 Nottscrowns and 100 Hantscrowns = 105 Nottscrowns, for if the exchange rate lay outside these limits it would be more advantageous for one of the parties concerned to send gold rather than make an exchange transaction.

In brief, then, though the phenomenon of exchange rates clearly arose under the gold currency standard, these rates were closely determined by the gold contents of the different countries' internal currencies. When however we come to consider the conditions prevailing in the world of the present day, when the internal currencies of virtually all countries are bank-notes and promises of bank-notes,[1] the monetary material itself, being merely paper, obviously has no significance in the determination of the relative values of different national currencies. What then does determine the exchange rates between different paper currencies? Let us tackle this question by first considering the facilities which exist for exchanging one paper currency for another.

The simplest way in which exchange facilities can be arranged is for the government of each country to adopt a *laissez-faire* policy and allow its nationals to buy and sell foreign currencies against the home currency, without official intervention or restriction of any kind. Under such a regime, competitive markets grow up in which each currency is exchanged against every other currency, and a single market price, or exchange rate, comes to obtain as between every possible pair of currencies. Since *laissez faire* implies that residents in any country may deal freely with foreigners as well as with their fellow countrymen, the market price of any one currency in terms of any other will tend to be uniform not only within each country but over the whole world. For if, say, the price of £1 were $4 in London but $3 in New York, all buyers of sterling for dollars would try to buy in New York, which would bid up the New York price of sterling, while all sellers of sterling for dollars would try to sell in London, which would depress the London price of sterling, and this process would continue until the two rates had achieved virtual equality.

---

[1] Apart from small change in the form of token coins which have a metallic value considerably below their face value, and which are minted only in exchange for paper money.

Moreover, not only would *laissez faire* result in the exchange rate between any pair of currencies being uniform throughout the world, but arbitrage operations would ensure that the rates established for different pairs of currencies would be 'orderly', in the sense that the 'direct' rate between any pair of currencies, A and B, (i.e. the rate at which currency A was actually being exchanged for currency B) would never differ appreciably from the 'cross rate' implied by the two direct rates (i) between A and some third currency and (ii) between B and the same third currency. A hypothetical example will make this point clear. Let us suppose that under *laissez faire* the direct pound-dollar rate happened to be £1 = $4 and the direct pound-franc rate £1 = fr. 1,000, the implied cross rate thus being $1 = fr. 250. Let us also suppose, however, that (for some reason which need not concern us here) the direct dollar-franc rate was not $1 = fr. 250 but $1 = fr. 200. It would then be profitable for me to undertake the following arbitrage operation. Beginning with a capital of £100, I could exchange it for fr. 100,000 (at the direct rate of £1 = fr. 1,000), then exchange my fr. 100,000 for $500 (at the direct rate of $1 = fr. 200), and finally exchange my $500 for £125 (at the direct rate of £1 = $4), thus making £25 profit on the operation. I and my fellow operators could profitably continue such transactions so long at the direct rates remained 'disorderly'. But as the result of the continuous bidding with sterling for francs, the sterling price of francs would tend to rise, and likewise the franc price of dollars and the dollar price of sterling. In this way an orderly pattern of direct rates would rapidly establish itself.

Though under *laissez faire* exchange rates would be uniform throughout the world and orderly, they would not of course be stable. If, for example, British people suddenly decided to buy more goods from overseas, a necessary preliminary would be for them to use their sterling to bid for increased quantities of foreign currencies, and this would have the effect of raising the sterling prices of these currencies, or (to put the same thing in a different way) of causing sterling to depreciate in relation to other currencies. Moreover sterling would go on depreciating until the balance of demand and supply was restored, either by the rising sterling prices of overseas currencies choking off the increased British demand for them, or by the increasing cheapness of sterling inducing foreigners to spend more of their currencies on purchasing sterling. Now, as we shall later see,[1] the conditions under

[1] Page 62.

which international trade is at present conducted are such that the short-run effect of a depreciation of any one currency, say sterling, may be to cause foreigners to spend less, rather than more, of their currencies on buying sterling, while the curtailment of British demand for foreign currencies may well occur rather slowly. Hence in practice a very large fluctuation in exchange rates may be required to maintain the balance of demand and supply, following an initial disturbance.

The instability of exchange rates under *laissez faire* might be aggravated by speculation. If for example the view became widespread that sterling was about to depreciate, there would be a rush by holders of sterling to exchange it for other currencies; this would bring about the expected depreciation, whether or not it would have occurred in any case. Thus a widely believed rumour, even if lacking any substantial foundation, would tend to justify itself, and consequently to gain added credence, and there might therefore occur variations in exchange rates which could be described as partially or even wholly self-generating.

The great instability of exchange rates which would be liable to arise under *laissez faire*, and the great inconvenience which would occur as a result, have been almost universally held to justify either official transactions in the exchange markets, or official restrictions on private exchange transactions, or a combination of both.

With official transactions but no official restrictions, exchange rates tend towards uniformity and orderliness, as under *laissez faire,* the only departure from *laissez faire* being that the monetary authorities[1] of the countries concerned undertake exchange transactions themselves, with the object of offsetting, partially or wholly, variations in exchange rates which otherwise would have occurred. An extreme case of official intervention of this kind was the gold *bullion* standard, the form in which the gold standard was restored in 1925, after a hiatus caused by the First World War. Under the gold bullion standard, the monetary authorities of each of the countries adhering to the standard undertake to buy and sell gold bullion against the country's internal paper currency in unlimited quantities at a fixed price.[2] Adherence to

---

[1] The institutions which should be classified as a country's monetary authorities differ slightly from country to country, but in all cases would include the central government and the central bank. In Britain the monetary authorities can best be taken as the Treasury and the Bank of England.

[2] This is a slight over-simplification, since the buying and selling rates were slightly different, to provide a small commission. In England the official purchase price was 77s. 9d. a standard ounce and the official selling price 77s. 10½d.

the gold bullion standard thus requires that each country's monetary authorities should hold a reserve of gold, which they add to or deplete according to circumstances, and the consequence of the standard is that the value of each country's currency is fixed within narrow limits in relation to gold (and thus in relation to each other country's currency) in much the same way as under the gold currency standard, so long as none of the countries is forced off the standard by the exhaustion of its gold reserve.

Under the gold bullion standard any international disequilibrium would, if sufficiently prolonged, eventually exhaust the gold reserve of the deficit countries, so that under this standard the question of dealing with such deficits is liable to pose itself in a rather dramatic form. The remedies which a country may adopt to deal with a persistent deficit, while continuing to maintain unchanged the gold value of its currency, we shall consider in Chapter 4; but sometimes these remedies have been so unattractive or impracticable that the countries concerned did in fact abandon the standard. A case in point was the abandonment of the gold standard by Britain in September 1931.

Britain's defection from the gold standard is interesting from our point of view in that it led to the development of a technique of *partial* stabilisation of a currency (in this case sterling) by official transactions. From September 1931 until 1940 the British monetary authorities did not commit themselves to maintain a fixed gold value of the pound, but instead they set themselves the task of 'ironing out' short-term fluctuations, which (as we have noted) might well have been very large under a regime of complete *laissez faire*. The new policy was carried out by the Exchange Equalisation Account, which was created in 1932 and thereafter administered by the Bank of England on behalf of the British Treasury. The Account was given an initial stock of sterling assets in the form of British Treasury Bills (which are in effect IOUs which the Bank of England is always prepared to exchange for new English paper money). The Account used its sterling assets to buy gold and foreign currencies whenever the pound seemed to be appreciating excessively; in doing so it increased the supply of sterling and thus depressed its value. Later on, when the Account had by such transactions accumulated a substantial stock of gold and foreign currencies, it was able to operate on a two-way basis and either exchange its sterling for gold and foreign currencies (when the pound appreciated excessively) or exchange its gold and foreign currencies for sterling (when the pound depreciated excessively).

A country's monetary authorities can, then, either determine or (less ambitiously) merely influence the external value of their own paper currency simply by undertaking transactions in the foreign exchange markets, provided that their stocks of gold and foreign currencies do not become exhausted. We have still to consider the much more drastic technique which can be used to the same ends, that of exchange control, or the official restriction of private exchange transactions. Exchange control may be imposed either on payments or on receipts or (more usually) on both. The present British exchange control, which is on both payments and receipts, represents the remains of the system imposed at the beginning of the second world war. In the preceding inter-war period, exchange control had been comparatively rare, except in the case of the USSR and of Germany and her allies.

Exchange control on *payments* usually imposes the rule that all purchases of gold or of foreign paper currencies (or of certain types of claims to foreign currencies) against the home currency need to be licensed by the home monetary authorities, who are given power to restrict, or even stop altogether, the issue of licences for particular types of transactions, such as the purchase of certain (or all) foreign currencies to pay for so-called 'luxury' imports or to buy foreign securities. In its effects exchange control on payments may correspond closely to quotas or prohibitions on the import of goods, since foreign currencies are bought *inter alia* as a preliminary to buying foreign goods. Hence restrictions on the purchase of foreign currencies can be made to reduce imports of goods just as effectively as import restrictions, while conversely restrictions on imports are an effective device for curtailing the demand for foreign currencies. Thus it is frequently only a matter of administrative convenience whether a given aim is attained by exchange control or by import quotas or prohibitions. The main cases where the two devices are not alternatives are where the purchase of a foreign currency would be associated with a purchase not of goods but of services or of securities or other capital assets. If for example I wish to buy dollars for the purpose of spending a holiday in America (where I would buy the services of American hotels, etc.) or of buying US government bonds, I cannot be restrained by import quotas or prohibitions, since I do not propose to import any American goods into this country, but I shall nevertheless be thwarted if the

British exchange control refuses my application for permission to buy dollars. An exchange control on payments may thus be rather more comprehensive in its scope than are quotas and prohibitions on imports of goods.

Exchange control on *receipts* is usually imposed, not to reduce exports or to prevent exporters from selling the foreign currencies they earn, but to force any home resident who obtains foreign currencies to sell them to the home monetary authorities. To this end it is usually made illegal for any home resident to hold gold, foreign currencies, or certain types of claims to foreign currencies, except under licence, and licences are issued only at the discretion of the authorities. The purpose of this kind of exchange control (which since the war has often been enforced more or less strictly by many countries) is simply to centralise a country's means of external payment in a common pool, in the hands of the monetary authorities.

In some cases exchange controls are enforced by suppressing the free markets in gold and foreign currencies, or at any rate in certain foreign currencies, and giving the monetary authorities the position of monopolistic dealer in all transactions in the currencies concerned. The authorities are then able to impose any terms they deem appropriate on any home resident wishing to buy or sell the foreign currencies in question. Alternatively the free market may not be suppressed but merely restricted, only certain classes of purchasers and sellers being allowed access to the free market.

The suppression of free dealings makes it possible for the monetary authorities to act as a *discriminating* monopolist in fixing exchange rates or, in the words of the International Monetary Fund Agreement,[1] to indulge in 'multiple currency practices'. They may quote widely different buying and selling rates for the same foreign currency, and also different buying (selling) rates according to the type of international transaction giving rise to the supply of (demand for) a particular currency. Even the restriction, as distinct from the suppression, of free dealings may facilitate multiple currency practices, in that it may give rise to two exchange rates for the same currency, the official rate, applicable to certain transactions, and the so-called 'free' rate, applicable to others. A good example of multiple currency practices is provided by Chile, whose exchange rates in 1950 are set out in Table 1 at the end of this chapter.

[1] See below, Chapter 7.

Just as the official licensing of overseas payments corresponds broadly to quotas or prohibitions on the import of goods, so multiple currency practices correspond broadly to the imposition of tariffs (i.e. customs duties) on imported goods. If, for example, the Australian monetary authorities suddenly abandoned their traditional policy of buying and selling sterling at virtually the same price in Australian money (at present approximately £100 stg. = $215 Australian), and imposed a higher selling price of £100 stg. = $258 Australian, this would mean that Australian purchasers would have to pay to the Australian authorities a levy of $43 Australian on every 100 English pounds' worth of goods imported, in exactly the same manner as if the Australian government had imposed an all-round 20 per cent *ad valorem* tariff on all imports. If a third exchange rate of £100 stg. = $A430 were imposed in respect of the overseas currency requirements of importers of 'luxury' goods, this would correspond to a new 100 per cent tariff on such goods. In other cases multiple exchange rates are equivalent in their effects to export taxes or subsidies. Thus if the Australian authorities began to enforce a new *buying* rate of £100 stg. = $A200 in respect of the overseas earnings of wool exporters, this would correspond to an export tax on wool, while had the rate been £100 stg. = $A250 this would have been the equivalent of an export subsidy on wool.

The suppression of free exchange markets, or even simply the suppression of arbitrage transactions, may also cause a divergence between the direct exchange rate between two currencies and the implied cross rate between them. As we have seen, so long as free dealings are permitted by all countries, private arbitrage operations ensure that the three direct exchange rates between any three currencies, A, B and C, are such that the cross rate between B and C implied by the direct rates between A and B and between A and C cannot differ appreciably from the direct rate between B and C. This multilateral orderliness of exchange rates is not affected by official transactions by the monetary authorities, but it can readily be upset by exchange control, with consequences which will be made clear by the example given below on pages 90-1.

There is considerable scope for international cooperation in the field of exchange rates once it is agreed that there is any case for departing from strict *laissez faire*. First, there is a minimum need for bilateral agreements on direct rates between each country and every other country, simply to ensure that the monetary authorities of two countries do not act at cross purposes and attempt to stabilise the same direct exchange rate at different levels. Second, if the monetary authorities of the countries concerned enforce exchange restrictions which effectively prevent arbitrage operations, multilateral agreement is necessary to ensure that direct rates are settled on an orderly basis, with cross rates in conformity with the corresponding direct rates. Third, as we shall see in Chapter 4, there is need for international action to reduce restrictions on payments, whether these restrictions are exclusively outright prohibitions of certain payments or categories of payments, or also include multiple currency practices.

Forward exchange rates

Thus far we have been concerned exclusively with *spot* exchange rates, that is to say, the price of one currency in terms of another in the case of an exchange transaction where the parties to the bargain each offers the immediate delivery of the currency he undertakes to sell.

We must now briefly consider *forward* rates, for these have become increasingly important since the reopening of the London foreign exchange market (see below, page 184). In a forward market, the two parties to any transaction promise delivery at a specified date in the future, usually between one and twelve months after the date of the transaction.

In a free exchange market, the forward rates typically differ, however slightly, from the spot rates, the former being quoted at a certain premium or discount as compared with the latter. For example, at a time of speculative pressure against sterling, towards the end of 1964, the *Financial Times* noted that 'continuing uncertainty about the longer-term outlook, however, was reflected in a further weakening in forward sterling—the discount against dollars for delivery in three months widening $\frac{1}{8}$ cent to 2 cents, equivalent to about $2\frac{7}{8}$ per cent per annum'.[1]

The forces which operate to influence the forward discount (or premium) of one currency in relation to another are too complex to be treated here, but one very important force is the expectation that one of the currencies is about to be devalued[2] in terms of the other. The chain of events which is touched off by such an

---

[1] *Financial Times*, 1 December 1964. It is a common practice to quote the discount (or premium) of a forward rate, in relation to the spot rate, as being the equivalent of so many per cent per annum
[2] Below, p. 56 et seq.

expectation is set out, for illustrative purposes, in an appendix[1] at the end of this chapter.

But accepting the fact that, in an exchange market like the London market since 1953, forward rates can (and do) vary (if only slightly) in relation to the corresponding spot rates, we may note that the forward rates prevailing in this and other markets (e.g. New York or Zurich) will tend to be uniform and orderly, as the result of arbitrage operations, in precisely the same way as in the case of the spot rates. This tendency to uniformity and orderliness of forward rates can however (as in the case of spot rates) be upset by exchange control, where this is operated in a way which prevents the arbitrage transactions which would otherwise be undertaken by dealers seeking to maximise their profits.

We may also note that a country's monetary authorities may undertake transactions in the forward market for their currency just as (as we have already seen) they can undertake transactions in the spot market. Recourse to official intervention in the forward market was noted by the Radcliffe Committee in its Report[2] published in 1959, but such intervention became much more important in the 1960s, as we shall see in the Appendix to Chapter 4. Hence it may well become increasingly necessary, in the forward market as in the spot market, for the monetary authorities of different countries to cooperate in order to avoid acting at cross purposes.

APPENDIX

Speculation and the forward exchange market

(1) Let us start from a position where a belief develops that sterling may be devalued in relation to the dollar. In these circumstances, anybody sharing this bearish sentiment will want to sell sterling, either forward or spot.

(2) In the case of anyone holding convertible spot sterling or acquiring it by current transactions, there will be a choice between selling spot and selling forward. If the discount on forward sterling is balanced by an interest rate differential in favour of London it will usually be more convenient to sell forward rather than sell spot.

(3) In the case of an operator who does not start with a supply

[1] The reader is recommended to omit this on his first reading of the book.
[2] *Committee on the Working of the Monetary System*. Its Report, dated August 1959, was published by HMSO as Cmnd. 827. See paragraphs 703 to 707.

of spot convertible sterling, he may of course be able to borrow some, but otherwise the *only* way he can operate as a bear is to sell forward.

(4) The consequence of forward sales is to drive the forward rate down and, except in so far that this process calls forth an increased demand for forward sterling, the forward sales will simply be choked off by the fall in the rate.

(5) Such an increased demand for forward sterling may arise from four sources:

(a) Intending purchasers of UK exports (or, more precisely, anybody who will shortly be needing sterling for commercial transactions) may be tempted (by its low price) to buy forward sterling immediately, rather than buy spot sterling later on.

(b) The Exchange Equalisation Account can buy sterling forward (i.e. sell dollars forward).

(c) Authorised dealers could likewise buy sterling forward (i.e. sell dollars forward) and cover themselves by buying spot dollars from the Exchange Equalisation Account. However, the maximum holding of spot dollars permitted to the authorised dealers as cover against forward transactions is only about £m 100 and the effective swing is much less than this, say £m 25.[1]

(d) Any holder of convertible spot sterling may buy sterling forward and cover himself by selling sterling spot: this will be profitable so long as the discount on forward sterling is greater than the interest rate differential in favour of London. The maximum purchase of forward sterling by such operators is presumably the total outstanding amount of External Account sterling, but presumably holders of External Account sterling would never want to run down their balances to zero, or anything like.

(6) What is the effect on the UK official reserve of gold and dollars of the transactions described in paragraph 5?

(a) If the forward sterling is bought for commercial purposes in lieu of a purchase of spot sterling at a later date, there will *until that later date* be no change in the official reserve.

(b) If it is the Exchange Equalisation Account which buys sterling forward (i.e. sells dollars forward) there is no change at all in the Account's published holding of spot dollars and gold. The Account will however have an uncovered position on forward dollars (the extent of which is not published).

(c) In so far as authorised dealers cover themselves by buying spot dollars, this depletes the Account's holding to a like amount.

[1] Radcliffe Report, paragraph 705, referring to 1958.

(d) In so far as holders of External Account sterling convert their holdings into spot dollars in order to cover themselves against their sales of forward dollars, the Account's holding of spot dollars and gold will be depleted to a like amount.

(7) Until 1951 forward transactions were monopolised by the Exchange Equalisation Account, which was prepared to buy and sell forward (though only for approved purposes) at published buying and selling prices. Since then the Account has not been under any obligation to deal forward in sterling, but has from time to time done so, occasionally on a large scale, as I explain in the Appendix to Chapter 4. The presumed purpose of official intervention, at any rate during the period from the last quarter of 1964 until the devaluation of sterling in November 1967, has been to support the forward rate and thus to meet the requirements of foreign investors prepared to invest in London but only on a covered basis. Unfortunately, however, such official support of the forward rate also provides great opportunities for bear speculators, who are enabled to sell sterling forward on a large scale without driving down the forward rate (and hence without thereby reducing the margin of speculative profits to be derived from selling sterling forward on the eve of a devaluation).

TABLE 1

MULTIPLE EXCHANGE RATES IN 1950[1] IN CHILE

All rates expressed in Pesos per US Dollar

Buying Rate	Applicable to:	Selling Rate	Applicable to:
19.37	Local currency requirements of large foreign-owned mining companies for current operating costs.		
		31.00	(1) Essential imports of goods. (2) Certain authorised imports of services.
37.00	Exports of such goods as hides, wool and fish products.		
39.40	Agricultural and industrial exports, with certain exceptions.		
41.20	Exports of wheat, beans, and produce of small mines.		
43.00	(1) Exports such as sodium sulphate and some foodstuffs. (2) Exports of services. (3) Capital transactions, including local currency requirements for capital investments of large mining companies.	43.10	(1) Non-essential imports of goods. (2) Other authorised imports of services. (3) Capital transactions.
100.77[2]	Local currency requirements of visiting tourists and diplomats.	100.77[2]	Non-licensed imports of services.
130.00[3]	Sales of newly mined gold.	130.00[3]	Authorised imports of luxury goods.

[1] Taken from page 98 of the IMF's *First Annual Report on Exchange Restrictions,* published in March 1950. Chile's exchange rates have been altered on several occasions since this *Report* appeared.
[2] Fluctuating free market rate.
[3] Fluctuating gold market rate.

3

INTERNATIONAL LIQUIDITY

Compensatory official financing

We have already noted the widespread recourse to official transactions in the foreign exchange markets, aimed at mitigating, or preventing altogether, the instability of exchange rates which would arise under *laissez faire*. Who undertakes such transactions, and in what media are they conducted? In Britain, as we have seen, the agency undertaking the transactions has been since 1932 the Exchange Equalisation Account, a fund operated on behalf of the Treasury by the Bank of England. Previously the agency had been the Bank of England itself, and these two British arrangements (post-1932 and pre-1932) typify those which are in use throughout the world today: in almost all countries the official agency charged with intervening in the foreign exchange markets is either the central bank itself or an off-shoot of the Treasury or Finance Ministry. Let us therefore for convenience apply a common label to both of these possibilities, and refer to the competent authority as the 'official monetary agency'.

Since the transactions of such agencies are designed to offset other transactions, the net balance of which would otherwise cause exchange rate fluctuations which the relevant agency judges to be undesirable, any transaction by an official agency in the exchange market may conveniently be labelled a 'compensatory official transaction'. How then are compensatory official transactions financed? Primarily they are financed by the agency holding a reserve of liquid international assets—gold, foreign currencies and 'safe' short-term claims to foreign currencies—

which can be added to when the home currency would otherwise appreciate unduly, or depleted when the home currency would otherwise depreciate unduly. This, as we have already seen, was how the British Exchange Equalisation Account came to operate, and all official agencies operate primarily in the same way.

The adverb 'primarily' is required on account of the fact that an official agency whose reserves would otherwise be in danger of exhaustion may be rescued by an international[1] loan or grant (or exchange of currencies) intended specifically for this purpose. The British Exchange Equalisation Account has for instance been rescued in this way, at various times in the post-war period, *inter alia* by Marshall Aid, by the famous Anglo-American Loan,[2] by a loan from the US government's Export-Import Bank negotiated after the Suez crisis in 1956, by purchases of dollars and other currencies from the International Monetary Fund, and by the so-called Basle arrangements.[3]

Thus, in the light of British experience, we see that the external value of a currency may be maintained by various kinds of compensatory official financing. Broadly speaking, three major species may be distinguished:

(1) the depletion of the official reserve (in Britain's case the Exchange Equalisation Account's own reserve of gold and foreign currencies).

(2) drawings on loans and grants from other countries (in Britain's case frequently the United States).

(3) the accumulation of the home currency by the official agencies of other countries and by international institutions (in Britain's case the accumulation of sterling by many other countries and by the International Monetary Fund and the European Payments Union).

Each of these three species of compensatory official financing may be regarded as the use of a corresponding 'official resource for international settlement', these resources being respectively:

(1) international reserves
(2) external drawing rights
(3) external 'accumulation facilities'.

Such resources collectively correspond to what is usually understood by the term 'international liquidity'.

---

[1] A transaction with an international institution such as the International Monetary Fund should (in addition to transactions between two countries) be classed as 'international'.
[2] Below, pages 173-5.
[3] Below, page 252 et seq.

None of these resources is infinite in amount. This is clear enough in the case of a country's own international reserves, but it is also usual for both accumulation facilities and drawing rights to be limited by prior agreement to a definite maximum, sometimes known as the 'swing', or alternatively the 'ceiling', of the agreement. There is however one circumstance in which accumulation facilities are neither the result of an agreement nor subject to a definite ceiling: this occurs when country A enjoys accumulation facilities with B by virtue of the fact that B has elected to adhere to A's currency as a standard, as for instance Australia and the other countries of the outer Sterling Area adhere to sterling as a standard, which means that B's monetary authorities follow a policy of offering to buy or sell A's currency without limit at a published price, just as countries on the gold bullion standard would always buy and sell gold at a published price. The accumulation facilities thereby offered by B to A would be limitless so long as B did not change her policy, which however she would be free to do on her own initiative.

It may be helpful at this stage to consider a statistical example of compensatory official financing. Table 2A below sets out the receipts which came to the United Kingdom from overseas in 1966 and the payments made overseas by the United Kingdom in the same year. Some of the receipts and payments were on current, others on capital, account. Current receipts comprise the sales proceeds of goods and services sold overseas, income received on British-owned overseas investments, and (usually a negligible item) incomes paid as gifts to Britishers by foreigners. Current payments comprise payments for goods and services supplied from overseas, income paid to overseas owners of investments in Britain, and transfer payments made overseas. The excess of current payments over current receipts, technically known as the United Kingdom's negative or 'unfavourable' *balance of current payments,* was (according to Table 2A) $170 millions in 1966.

The same table gives the balance of the capital items, excluding compensatory official financing, as unfavourable to the extent of $1,400 millions;[1] this amount added to the balance of current payments gives Britain's total *external deficit* for the year—$1,570 millions. This deficit was financed as is shown in Table 2B.

The compilation of a statement like that on page 42 presupposes that all international transactions can be classified according as to whether or not the item in question is compen-

[1] Namely items 13 to 18 (total $m. 2,190) minus item 5 (total $m. 790).

TABLE 2A[1]
UK BALANCE OF PAYMENTS IN 1966
(*all figures in* $ *millions*)
CURRENT ITEMS

Receipts		*Payments*	
1. Exports of goods[2]	14,310	7. Imports of goods[2]	14,620
2. Transportation (net)	130	8. Payments for US military aircraft	120
3. Investment income (net)	1,040	9. Travel (net)	220
4. Non-government services (net)	770	10. Government expenditure on services	780
		11. Private transfer payments	170
		12. Government transfer payments	510
Total current receipts	16,250	Total current payments	16,420

CAPITAL ITEMS
(*long term*)

5. Private investment (net) in the UK	790	13. Government lending and other capital transactions	230
		14. Private investment abroad	890

(*short term*)

6. Balance covered by compensatory official financing (=external deficit)	1,570	15. UK net liabilities in OSA[3] currencies	120
		16. UK banks' net liabilities in non-SA[3] currencies	450
		17. Sterling liabilities other than to official monetary agencies	370
		18. Miscellaneous capital	130
Grand total	18,610	Grand total	18,610

TABLE 2B[1]
UK COMPENSATORY OFFICIAL FINANCING IN 1966
(*all figures in* $ *millions*)

Sterling liabilities to official monetary agencies (a) in OSA[3] countries	−75
(b) in non-SA[3] countries Central bank assistance	} 860
Transactions with IMF	−10
Depletion of UK's official reserve of gold and foreign currencies (including UK official portfolio of dollar securities)	795
Total	1,570

[1] These two tables are adapted from the IMF's *Balance of Payments Yearbook*, as re-issued in November 1967.
[2] Calculated at their value when loaded on board ship, i.e. net of all shipping costs.
[3] OSA means Outer Sterling Area; non-SA means non-Sterling Area.

satory official financing. In practice however the distinction is not always easy to draw.

In principle the criterion to be applied is one of motive: 'the distinguishing mark of a compensatory transaction is that it is undertaken broadly to balance international transactions during the reporting period',[1] whereas a non-compensatory transaction is one which is undertaken irrespective of the size of the surplus or deficit which would otherwise occur. A case in point is Marshall Aid. Was the primary aim of this Aid to relieve Europe's shortage of dollars by supplying *gratis* goods which otherwise would have had to be bought for dollars, or was it simply a relief measure which would have been undertaken even if the European countries had not been short of dollars? The answer is uncertain, but since the amount and the allocation of the Aid was based on estimates of the 'dollar gap' of each of the recipient countries, the presumption is that the United States intended it primarily as an act of compensatory financing. A very thorough explanation of the statistician's problem of deciding what is, and what is not, 'compensatory official financing' is given in an article on page 276 of the Bank of England's *Quarterly Bulletin*, December 1964.

Another question which we have to face is this: though every item entered in the statement on page 42 represents a transaction between Britain and some other country, can we be sure that any item classed as compensatory official financing from Britain's point of view will necessarily be similarly regarded by the other party to the transaction? The answer, unfortunately, must be negative: 'unfortunately', that is, because we are thereby forced to admit exceptions to the simple rule that compensatory official financing must necessarily cancel out for the world as a whole, the total of external deficits necessarily balancing the total of external surpluses. An exception to this rule would have arisen, for example, if the British government had drawn on a dollar credit made available by a group of Wall Street banks, for the transaction from the American standpoint could then not possibly be regarded as compensatory *official* financing, even though it would have been so regarded by Britain. A similar case is that of *newly mined* gold: if South Africa sends newly mined gold to America, there occurs an increase in American official reserves without any corresponding decrease in any other country's official reserves.

Thus it is possible for one country to have a balance of payments surplus without another country having a deficit, and conversely.

[1] The IMF's second *Balance of Payments Yearbook*, page 23.

I shall however, following Professor Meade, take it that 'This possibility is not unreal; but it is unlikely in fact to be quantitatively as important as the fundamental disequilibria which develop when one country's surplus is matched by another's deficit. Accordingly, in what follows we shall neglect this case unless we make specific mention of it.'[1] More specifically I shall in Part I assume the equality of total surpluses and deficits: in Parts II and III it will be necessary to take account of significant deviations from such a state of equality.

Settlement in conditions of equilibrium

Arrangements for international settlements range from the strictly bilateral to the fully multilateral. So long as no exchange controls exist, the exchange markets provide the necessary facilities for fully multilateral settlements, since the owner of any one currency can obtain any other currency simply by bidding for it. There therefore remains to consider only the kinds of arrangements which may prevail under a regime of exchange controls.

Let us begin with the extreme case of complete bilateralism, which is unlikely to arise in practice unless the monetary authorities of either or both of the countries concerned enjoy a monopolistic status as dealer in the other's currency.[2] In these particular circumstances a purely bilateral arrangement can be concluded, like the agreements made between the United Kingdom and various European countries soon after their liberation, consisting essentially of an agreement to fix the exchange rate between the two countries' currencies and to create accumulation facilities on either a one-way or a reciprocal basis. (Such agreements are described in Chapter 11.)

A step towards multilateralism can be achieved on the basis of bilateral accumulation facilities if a group of countries, all of whom have bilateral agreements with one another, agree among themselves to undertake circular offsetting. This is possible and advantageous when facilities have been used in a closed circuit— for example if country A has been running a bilateral deficit with B, B with C and C with A—and when in addition the facilities are in each case subject to a risk of eventual exhaustion. In such a case the countries in the circuit will each find it advantageous if they can

---

[1] Meade: *The Balance of Payments*, p. 20.

[2] In this case compensatory official financing may not correspond to compensatory official dealings *in a foreign exchange market* (since there may be no 'market' in the ordinary sense of the word). Instead it must be taken to be simply the net balance of each country's official dealings in the other's currency.

arrange that each one of them should write down its holding of the 'preceding' country's currency in return for a similar cancellation of its own currency in the hands of the following country in the circuit, the amount of each of the cancellations being equivalent in value to the smallest of the holdings in the circuit. For by virtue of the offsetting operation each country in the circuit would enjoy an increase in its outstanding accumulation facilities available for use against the following country in the circuit.

In the special case of world-wide international equilibrium (i.e. where no country is in *overall* surplus or deficit, each country's bilateral deficits being precisely balanced in total by its bilateral surpluses) it is possible to arrange all countries' bilateral deficits into a series of closed circuits, and to cancel the lot by circular off-setting.[1] Such a state of affairs corresponds perfectly to the ideal of international settlement on a fully multilateral basis, for if all deficits can be offset as they arise, or with only a short delay, no country has any reason to care with whom it runs deficits and with whom it runs surpluses, provided that (in conformity with our hypothesis) its deficits and surpluses are in overall balance. If however our perfect equilibrium gives way to disequilibrium, with some countries developing overall deficits and others overall surpluses, the proportion of deficits which can be arranged in closed circuits and offset undergoes a progressive decline. Disequilibria of the magnitude which occurred in practice in the immediate post-war years may well reduce the possible amount of circular offsetting to almost negligible proportions.[2]

Another device for facilitating settlements on a multilateral basis is that of transferable currencies. If for instance country A has acquired a stock of country X's currency, the monetary authorities of the latter country may refrain from placing any obstacle in the way of A using this currency to make payments to country B. In such a case X's currency qualifies as a 'transferable currency'. Transferability may be unconditional, as in the case of transfers of *any* sterling between *any* countries before the last war, or it may be conditional. A conditionally transferable currency may be subject to conditions clearly laid down in advance (e.g. that the currency may not be transferred to finance capital transactions or payments to particular countries), in which

[1] See Ekker: Equilibrium of International Trade and International Monetary Compensations in *Weltwirtschaftliches Archiv*, Band 64, Heft 2, 1950. This authoritative article provides the basis for many of the arguments in the remainder of this chapter, and should be consulted by readers who want a more rigorous exposition.
[2] Ekker, op. cit.

case it may be said to enjoy conditional but automatic transferability; or it may be necessary for each transfer to be authorised
by the exchange control authorities of the country issuing the
currency, in which case the transferability is said to be discretionary or 'administrative'.

It is easy to see that circular transfers of X's currency could
serve the same purpose as circular offsetting. For (to adapt our
previous examples) suppose that X is Britain and that A's deficit
with B, B's with C and C's with A are each the equivalent of £10
millions sterling. Then instead of each country using its bilateral
accumulation facilities against the next country in the circuit, the
status quo then being restored by circular offsetting, it would be
equally satisfactory if the circuit of deficits had been cleared by the
payment of £10 millions sterling each from A to B, B to C and C
to A. It therefore follows that, provided that each country is in
overall equilibrium, circular transfers of one or more unconditionally transferable currencies can, like circular offsetting,
provide a completely satisfactory means of achieving international
settlement on a fully multilateral basis within a group of countries,
but that the scope for such transfers is progressively curtailed to
the extent that this condition is unfulfilled.

Settlement in conditions of disequilibrium
Now let us consider settlement within a group of countries *not* in
equilibrium, i.e. where some countries have overall deficits and
others overall surpluses. Here again, in the absence of exchange
controls, fully multilateral settlement will be automatically
ensured by the working of the foreign exchange markets. The only
difficulty that can arise is that the deficit countries will in due
course fear the possibility of running out of reserves and hence of
losing their influence over the external value of their currency.
This fear may become acute in a period of large and sustained
disequilibrium, as in the years immediately following the last
war, and may well induce (as in the ten years or so after the war)
widespread recourse to measures of exchange control. Hence it is
pertinent to consider how settlements are likely to be effected in
conditions of disequilibrium under a regime of widespread
exchange control. Let us suppose, therefore, that these circumstances prevail, and also that the various countries comprising the
world economy have, in respect of a given period,[1] already (by

[1] The choice of an accounting period for calculating bilateral deficits is necessarily
arbitrary. It should be noted that a lengthening of the accounting period may

circular offsetting) eliminated all closed circuits of bilateral deficits. What deficits would then remain and how could they be settled? This question can best be tackled as follows. It can be proved[1] that after all circular bilateral deficits have been eliminated, one country will necessarily emerge as having bilateral surpluses with some or all of the other countries and deficits with none. Let us call this the 'strongest' country.[2] There will also necessarily be a second strongest country with a bilateral deficit with the strongest country but with bilateral surpluses with all the other countries. Similarly a third strongest country will have bilateral deficits with the first and second strongest countries but surpluses with all the remaining countries. These remaining countries can in their turn be arranged in a definite order of 'strength', the weakest country having bilateral deficits with everybody else.

A numerical illustration will help to clarify this point. Suppose that there are only eight countries in the world: Canada, the USA, the UK, Britannica, Europa, Imperia, Latinnia and Miscellannia, and that we have estimated the bilateral balances obtaining between each of the 28 pairs of countries in some particular year. We could then present our estimates in the form of a table with each of the 28 bilateral estimates classified according to both the surplus partner and the deficit partner. If we did no more than this our entries would be scattered over the table without forming a simple pattern, but if in addition we eliminate all closed circuits of deficits and then arrange our countries in the order of their strength, we shall find, as in Table 3(A), that all the entries fall on one side of one of the diagonals, in the form of a compact 'wedge'.[3] The significance of this pattern of entries is that the settlements required to meet all the bilateral deficits

reduce, not increase, the bilateral deficit of one country with another: for example, A's deficit with B in January may be partially balanced by B having a deficit with A in February, in which case A's bilateral deficit for the two months together will be less than for January alone. The more months we consider at a time the more important is the cancelling out of 'reciprocal deficits' (as we call them in Chapter 11) likely to be. See below, page 146.

[1] See Ekker, op. cit.

[2] The label 'strongest' is purely for purposes of identification and does not imply that it is praiseworthy to be 'strong'. For a somewhat similar use of the term, see Professor J. M. Fleming's article 'On Making the Best of Balance of Payments Restrictions on Imports' in the *Economic Journal*, March 1951.

[3] The figures in Table 3 are actually taken from the first half of Table 88 of the ECE's *Economic Survey of Europe in 1949*, page 167, except that closed circuits have been eliminated and the names of imaginary countries substituted for certain groups of countries. Thus Latinnia corresponds to the Latin American republics, Britannica to the outer Sterling Area, and so on.

represent a uni-directional flow from the weaker to the stronger countries. Thus the weakest country, Europa, has to settle bilateral deficits with the seven countries which are stronger than she is, Britannica with her six superiors in strength, the UK with her five superiors in strength, and so on, until we reach the strongest country, the USA with no deficits at all.

The summary table, Table 3(B), tells us that of the eight countries, three have overall surpluses, totalling $m 7,290, while the other five have overall deficits, which total the same amount.[1] The total of the 28 individual bilateral deficits (or surpluses), two of which are so small as to be shown as nil, is of course greater than the total of the overall deficits (or surpluses)—the figure being, from Table 3(B), $m 11,040.

The interesting lesson which can be learned from Table 3 is that though bilateral deficits equivalent to $m 11,040 have to be settled, means of settlement equivalent to only $m 7,290 could suffice, provided (1) that a currency could be used which was freely transferable to, and acceptable to, all countries and could therefore flow freely from the weaker to the stronger countries and (2) that this currency was available to the five deficit countries in amounts sufficient to cover their respective overall deficits. For let us suppose such an international currency to exist. Then Europa, as the weakest country, would have to provide enough of the international currency to settle all her bilateral deficits—a total of $m 5,230. Britannica, however, whose bilateral deficits total $m 1,660, would have to provide only $m 1,160 since she would in addition pass on the $m 500 received from Europa. Likewise, the UK, Imperia and Miscellannia would need to provide the international currency only to the extent of their respective overall deficits, while Canada and Latinnia (and of course the strongest country, the USA) would not need to provide any of the international currency at all.

The 'saving' of $m 3,750 of the means of settlement ($m 11,040 minus $m 7,290) is the measure of the extent to which, in our example, bilateral deficits could be cleared by 'passing on' currencies, received in the same year—instead of 'passing round' currencies, as in the case of circular transfers. It follows that if overall deficits could be settled in currencies which could be both

---

[1] It is not logically necessary that all countries with overall surpluses should in all circumstances be stronger than countries with overall deficits. If for example in Table 3(A) Europa's bilateral deficit with the UK had been 1,200 instead of 200, the appropriate order of the countries would be unchanged, but the UK would then have had an overall surplus, not an overall deficit.

TABLE 3

AN ILLUSTRATION OF THE PATTERN OF BILATERAL DEFICITS,
WITH ALL CLOSED CIRCUITS OF DEFICITS ELIMINATED

(*The figures are expressed to the nearest million of US dollars, and relate
to some particular year*)

TABLE 3(A): The Individual Bilateral Deficits and Surpluses

Countries with their bilateral Deficits	Countries with their bilateral Surpluses:							
	USA	Latin-nia	Canada	Miscel-lannia	Imperia	UK	Brit-annica	Europa
USA								
Latinnia	1,000							
Canada	400	10						
Miscellannia	800	100	80					
Imperia	100	300	10	80				
UK	200	500	500	10	60			
Britannica	400	0	100	200	0	960		
Europa	3,300	700	200	30	300	200	500	

TABLE 3(B): Summary

Country	Total Bilateral Deficits	Total Bilateral Surpluses	Overall Deficits	Overall Surpluses
USA	0	6,200		6,200
Latinnia	1,000	1,610		610
Canada	410	890		480
Miscellannia	980	320	660	
Imperia	490	360	130	
UK	1,270	1,160	110	
Britannica	1,660	500	1,160	
Europa	5,230	0	5,230	
	11,040	11,040	7,290	7,290

'passed on' and 'passed round' this could facilitate the clearing not
only of the overall deficits themselves but also of all so-called
'compensable' deficits—i.e. of all bilateral deficits in excess of the
total of overall deficits. Under such arrangements, all international settlement would proceed on a fully multilateral basis,
for no country would mind with whom it ran deficits and with
whom surpluses, but would be concerned solely with its overall
position.

Unfortunately however a pattern of bilateral deficits which, as

in Table 3, calls for a passing on of means of settlement inevitably
leads to difficulties which do not arise where deficits can be
arranged in closed circuits. That such is the case can best be seen
by considering first the strongest country, the USA in our
example. Since the USA does not have to make any settlements,
it has no incentive to accept currencies with the idea of passing
them on, except possibly in a later period when the pattern of
bilateral deficits may have changed. The USA is therefore likely
to be somewhat cautious in deciding what currencies she will
accept in settlement of her surpluses. Let us suppose that she
accepts without limit only her own currency (US dollars) and
gold, other currencies being accepted only up to the limits of pre-
arranged 'swings'.[1] If therefore the USA be assumed to continue
for a long period as the strongest country, she will steadily drain
the five deficit countries of gold and US dollars, until these
became scarce or 'hard'. The evil day may be postponed by dollar
gifts and credits, but not indefinitely. Thus there will develop an
incentive, beginning probably with Europa but spreading to the
other relatively weak countries, to try to settle in a 'softer'
medium, and to discriminate in favour of countries which will
accept it. For example, Europa may try to persuade Britannica
to accept settlements in a 'softer' currency (which the USA
would not accept) by using the argument: 'We cannot pay you
in dollars, because we are running short of them, so if you do not
accept a softer currency, we shall perforce have to buy less of
your goods.' If Europa's policy succeeds against Britannica and
other countries, and if these in turn attempt to follow her example,
there will develop a 'soft-currency area' wherein settlements are
made in currencies not acceptable to the USA. This development
will undermine the multilateral basis of settlement, since countries
will have an incentive to attempt to run bilateral surpluses with
the hard currency countries rather than with the soft currency
countries, and to run bilateral deficits with the soft currency
countries rather than with the hard currency countries.

If, as we have assumed, the USA will accept certain other
countries' currencies up to a limited swing, the hardening of the
US dollar may induce the countries enjoying these facilities to
restrict the transferability of their currencies. The UK might for
instance try to stop other countries from settling with the USA in
sterling, since such settlements would use up the accumulation

_____

[1] In fact the USA did not, prior to 1961, accumulate the currencies of any other
countries. See below, page 256.

facilities which would otherwise be available to settle the UK's own bilateral deficit with the USA. In such circumstances countries holding sterling would have an incentive to prefer to run deficits with the UK and with countries to which sterling could be freely transferred, rather than with the USA. Thus here again the multilateral basis of international settlement would be undermined.

In brief, then, the free flow of means of settlement from the weaker to the stronger countries in Table 3 is liable to be interrupted in two ways:

(1) in some parts of the world, certain currencies may become too hard for general use in making settlements, and
(2) the soft currencies used instead may, since they enjoy at best only limited acceptability in the hard currency area, suffer a restriction of their transferability,

and in such a case the multilateral basis of international settlement will be undermined. Moreover, the process which has just been described can be repeated in respect of some other currency, say the Canadian dollar, which would be unlikely to become harder than the US dollar (since no currency could be more acceptable to Canada than one which, like the US dollar, could be used for settling her deficits with both USA and Latinnia[1]) but might however come to occupy a position somewhere between the US dollar and the soft currencies. There might indeed develop almost as many degrees of hardness as there are currencies, which would eventually lead to a reversion to complete bilateralism.

It must not be concluded from this section that prolonged international disequilibria make settlement on a multilateral basis quite impossible, but only that they lead to difficulties whose seriousness depends on the circumstances. It is for instance possible for the currency of a relatively weak country to remain reasonably hard if it is widely believed that she will in due course become much stronger, and the hardness will be further increased if the currency has long enjoyed the status of a world-wide international currency.

The scope for international cooperation
International cooperation is desirable in order to ensure that resources are available for compensatory official financing on a

[1] Since Latinnia has a deficit only with the USA, there could be no currency more acceptable to her than US dollars.

scale sufficient to accommodate international disequilibria until they either disappear of their own accord, or can be dealt with by any of the means discussed in the next chapter.

If means of settlement can be made available only on a strictly bilateral basis, more liquidity will probably be needed than if settlement can be arranged on a multilateral basis. Apart from this consideration, settlement on a multilateral basis is also desirable in itself, since it enables each country to allow its traders to buy and sell in whichever foreign market offers the best terms, irrespective of the bilateral deficits and surpluses which ensue.

So long as no exchange controls exist, the exchange markets automatically provide the necessary facilities for fully multilateral settlement. However, such a satisfactory state of affairs presupposes that deficit countries have adequate resources for supporting their national currencies in the exchange markets at whatever exchange rate they deem appropriate: for if their resources are inadequate (that is, in danger of running out) they must needs either revise their ideas about the exchange rate they should seek to maintain or adopt some other measure for dealing with their deficit. One such measure is the imposition of exchange controls, and this device was indeed very widely adopted in the early part of the post-war period, while the so-called 'dollar shortage' prevailed. In a regime of exchange controls, particularly of the stringent kind which obtained in the early part of the post-war period, multilateral settlement is unlikely to be achieved except by the provision of special facilities for clearing compensable bilateral deficits. Such facilities are easy to provide where the bilateral deficits can be arranged in closed circuits: circular offsetting or circular transfers of a national currency are, for example, perfectly suitable in such cases. Where, however, the bilateral deficits cannot be so arranged, the provision of satisfactory clearing arrangements presents much greater difficulties. In this chapter we have explored the difficulties which arise with one particular clearing mechanism, that of transferable currencies. In Chapter 13, dealing with sterling, we shall see how these difficulties show themselves in practice. Another possible mechanism consists of the 'compensations' which were provided for under various monetary agreements between the western European countries in the period 1947–50. Here too, however, difficulties were encountered, as will be described in Chapter 11.

4

THE ADJUSTMENT PROCESS

The feasibility of settling accounts between the different countries of the world depends not only on the availability of suitable means of settlement but also on the size of the accounts which have to be settled. Since in practice the means for international settlement are never indefinitely large, even in cases where accumulation facilities are not subject to a pre-arranged limit, it follows that international liquidity is only a device for accommodating *temporary* deficits; hence in cases of persistent deficits there arises for the deficit countries the problem of how to correct them before their reserves become exhausted. (If their reserves did become exhausted, and still they took no steps to correct their deficits, there would inevitably occur a depreciation of their currencies.)

In this chapter we shall consider the problem of dealing with international disequilibria in the sense of overall deficits and surpluses, and pay little attention to the question of bilateral deficits. This limitation is appropriate because, as we have seen, bilateral deficits and surpluses can easily be cleared provided that all countries can be brought into approximate overall equilibrium.

An individual county, such as Nottinghamshire, is fortunate, not only in having a generous supply of the means of settling her external accounts (due to having a common currency with the other British counties), but also in the fact that an outflow of cash has a strong tendency to be self-correcting. In an independent country, however, the problems arising from the more limited availability of means of settlement are aggravated by the relative inefficiency of the available means for correcting a deficit.

The reasons for the latter can best be seen if we again give rein to our imagination and this time suppose what would happen if Nottinghamshire were completely independent, with its own separate paper currency, the 'Nottspound', and arranged its external payments by adhering to *sterling* as a standard, as Australia does.[1] Let us however assume for the time being that neither Nottinghamshire nor the rest of the United Kingdom has imposed any restrictions on trade, on capital transactions, or on payments, between the two economies. In these hypothetical circumstances it is clear that despite the absence of any such restrictions, Nottspeople's capital transactions with the rest of Britain would be much less helpful, from the point of view of correcting external disequilibria, than at present.[2] The existence of the two currencies, the Nottspound and the pound sterling, would be a deterrent to investors, whose future profits would be more uncertain if there was a risk that the official exchange rate might eventually be changed or that exchange restrictions might be imposed. Moreover, such borrowing and lending as remained would be considerably distorted by factors which are at present largely absent. Political and social changes affecting only one of the two economies, such as changes in taxation or in official regulations, a change of government, a deterioration of industrial relations, or an increase in social unrest, might greatly upset the balance of borrowing and lending between the two economies. Even the fear that such changes might occur would act in the same way. In addition there might be speculative movements of securities, in anticipation of changes in the exchange rate, or panic sales of securities due to fears that exchange controls might be imposed. It is easy to imagine that movements of securities between independent economies, far from being an equilibrating factor, might well be the reverse. Such, at any rate, seems to be the view of many governments, for controls of one kind or another on international capital movements have frequently (though not always effectively[3]) been maintained, by Britain and many other countries, during the post-war period, and more recently there have been attempts (again not altogether effective, as will be briefly explained in an appendix to this chapter) to use Bank Rate and official intervention in the forward exchange market to influence international capital movements.

Since Nottspeople's capital transactions with the rest of

[1] Above, p. 41.
[2] Above, p. 22.
[3] See Chapter 14.

Britain would probably no longer be equilibrating if the county achieved independence, we must now pursue the question (which we rather neglect in Chapter 1) of whether, and in what circumstances, the county's external *trade* would be equilibrating.

An external deficit due to a falling off in an independent Nottinghamshire's exports to the rest of Britain would be to some extent self-correcting if no steps were taken to offset the depression (and the consequential reduction in imports) due to the decline in exports and also to the resulting decline in Nottspeople's demand for goods and services.[1] Indeed, the decline in exports might cause an even greater decline in imports, in which case the Nottinghamshire government could, without danger to the county's sterling reserves, take steps to stimulate an appropriate degree of recovery. On the other hand, if the automatic decline in imports proved to be inadequate, the Nottinghamshire government could always take steps to aggravate the depression, for example by requiring a contraction of bank credit.

But curing an external deficit by means of an internal depression is (as we noted in Chapter 1) an unpleasant treatment and we are naturally more interested in the other available remedies. One such remedy might arise merely with the passage of time and the pressure of circumstances, for the depression might well in due course become unnecessary (as a means of dealing with the external deficit) if the effect of the unemployment in Nottinghamshire was to depress the level of wages, and thus to cheapen the prices of Nottinghamshire's goods in relation to goods produced elsewhere. For this outcome would be similar to that of a depreciation of the Nottspound in relation to the pound sterling, which (it will be shortly shown) would in favourable circumstances reduce Nottinghamshire's deficit.

If however a depreciation of the Nottspound could cure the external deficit, why wait for unemployment to act on the level of wages? Workers would obviously resist the reduction of their wages, probably with partial or even complete success, the necessary negotiations would be prolonged and bitter, and unemployment would have to continue until an adequate fall in the wage level had occurred.[2] Why not instead simply depreciate the Nottspound straight away?

[1] cf. above, p. 21, and my *Wealth and Income*, Part Three.
[2] The acceptance of this argument against attempting to cure an external deficit by depressing the level of prices does not of course imply that Nottinghamshire should not attempt to prevent her price level from rising. Rising prices would unnecessarily aggravate her deficit and her problem of dealing with it.

Devaluation in favourable circumstances

If the Nottspound were reduced in value from one pound sterling to (say) 19 shillings, this would increase the prices in Nottspounds which Nottspeople would have to pay for imported goods. When imported goods became dearer, Nottspeople would buy less of them and consequently need less sterling to pay for them. If, as is likely under free trade, the total expenditure of Nottspeople has been directed in goodly proportion towards imported goods of all kinds, including luxury goods and goods for which passable substitutes can be made locally, and if in addition the prices (in Nottspounds) of locally produced goods do not appreciably rise (whether through being bid up by the diversion of demand from imported goods or through the operation of the so-called 'wage-price spiral'[1]), the reduction in sterling expenditure on imports would be considerable. In technical language we can say that a devaluation of the Nottspound would be particularly efficacious because of Nottinghamshire's high price-elasticity of demand for imports, i.e. because her imports would be choked off rapidly by a rise in their prices.

Let us turn now from Nottinghamshire's imports to her exports. It is likely that under free trade the demand for Nottinghamshire's exports would also be highly price-elastic, partly because Nottinghamshire's customers (counties importing Nottinghamshire's exports) would, like Nottinghamshire herself, have a high price-elasticity of demand for imports, and partly because a reduction in the sterling prices of Nottinghamshire's exports would enable her to underbid her competitors and thus to supply a higher proportion of her customers' import-requirements. Hence, provided that the competitive advantage afforded to Nottinghamshire's exports is not offset by a rise in their prices (in Nottspounds), the effect of Nottinghamshire's devaluation would be to increase the volume of her exports in a much greater proportion than the reduction in their sterling prices,[2] so that her total sterling earnings from her exports would considerably increase.

---

[1] The rise in the prices of imported goods, and particularly of necessities for which no suitable locally produced substitute is available, may induce workers to press for higher wage rates. If workers do exact higher wage rates, producers are likely to pass on their extra costs to their customers in the form of higher prices, and these higher prices may be held to justify a second round of wage increases. This process could continue through many rounds.

[2] If export prices in terms of Nottspounds remained unchanged, they would fall in terms of sterling to the same proportionate extent as the devaluation of the Nottspound in relation to sterling.

Devaluation in unfavourable circumstances

On the assumptions we have made as to the conditions governing Nottinghamshire's demand for imports and supply of exports and those governing the demand for her exports[1] we can conclude that devaluation would be a highly efficient way of improving Nottinghamshire's balance of current payments and thereby correcting her external deficit. Let us now consider how much less efficient devaluation would be if the relevant conditions were otherwise. To start with, let us reverse our previous assumptions as to Nottinghamshire's demand for imports and supply of exports by supposing Nottinghamshire to be (1) liable to suffer excess demand, (2) highly inflexible in her economy, (3) subject to certain kinds of official restrictions, and (4) subject to the wage-price spiral—wage-rates being in some degree geared to the workers' cost of living. Then, when we have followed through the implications of these possibilities, we can complete the story by reversing our previous assumptions about the demand for Nottinghamshire's exports.

(1) If the level of demand for Nottinghamshire's goods were already so high that output was nearly at its maximum, both the diversion of demand from imported to locally produced goods and the increase in the demand for exports would probably result in the bidding up of home prices, thereby offsetting the effect of the devaluation. It would then be up to the Nottinghamshire authorities, if they wished the devaluation to be successful in its objective, to eliminate the excess demand, either by restricting credit, or by increasing taxation, or by some other suitable means. (It would be useless to keep prices down by official controls if excess demand prevented the volume of exports from increasing: such a policy would merely make Nottinghamshire's sterling earnings lower than ever.)

(2) Unfortunately the avoidance of an excess of *overall* demand for locally produced goods is not a sufficient condition for the avoidance of a serious rise in home prices. Devaluation stimulates the demand for specific types of goods, namely those which are the closest substitutes for imported goods and those which are

---

[1] I do not make any explicit assumptions as to the conditions governing the supply of Nottinghamshire's imports, because the conditions to be found in practice would almost never be unfavourable to the success of devaluation as a cure for an external deficit. In so far as Nottinghamshire's demand for imports fell off as the result of devaluation, this would tend, if anything, to reduce the sterling prices of imports, never (in any likely circumstances) to increase them.

suitable for export. If the output of these particular types of goods can be increased only with difficulty, and if the home demand for them cannot be much reduced, then a relatively large devaluation will be required to effect a given improvement in the balance of current payments. An increase in the output of the relevant types of goods may well be difficult to achieve if the industries producing them are already operating to the limit of their existing resources of manpower, land, or equipment, since the expansion of output would then require that additional resources of a suitable type should be attracted from other industries—which would be impossible if such resources simply did not exist or if they were located in the wrong place and immobile. A reduction in the home demand for the relevant types of goods would be difficult to achieve if these goods happened to be necessities or, in the case of exportable goods, if the proportion of output sold on the home market was in any case very small.

(3) If we drop our previous assumption of free trade and imagine that our 'independent' Nottinghamshire follows the practice (not unknown among independent countries) of drastically restricting imports by tariffs, quotas, exchange controls and similar devices, then there is less likelihood of the county's demand for imports being highly elastic. For if official restrictions have already reduced imports to bare necessities which cannot be produced locally, only a drastic devaluation would effect much further reduction.

(4) In so far as wage rates are geared to the wage earner's cost of living, a devaluation (by raising the prices of imported goods consumed by wage earners) is liable to provoke a wage-price spiral, thereby reducing the competitive advantage afforded by the devaluation.

Let us now reverse our previous assumption of a highly elastic demand for Nottinghamshire's exports. The lower the elasticity of demand for Nottinghamshire's exports the larger the devaluation needed to achieve a given increase in the county's sterling earnings from her exports. Indeed, below a certain critical elasticity, technically known as the point of 'unit elasticity', Nottinghamshire's sterling earnings would actually fall, the increase in the volume of exports being insufficient to compensate for the reduction in their sterling prices. In such circumstances, it would be best for the Nottinghamshire authorities to tackle an unfavourable balance of current payments not by attempting to stimulate exports by devaluation (or other means), since this would merely represent so much wasted effort, but to concentrate on reducing imports, for example by imposing restrictions on imports or on current payments.

The incentive to impose restrictions, rather than to devalue, would still be present (though not quite so strong) if the demand for Nottinghamshire's exports were of more than unit elasticity, but not much more, that is, if devaluation would have increased Nottinghamshire's sterling earnings but not by very much. For if (to give a hypothetical example) the conditions of export demand were such that a 10 per cent reduction in the sterling prices of Nottinghamshire's exports would cause an increase of only 12 per cent in the quantity bought, and therefore an increase of less than 1 per cent in the total sterling value of Nottinghamshire's exports,[1] it might well be thought that the extra sterling earned by an increase in export production provided an inadequate return for the extra effort involved—so that it would still be advantageous to deal with external deficit solely by reducing imports.[2]

The advantage to be gained by resorting to restrictions, rather than to devaluation, when the elasticity of demand for exports is low, is not very great when circumstances are such that imports are rapidly choked off by devaluation, for then a comparatively small devaluation will do the trick and the amount of 'wasted effort' in export production will not be serious. If however imports do not readily respond to devaluation, a low elasticity of demand for exports is a strong argument for preferring restrictions to devaluation.

Factors affecting the elasticity of demand for exports

Let us now abandon our imaginary 'independent' Nottinghamshire and consider as realistically as possible the conditions which determine the elasticity of demand for an economy's exports. The elasticity of demand for our country's exports depends on (1) the elasticity of demand for imports by the various foreign countries which buy our exports, (2) the importance of the home country as an exporter, compared with rival countries exporting the same kind of goods as we do and (3) the extent to which our rivals

---

[1] If prices change in the ratio of 100:90 and quantity bought in the ratio of 100:112, total value will change in the ratio of $100 \times 100 : 90 \times 112$ or $100 : 100.8$.

[2] In technical terms this proposition would be translated thus: Nottinghamshire might consider that the advantage of the greater *volume* of external trade achieved by devaluation would be more than counterbalanced by the simultaneous adverse change in her *terms* of trade (an economy's terms of trade being the ratio of its export prices to its import prices).

retaliate against a cut in our export prices by cutting theirs too, for instance by following our example and devaluing their currencies.

(1) What might prevent our foreign customers from buying more imports when we reduce our prices, measured in foreign currencies? The most serious obstacle is the use of drastic official restrictions on imports.

The reason why drastic official restrictions operate to reduce the responsiveness of consumers in the importing countries to any reduction in the prices of our exports is clear enough when the restrictions take the form of quotas, exchange rationing or outright prohibitions, for here the importer is presented with a rigid ceiling to the volume or value of his turnover. The reason is also apparent in the case of specific tariffs,[1] since a duty of so much per ton means that a cut of x per cent in the price of imports net of duty causes a cut of less than x per cent in the price gross of duty, so that the final consumer has so much less incentive to increase his purchases. *Ad valorem* duties are less objectionable than other types of restrictions, in that a cut of x per cent in the price of imports net of duty does in this case allow a cut of x per cent in the price gross of duty. But even in this case it would seem that a country with a high *ad valorem* tariff on an extensive range of commodities may thereby have, on the average, a low elasticity of demand for imports. For the effect of the tariff may be to distort the composition of the country's imports, by causing a complete exclusion of many commodities in highly elastic demand. *Ad valorem* tariffs are also just as restrictive as other restrictions where (as sometimes happens) the tariff-making body makes a practice of stepping up the tariff whenever it proves to be incompletely restrictive. It would seem then that all official restrictions are obnoxious from the point of view we are now considering, but some are more obnoxious than others, the least obnoxious kind being the *ad valorem* tariff.

It is of course true that in a restrictionist world international disequilibria could be corrected by a reduction in the restrictions imposed by the surplus countries rather than by an increase in those imposed by the deficit countries. Unfortunately, however, though deficit countries are sooner or later compelled, by the fear of exhausting their liquidity, to attempt to deal with a persistent disequilibrium, surplus countries are under no such compulsion, and therefore tend in practice to leave on the deficit countries the

[1] A specific tariff is a levy of so much money per physical unit of the goods imported, an *ad valorem* tariff is a percentage levy on the value of the goods imported.

onus of making the necessary adjustments. This at any rate is what tends to happen if there are no deliberate attempts at international cooperation.

(2) We must now take into account the fact that our country may still enjoy a highly elastic demand for exports, even if each of our customers has an inelastic demand for imports, provided that a reduction in our export prices would enable us readily to undercut our rival suppliers in the export markets. This situation would arise only if our country contributes only a small proportion of the world total of exports of each of the commodities she exports. If, for example, our country is an exporter of (let us say) coal, but in small quantities compared with the total coal exports of all countries, a small cut in our export price will probably be sufficient to enable us to undercut our rival exporters to an extent which will represent a large proportionate increase in our export tonnage. We might perhaps double our export tonnage by a (say) 5 per cent reduction in our export price, even if the coal-importing countries had imposed such drastic trade restrictions that the tonnage imported from all sources did not increase at all. If on the other hand our country were the *only* coal exporter, we should have no rival exporters to undercut and a 5 per cent price reduction would decrease our foreign currency earnings unless there followed an increase in total coal imports of over 5 per cent. In general, therefore, countries whose exports are small in amount and widely diversified are likely to experience a much more elastic demand for their exports than are countries whose exports are large in amount and confined to a narrow range of products.

(3) Even when our country would enjoy a highly elastic demand for her exports if we alone reduced our prices (measured in the importing countries' currencies), we may nevertheless effect little or no increase in our export earnings if the action we take to reduce our prices—in this case currency devaluation—is also taken by our rival exporters. If for example Britain devalued her currency in an attempt to sell more exports, she would always have to face the possibility that other exporters of manufactures—for instance Belgium and Germany—would follow suit.

Another consideration which is relevant to the elasticity of the demand for our country's exports is the period which is allowed for the adjustment of demand to occur. For example, a 5 per cent cut in our export prices, taking effect as from (say) January, would almost certainly be less effective in increasing the volume of our exports in the following month than in increasing it in the following January, simply because it would take time for the purchasers of our goods in the importing countries to change their trading arrangements so as to take advantage of our lower prices. This delay in the reaction on the part of our customers would be longest if we specialised in the export of finished goods, particularly manufactured articles, rather than of primary commodities. The purchaser of almost any kind of manufactured article tends to be loyal to the brand, or the design, or the producing firm, with which he is already familiar, and in consequence he is not readily induced to transfer quickly his allegiance to another source of supply merely by the quotation of a lower price. For this reason the countries specialising in the export of manufactured articles (Britain, for example) are almost certainly faced with a relatively low short-term elasticity of demand for their exports, and when the other relevant conditions (e.g. the trade restrictions of customers' countries) are also such as to make for a low elasticity, then demand in the short term may well be of less than unit elasticity. It is for example possible that a country such as Britain would in the short run reduce, rather than increase, her foreign currency earnings by a reduction in the foreign-currency prices of her exports[1] even though in the longer run earnings would recover and in due course appreciably surpass their original level. This line of argument is undoubtedly supported by the course of events following the devaluation of sterling from $2.8 to $2.4 in November 1967. (Admittedly, as we shall see in Chapter 18, the argument is not supported by the course of events immediately after the British devaluation in September 1949, when British export earnings *quickly* increased, but this outcome can reasonably be attributed to speculation and other factors which we have not so far taken into account.)

Summary and conclusions

It may be useful to summarise our arguments as to the efficacy of devaluation (and incidentally of other forms of currency deprecia-tion[2]) by listing as follows the circumstances in which it is unlikely

[1] If Britain allowed sterling to depreciate and thereby brought about a reduction in the foreign-currency prices of British exports, it is conceivable that the short-term reduction in her foreign-currency earnings might be greater than the short-term reduction in her foreign-currency expenditure on imports (induced by the rise in the sterling prices of imports). In this case the short-term effect of depreciation would be not to cure an external deficit but to aggravate it.
[2] The term 'devaluation' is usually reserved for those cases of currency depreciation where, as we have assumed in our examples, the value of the currency is stabilised by official intervention both before and after the depreciation.

to appear attractive as a means for improving a country's balance of current payments[1]

(1) Devaluation is ineffective in so far as the competitive advantage it affords our producers is offset by a rise in the home-currency prices of our goods. Such a rise in our prices may arise from the pressure of excess demand in our home economy, or through the inflexibility of the home economy, or again from the operation of the wage-price spiral.

(2) If, however, our devaluation would not be rendered ineffective for these reasons, so that our supply of exports could be increased without a serious rise in their home-currency prices, the case for devaluation as against restrictions turns on the elasticity of demand for our exports. For devaluation imposes an entirely fruitless burden on our export industries if the demand for our exports has less than unit elasticity and a largely fruitless burden if the elasticity is not much greater than unity. The elasticity of the demand for our exports depends partly on our ability to under-cut our competitors, but (especially if we take account of the possibility of retaliation) it is unlikely to be very high if other countries do not permit their imports to increase when these become cheaper in terms of their own currencies. The main reason why our customer-countries should not take more imports when they become cheaper is the existence of official restrictions.

(3) There is in the short run the additional complication that the elasticity of demand for exported *finished* goods (particularly manufactured articles) is liable to be low, due to the loyalty of the consumer to the brand, design or producing firm with which he is already familiar. For this reason devaluation may appear an unsatisfactory remedy to a country when balance of payments difficulties call for (as in practice they frequently do) a *quick* remedy.

If it is conceded that in certain circumstances international disequilibria may be dealt with by the deficit countries imposing restrictions, rather than by a change of exchange rates, it is preferable that the restrictions imposed by the deficit-countries should be discriminatory, in the sense of being directed against the main surplus countries. In so far as deficit countries impose restrictions directed against each other they merely harm each

[1] It must not be concluded from the foregoing that all arguments for and against devaluation rest exclusively on its effect on a country's balance of current payments, since devaluation may have substantial effects on the capital (as well as on the current) items of a country's balance of payments. Some of these effects will be considered in Chapters 14 and 18.

other, without in any way correcting the original disequilibria.[1] It is however unhappily a feature of multilateral means of international settlement (so admirable in other respects) that they provide an incentive for indiscriminate restrictions, since if country A can by means of new restrictions push B into deficit, A will thereby obtain the means of settling part of her own deficit with C, the original surplus country. However, as we have seen, persistent disequilibria tend to undermine the basis of multilateral settlement by leading to the emergence of hard and soft currencies, and this development, in a very rough and ready fashion, calls forth the kind of discrimination that the disequilibrium requires.

It will by now be clear that the scope for international action designed to deal with persistent international disequilibria is very extensive. First, there is the need for agreement to make reciprocal reductions in restrictions on international trade and on international payments. Such measures not only allow each country to obtain greater benefit from its comparative advantages in different fields of industry but also improve the efficacy of variations in exchange rates as a means for correcting persistent disequilibria. Second, in so far as restrictions still need to be used for dealing with disequilibria, surplus countries must be persuaded that the correction can be better made by them reducing their restrictions than by deficit countries imposing additional restrictions. Third, if restrictions do have to be imposed by deficit countries, such countries must be permitted to discriminate against countries in serious and persistent surplus. Finally, in so far as use is made of Bank Rate to combat disequilibrating capital movements (see the final section of this chapter and the appendix which follows it), international agreement is desirable to avoid a competitive bidding up of interest rates (such as actually took place in the course of the year 1966[2]).

---

[1] If the deficit countries had chosen to cure their deficits by devaluation and had all devalued by the same percentage, the relative values of their currencies would have remained unchanged, and trade between them would not have suffered any reduction.

[2] Hence the meeting at Chequers on 21 January 1967, of the finance ministers of the USA, the UK, Germany, France and Italy to 'agree to cooperate on lower interest rates'. See *Financial Times*, 23 January 1967. However the consequences of this cooperation were short lived, and the competitive spiral of interest rates resumed its course later in 1967. In January 1970, Professor Karl Schiller, the West German Economics Minister, announced his intention to seek an international conference of the most important Western countries with the aim of reaching agreement on bringing down interest rates. See *Financial Times*, 23 January 1970.

The concept of 'suppressed disequilibrium'

There remains to be considered an important question of terminology. So far we have described a country as being 'in disequilibrium' only when it has an overall deficit or surplus. We have now to recognise that the same term is sometimes used in a wider sense, to include what might be termed 'suppressed' disequilibria as well as the 'open' disequilibria of overall surpluses and deficits. The notion of a suppressed disequilibrium is based in effect on the acceptance of a distinction between 'satisfactory' and 'unsatisfactory' ways of dealing with an open disequilibrium. If an open disequilibrium is eliminated by a satisfactory means, it is taken to be cured, but if it is eliminated by an unsatisfactory means it is merely 'suppressed'. Unfortunately the criteria by which satisfactory treatments can be distinguished from unsatisfactory ones are rarely made explicit, but the most plausible interpretation of the distinction is that unsatisfactory treatments comprise:

(1) a serious increase in unemployment in the deficit countries.

(2) the imposition by the deficit countries of additional restrictions on international trade[1] or on international payments on current (as distinct from capital) account.

On this basis, satisfactory treatments would include adjustments of exchange rates, a reduction in the restrictions imposed by surplus countries, the adoption of measures (e.g. exchange control or a change in Bank Rate) to influence capital movements, and finally a curbing of demand in the deficit countries sufficient to stabilise, or even to depress, the prices of their products. (However, a curbing of demand sufficient to depress, and not merely to stabilise, the prices of the deficit countries' products can perhaps claim to be 'satisfactory' only when prices have actually been reduced to the required extent, for the process of reduction may cause much more social discord and hardship than the other 'satisfactory' treatments.)

Unfortunately the concept of suppressed disequilibria, though useful for theoretical analysis, is difficult to apply in practice. Who shall say, in respect of any country suffering unemployment,

---

[1] The following excerpt from Article 21, paragraph 6 of the ITO Agreement (see Chapter 8 below) illustrates the use of the word 'disequilibrium' to mean 'suppressed disequilibrium':

'If there is a persistent and widespread application of import restrictions under this Article, indicating the existence of a general disequilibrium which is restricting international trade, . . .'

I.M.C.—C

how much of its unemployment can be attributed to the need for reducing, or eliminating, an external deficit, and how much is attributable to other factors? Happily this awkward conundrum has not given much trouble in the post-war period, for serious unemployment has been rare.[1] There is also a practical problem in identifying suppressed disequilibrium in the form of restrictions on trade or on current payments, for such restrictions are also used for purposes other than preventing deficits, and it may be difficult to distinguish an unambiguous purpose behind any particular set of restrictions.[2]

Bank Rate and capital movements

Thus far in this chapter I have said little about international transactions on *capital* account, except to point out that, though such transactions are an important part of the adjustment process as between different counties, they are much less so as between different countries. However, in circumstances where exchange rates are stable, and are confidently expected to remain so, and when exchange control is not only absent but unthinkable, then capital movements can make a useful contribution to international adjustment. Unfortunately in the post-war world circumstances have usually been quite otherwise and though (as I explain in the appendix which follows) attempts have been made, by official intervention in the forward exchange market, to make capital movements less *dis*equilibrating, I do not believe that such movements can reasonably be represented, in the circumstances of the post-war world, as playing a positive part in the adjustment process.

Under the regime of the nineteenth-century gold standard, circumstances were much more favourable, and there can be no doubt that Britain was then able, when in balance-of-payments deficit, to rely on compensatory movements of private short-term capital. Such movements were encouraged by raising Bank Rate, which raised the level of short-term interest rates prevailing in London and hence made London a relatively more attractive home for mobile capital. In the period since the first world war, except perhaps to a very limited extent in the 1920s, this traditional device for equilibrating our balance of payments has not been effective, and other countries' experience has not been conspicuously more favourable. The most that can be said is that

[1] See below, Part III.
[2] See below, pp. 226–7.

disequilibrating capital movements have sometimes, and to a limited degree, been mitigated by a timely increase of interest rates in the deficit countries or by a timely decrease in the surplus countries, or by a combination of both. But even then, the success of such measures has usually depended on their being backed up by appropriate official intervention in the forward exchange market, as will be explained in the Appendix below.

A more widely used device for influencing capital movements in the post-war period has been that of exchange controls on capital movements. In particular, such controls have been imposed by the UK ever since the outbreak of war in 1939. Nor has Britain been very unusual in this respect: except for North America the control of capital movements was fairly general in the earlier part of the post-war period and has been progressively relaxed (with occasional backsliding) by the countries of Continental Europe only in the period since 1959. This same period has however seen the imposition of US exchange controls on capital movements, as will be explained in Chapter 16.

However, the controls imposed have always been less strict *de facto* than *de jure*, since they are extremely difficult to enforce, especially in so far as they apply to non-residents. Some of the difficulties encountered in enforcing the controls on sterling are considered in Chapter 14.

APPENDIX

Official intervention in the forward market

As we have just seen, the traditional weapon for preventing an outflow of capital from London, and indeed for inducing an inflow, was to raise Bank Rate, which raised the level of short-term interest rates prevailing in London and hence made London a relatively more attractive home for mobile capital. But, as the Radcliffe Committee reported in 1959: 'The general tenor of the evidence submitted to us was that in post-war conditions no large-scale transference of funds was to be expected in response to changes in short-term interest rates unsupported by other measures. Two important influences limiting this response have been the fear of official interference with the movement of funds and fear of depreciation of sterling.' The consequence of these fears was that 'such movement of funds as there has been has almost always, at least until lately, been covered in the forward market; that is to say, the foreign holder of sterling has generally taken the precaution of selling it forward at a discount so as to avoid any larger loss through a possible devaluation of the pound'.[1]

If however all owners of mobile funds are prepared to invest in London only on such a covered basis, the outcome will be, in the absence of official intervention in the forward market, a rapid fall in the forward value of sterling to the point where the discount on forward sterling will counterbalance the extra interest to be earned in London, and once this has happened the profitability of *covered* investment in London will no longer be greater than investment elsewhere. The monetary authorities can maintain the attractiveness of London only by supporting the forward pound, i.e. by contracting to buy pounds with dollars (or other foreign currencies) at some agreed date in the future (say three months hence), but this leaves the Exchange Equalisation Account with a short (i.e. oversold) position on forward dollars. Hence the conclusion of the Radcliffe Committee (in paragraph 439 of the Report) that 'a real strengthening of Britain's international balance sheet occurs only if lenders are not universally covering themselves by hedging in the forward exchange market'. However, this generalisation is perhaps rather too sweeping, as the Report itself implies in a later paragraph:[2] though the attraction of volatile or speculative funds to London (whether by a high Bank Rate or by officially supporting the forward price of sterling) does not result in a real strengthening of Britain's international balance sheet, the attraction into sterling securities (even short-term ones) of foreign funds which will remain thus invested for a period of months or years is surely not open to the same objection. Hence, if the official support of forward sterling is expected to attract a reasonably loyal clientele of foreign investors, there is surely a case for providing such official support. Unfortunately, however (as we saw in the Appendix to Chapter 2 on page 35), the official support of forward sterling also serves to facilitate the bear speculation which always occurs when a devaluation of sterling is thought to be imminent.

[1] Both quotations are from paragraph 697 of the Radcliffe Report.
[2] 'While operations in the forward exchange market would not be an effective method of countering speculation against the pound, they could play an important part at times when there was confidence in the pound and a divergence between interest rates abroad and in the United Kingdom. Under such conditions there might be good reasons why interest rates should not be brought into line with those in foreign centres; and it would be easier to maintain the divergence without giving rise to a movement of funds if the authorities could maintain an appropriate premium or discount in the forward market.' (Radcliffe Report, para. 707.)

The Radcliffe Committee's views about official intervention in the forward market led them to conclude: 'we see no reason why the authorities should refrain from supporting the forward rate when they see fit: the Exchange Equalisation Account does in fact participate in the market'. It would appear, however, that official participation was on a small scale up to the time of the prolonged sterling crisis which began in the last quarter of 1964. Thereafter, however, until the devaluation of sterling on 18 November 1967, the Account intervened so as to prevent the forward rate falling to a serious discount, and the intervention is believed to have been on some occasions on a massive scale. Unfortunately a policy originally adopted mainly with the object of retaining a loyal clientele of foreign investors ended up, in the weeks immediately preceding devaluation, by affording almost unlimited opportunities for bear speculation, so that after the sterling spot rate had been reduced to $2.4 on 18 November, the Account found itself committed by outstanding forward contracts to the purchase of large amounts of sterling at a price near to the old parity of $2.8 per pound. After devaluation, the Account apparently reverted to its earlier policy of severely limiting its intervention in the forward market.[1]

Other countries, including the United States, have also on occasions in the post-war period intervened in the forward exchange market with the object of reducing the forward discount on their currencies, and of thereby retaining internationally mobile capital which might otherwise have moved to other centres.

Yet other countries, for example Germany and Italy, have on occasions intervened in the forward market in the opposite sense, i.e., to prevent a forward premium on their national currencies in relation to the dollar. The motives for such interventions have been various, but usually have been related to the objective of inducing the local banking system to lend less freely in the home currency.[2]

---

[1] Bank of England, *Quarterly Bulletin*, March 1970, p. 39.
[2] On this see Arthur L. Bloomfield, 'Official Intervention in the Forward Exchange Market: Some Recent Experiences', in the March 1964 issue of the *Quarterly Review* of the Banca Nazionale del Lavoro. For more up to date information about US forward operations, see the article on 'Treasury and Federal Reserve Foreign Exchange Operations', in the *Federal Reserve Bulletin*, March 1969, p. 210, and corresponding articles in the March issue in previous years.

5

THE INTERNATIONAL TRANSMISSION OF

DEPRESSIONS

Depressions may be transmitted from one country to others in the following ways:

(1) A certain country, A, develops a business depression, due to a recession of home demand. In consequence A's imports of goods from the rest of the world fall off, and her depression thus spreads spontaneously to other countries.

(2) Country A may then attempt to restore her own prosperity by imposing trade or payments restrictions, or depreciating her currency, with the object of diverting home demand from imported to home-produced goods or of stimulating exports (or of doing both). Since one country's imports are another's exports, such a policy, if successful, must reduce the level of demand in other countries; hence it is a 'beggar-my-neighbour' remedy for unemployment.[1]

A large reduction in A's imports (whether due to a recession in A's home demand or to A's adoption of beggar-my-neighbour remedies for her unemployment) may undermine not merely her neighbours' prosperity but also their liquidity, for such an improvement in A's balance of external trade cuts down her neighbours' supply of the means of settling their accounts with A. On the other hand, in so far as A inflicts depression on her neighbours they will normally not wish to import so much from A, which tends to relieve the drain on their means of settling with A. On balance, therefore, the drain of means of settlement to A

---

[1] See Joan Robinson: *Essays in the Theory of Employment*, p. 210.

from her neighbours may not be serious[1]—provided that A's neighbours take no steps to offset the decline in their prosperity.[2] But if they do attempt to restore their prosperity, and elect to do so by stimulating their home demand (for example by increasing expenditure on public works), this will tend to reverse the decline in their imports from A, and consequently in their payments to A. Thus even if the *immediate* problem which besets A's neighbours is solely that of depression, without serious loss of liquidity, there is still the possibility that the problem of illiquidity may arise when action is under consideration for combating the depression.

As we have seen, the problem of depression may arise among A's neighbours either because of the spontaneous spread of a depression originating in A or because A has adopted beggar-my-neighbour remedies for her unemployment. Beggar-my-neighbour remedies for unemployment are not quite as harmful to other countries as it might at first appear, for in so far as they are successful in restoring prosperity in the country adopting them they will reverse the fall in her imports attributable to the depression (though they will not of course reverse such improvement in her balance of current payments as is due to the imposition of restrictions or to the depreciation of her currency). Nevertheless, beggaring one's neighbours remains reprehensible, even though they are not beggared quite as badly as might at first seem to be the case.

The spontaneous spreading of depression from one country to another raises rather more complicated issues of international morality. What is liable to happen in practice is that the 'victim' countries attempt to insulate themselves by taking steps to cut down their imports more or less in line with the decline in their exports. In this way they hope to balance the reduction in the export demand for their goods by a diversion of internal demand from imported to home-produced goods, thereby restoring their prosperity without however imposing any additional strain on their liquidity. But if A's neighbours react in this way, there will be unfortunate consequences. First, if they reduce their imports by means of additional restrictions and not by currency depreciation, there is a danger (as we have seen) that the restrictions may be imposed without discrimination against A, in which case the

---

[1] This is particularly true if A has previously been running an external deficit, or if her neighbours hold substantial reserves of suitable means of settlement.
[2] See above, p. 55.

victim countries will quite unnecessarily harm each other. (This would not happen if the victim countries all depreciated their currencies by the same percentage in relation to A's currency, so that the *relative* values of their own currencies remained unchanged.[1]) Second, any restrictions imposed on such an occasion create a permanent vested interest in favour of their indefinite retention, long after the original reason for them has passed away. Third, in so far as the victim countries reduce their imports from A, whether by imposing restrictions or by currency depreciation, this will aggravate A's depression; A may consider this an unfriendly act and attempt to retaliate.

It is difficult to resist the conclusion that A's neighbours should tolerate the import of unemployment and attempt to combat it by an increase, not simply a diversion, of their internal demand; in this way they would alleviate, instead of aggravate, A's misfortune. If, however, they adopted such a policy this would tend to deplete their means of settlement with A. A could of course assist by providing her good neighbours with additional means of settlement, for instance by extending to them additional drawing rights in the form of official grants or loans, but even so the flow of settlements to A from her neighbours could not go on indefinitely. What therefore A's neighbours would have to demand of A, in return for their adoption of a policy of stimulating the level of internal demand in their own economies, is that A in turn should make prompt and strenuous efforts to stimulate her own internal demand, and thereby deal effectively with the root cause of all the trouble.

The scope for coordinated international action against business depressions is thus seen to be extensive. The following list of possibilities is derived mainly from two post-war international reports on the subject of unemployment:[2]

(1) There should be agreement to outlaw beggar-my-neighbour remedies for unemployment.

(2) Each country should prepare in advance domestic measures which would come into operation at the onset of a depression.

---

[1] See footnote 1 on p. 64.

[2] *National and International Measures for Full Employment*, a report presented in 1949 by a group of experts to the Secretary-General of the United Nations, and *Action against Unemployment*, a study published in 1950 by the International Labour Office.

The detailed recommendations of these reports are well worthy of study but must be regarded as controversial.

(3) International arrangements should be made to restore the liquidity of victim countries.

(4) Reassured by these arrangements, countries which fear the possibility of contagion from external depression might be both able and willing to forgo the practice of insulation.

(5) Lastly, there might be international action to assist the depressed country in taking measures to stimulate her internal demand.[1]

It may be wondered why, with such widespread concern at the phenomenon of the international transmission of depressions, there should be so little interest in the contrary phenomenon of the international transmission of inflation, for an inflation in one country spreads to its neighbours in exactly the same way as a depression.[2] This relative lack of interest can be attributed to the following factors. First, in a situation where most countries are depressed (even though only mildly) the occurrence of inflation in one country, or several countries, is beneficial to the rest of the world. Only in a situation of world-wide full employment (whether of labour or of productive capacity) is inflation in one country a cause for misgivings among its neighbours. Second, if a country is experiencing an inflation, the rest of the world gains, rather than loses, in liquidity, so here again there is usually no cause for complaint.[3]

Nevertheless, it may be that too little attention has been paid to the international propagation of inflation. With so many governments committed, not only to full employment policies as such, but also to ambitious social and defence policies whose net effect is inevitably to increase demand, it seems likely that inflationary tendencies are here to stay, and that the periodic recessions of demand which characterised all capitalist economies prior to the second world war will henceforth occur only rarely and even then in only a comparatively mild form.

Countries suffering from excess demand may adopt remedies (e.g. currency appreciation or restriction on exports) aimed at reducing exports, stimulating imports, or a combination of both, so as to provide their home market with more goods on which their excessive home demand can expend itself. Examples of such

---

[1] See *Action against Unemployment*, Chapter VIII.
[2] The IMF has been greatly concerned with problems of inflation (see Chapter 8) but in another context, namely as a cause of external disequilibria.
[3] Admittedly there have from time to time in the 1960s been complaints by certain European countries, particularly by France, about the increase in their reserves which has occurred as the counterpart of the US deficit. However, this particular deficit cannot in most of the period be attributed to inflation in the US economy.

policies are to be found in the post-war period[1] and, though they have usually been kept in check by the need to moderate the resulting depletion of official reserves, they could in conceivable circumstances prove an embarrassment to neighbours who were also struggling to combat inflation in their own economies.

[1] See below, pp. 220–1 and 232.

Part II

The machinery of international monetary cooperation

6

GENERAL SURVEY

Most of the possibilities for international monetary cooperation which were noted in Part I have been exploited, though with varying degrees of success, by the statesmen and officials who have had responsibility for international economic affairs in the period since the second world war. The form which cooperation has taken has been different in different cases. In some cases it has been bilateral, in others multilateral; in some cases it has been *ad hoc*, in others institutionalised in some continuing international agency such as the International Monetary Fund; in some cases it has amounted to mere consultation, in others it has taken the form of treaties or agreements, such as the Articles of Agreement of the International Monetary Fund. The most advanced kind of cooperation in this period is to be found in the field of international liquidity arrangements, where international institutions have been established (again the IMF is a good example) for undertaking financial transactions on a large scale. Let us look briefly at how cooperation has in fact been achieved in the various fields we have already noted.

Exchange rates

In the field of exchange rates, the IMF's Charter (the Articles of Agreement) lays down the post-war rules of the game and gives the Fund the task of enforcing them, so that virtually the whole story will be told in the chapter concerned with the Fund's activities in this field (Chapter 7).

The adjustment process

As regards the adjustment process, an important part of the story is of course subsumed under 'exchange rates', since changes in exchange rates are an important device for achieving adjustment. The only other aspect of the adjustment mechanism which has given rise to intensive international cooperation in the post-war period has been concerned with the rules of the game for recourse to restrictions on payments and trade by countries in balance of payments difficulties. Here the main responsibility has rested on the IMF in respect of payments restrictions and on the GATT[1] in respect of trade restrictions (see Chapter 8) though in Western Europe the Trade Liberalisation activities of the OEEC[2] were in part of the post-war period of great importance. Other devices for facilitating adjustment (for example, variation in interest rates, and fiscal and monetary policies designed to influence the pressure of effective demand) have been the object of international cooperation, especially since the establishment in 1961 of the OECD,[3] but so far such cooperation has not progressed beyond 'multilateral surveillance', which, in the jargon of today, means close consultation and examination of statistics. The one case where the frontiers of mere consultation may possibly have been transgressed arises as a by-product of the financial transactions of the IMF: a country proposing to make substantial use of its drawing rights on the Fund (as for instance the UK in 1969) is asked for a Letter of Intent, specifying the remedial policies she intends to adopt to reduce her external deficit, and may in addition be required to adhere to certain performance criteria.[4]

The international transmission of depressions

As regards international cooperation to prevent the spreading of depressions from one country to another, there was at one time a proposal to incorporate agreed rules of the game in the GATT Charter, but in fact no action was taken (below, page 106). Such cooperation as has in fact occurred has taken the form of multilateral consultation, mainly between the members of the OECD or within the more intimate forum of the European Economic Community (below, Chapter 12). But little cooperation has in fact

[1] General Agreement for Tariffs and Trade.
[2] Organisation for European Economic Cooperation (see Chapter 12).
[3] The Organisation for Economic Cooperation and Development, the successor to the OEEC. See below, p. 162.
[4] Below, p. 117.

been called for in this field in the highly prosperous post-war world, which has never been seriously threatened with the evil of widespread unemployment. Indeed the problem of the post-war world has usually been excessive demand, not inadequate demand, and much of the international consultation, in the OECD and elsewhere, to which reference was made in the preceding paragraph, has centred on the need for countries in external deficit to moderate the excessive pressure of their inhabitants' demand for goods and services.

International liquidity

On the eve of the second world war, international liquidity took almost exclusively the form of the reserve assets held by central banks (or exchange equalisation accounts) and with these assets taking the form of gold, US dollars and sterling. The only international institution concerned with liquidity arrangements was the Bank for International Settlements, set up in Basle in 1930 as the result of the same conference at The Hague which drew up the Young Plan for dealing with German reparations: however, this institution had (after a very promising start) lapsed into virtual inactivity following the financial débâcle of 1931.

These liquidity arrangements of the late 1930s continued in the post-war period but were backed by new devices which supplemented the owned reserve assets of the three traditional kinds with new arrangements for borrowed reserves, drawing rights and other facilities. Such facilities were sometimes ad hoc and bilateral, but more frequently they were institutionalised. Much the most important institution for the provision of liquidity came to be the IMF, which began to do business in 1947, though on a modest scale until 1956. In the 1950s, however, there were important, though short-lived, Western European arrangements, notably the Intra-European Payments Schemes (Chapter 11) and the European Payments Union (Chapter 12).

The Bank for International Settlements also staged a spectacular recovery. It acted as Agent for the West European arrangements I have just mentioned. Its monthly meetings at Basle[1] also provided an occasion for the Governors of the central banks of the larger West European countries and of the United States to consult on

---

[1] The countries represented on the BIS Board of Directors were the UK, France, Germany, Italy, Belgium, the Netherlands, Sweden and Switzerland, but in the 1960s other countries (the United States since 1961 and more recently Japan and Canada) have participated in the informal discussions which are always held on the same day as the Board meetings.

matters of common interest and (in the 1960s) to concoct rescue operations (particularly for the lira, the pound, and later the French franc) which in due course came to be known as Basle-type operations.[1] Finally, the banking business of the BIS also began to thrive. The intention of the founders of the BIS was that it should be a bank for central banks, accepting deposits, making advances, discounting bills, exchanging currencies and indeed undertaking all kinds of banking business—but with a clientele limited to central banks, especially those in Europe and North America. After a promising start in 1930, this banking business later dwindled as a consequence of the 1931 financial débâcle, and did not begin to recover until the 1950s. By 1960 the balance-sheet total of the BIS had reached the equivalent of nearly $1,000 million: by 1970 it had grown to about $6,900 million. The development of the Euro-dollar market (see Chapter 16) has opened up new opportunities for the BIS: in recent years it has operated extensively in this market, both on its own account and also as a kind of open-market manager on behalf of various central banks. It is a sign of the growing importance of the BIS as a bank that it participated as a principal in most of the 'Basle-type' operations of the 1960s, as well as providing the forum in which they were negotiated.[2]

Sub-divisions of the post-war period

Part III of this book provides a brief historical narrative of the post-war period, but it may none the less be helpful at this stage to have an even briefer note of the various phases through which international monetary arrangements have passed since the end of the second world war.

Phase One, corresponding very roughly to the second half of the 1940s, may be called the bilateral phase, in that it was in these years that an impoverished and devastated Europe improvised international settlement arrangements on a largely bilateral basis (Chapter 11) and during which the UK, despite a premature dash to convertibility in July 1947, was obliged to conduct sterling settlements, outside the Sterling and Dollar Areas, mainly on the basis of bilateral monetary agreements. Within the Sterling and Dollar Areas, multilateral settlement obtained, but strict exchange controls regulated payments from the former area to the latter.

[1] See Chapters 15 and 21. On the role of the BIS in providing facilities for discussions and negotiations between central banks, see the interview with its General Manager, M. Gabriel Ferras, in *The Banker*, September 1966.
[2] See BIS, *39th Annual Report*, 1969, p. 164 et seq. and the *40th Report*, 1969, p. 171 et seq.

Phase Two, corresponding, again very roughly, to the 1950s, may be called the two-area phase, in that what had previously been the area of bilateral settlements coalesced with the Sterling Area to form a single area, which we may call the 'soft-settlement' area, within which multilateral settlement proceeded without much interference from exchange controls, at any rate on current transactions, but which was partially sealed off from the Dollar Area (or 'hard-settlement' area) by restrictions on payments and trade. Within the latter area international settlement and liquidity were based on gold and the US dollar, the two media being mutually convertible by virtue of the willingness of the US authorities to deal in gold (with other central banks) at a fixed price of $35 an ounce. In this Area sterling was also in use, but only in the form of so-called 'American Account' sterling, which was as far as possible[1] segregated from other sterling by the regulations enforced by the sterling area exchange controls.

Within the soft-settlement area, settlements and liquidity were based on sterling (other than American Account sterling) and on the European Payments Union.[2] Gold and US dollars were used as sparingly as possible for settlements within the area, since countries within the area naturally preferred to retain them for the purpose of settling their debts with the hard-settlement area. Moreover, in order to conserve their exiguous supplies of gold and dollars, countries in the soft-settlement area imposed severe discriminating restrictions on their imports from the hard-settlement area and resorted to such devices as dollar retention quotas.[3] Despite all these and other devices, the soft-settlement area, taken as a whole, was until the early fifties in enormous deficit with the hard-settlement area, this deficit being financed, *inter alia*, by a running down of gold and dollar reserves in the former area and by American aid in various forms, especially Marshall Aid.

Phase Three of the post-war period, which may very roughly identify with the 1960s, is the post-convertibility phase. Though sterling had been de facto convertible since 1955,[4] neither the UK nor the other major European countries undertook any commitment to convertibility until December 1958,[5] and most of them delayed the commitment to Article VIII in the Fund until

[1] In practice there developed from time to time serious 'leaks' and 'black markets', as will be explained in Chapter 14.
[2] Below, Chapter 12.
[3] Below, p. 95.
[4] Below, p. 187.
[5] Below, p. 187.

February 1961,[1] by which time discriminatory import and payments restrictions and dollar retention quotas had virtually disappeared.

The characteristic feature of Phase Three is that the world became united in a single settlement area. The US dollar's official value in terms of gold was maintained at $35 an ounce, and sterling and most other major currencies became convertible (at any rate for non-residents) into US dollars. The various brands of non-resident sterling were assimilated into one and given the same privileges as had previously been enjoyed only by American Account sterling. The EPU was wound up.

The transition from Phase Two to Phase Three was made possible only because the major disequilibrium which came to be called the 'dollar shortage' or 'dollar gap' was reduced and eventually closed, *inter alia*, by the landslide of devaluations precipitated by the devaluation of sterling in September 1949.[2] Nevertheless other disequilibria emerged which were a constant threat to convertibility. In the first place, the chronic weakness of the British balance of payments from 1955 onwards meant that the convertibility of sterling into dollars was rarely completely above suspicion. A series of rescue operations, beginning with a substantial drawing on the IMF in 1956, succeeded in maintaining non-resident covertibility at an unchanged parity of $2.8 to the £ until November 1967 when, after two years of recurrent crises, the defenses failed and the exchange rate had to be dropped to $2.4.

In the second place, convertibility in the 1960s was menaced by the fact that the allegedly incurable dollar scarcity of the earlier post-war years gave way to an equally intractable dollar surplus: the large US external surplus of the early post-war years gave place in the late 1950s to a large external deficit. In consequence there was a heavy drain of gold from the US reserves and (as from 1960) an increasing anxiety as to the convertibility of the US dollar into gold at the price of $35 an ounce. A formidable array of devices was mobilised for the defence of the dollar, for example dollar swaps and Roosa bonds.[3] The gold pool was set up to stabilise the price of gold in the free market. Then, when the private demand for gold appeared to be insatiable, the free

[1] Below, p. 101. Commitment to Article VIII submitted a country to a much stricter discipline by the Fund with respect to payments restrictions.
[2] An important impact on the US balance of payments of the 1949 devaluations was the stimulus it gave to US direct investment overseas—in Europe in particular.
[3] Below, pp. 257-8.

market was in March 1968 divorced from the official market, and now (July 1970) seems likely to remain so.[1] The United States government adopted a series of measures (some with the force of law) which amounted to an exchange control on capital trans-actions by residents, as will be explained in Chapter 16.

Guide to subsequent chapters

The main expository problem in describing how international monetary cooperation has actually operated in the post-war period is that some kinds of cooperation have been highly institutional-ised, with substantial powers vested in continuing institutions, whether national or international, while other kinds have been the outcome of relatively informal consultations conducted in what-ever international forum seemed to be most convenient at the time. The former kinds of cooperation are most readily described by recounting the post-war story of each institution in turn, the latter kind by a chronological account of the post-war period, subdivided into convenient sub-periods. My own solution to this expository problem has been to adopt both approaches, the former in Part II and the latter in Part III. Thus the succeeding chapters in Part II give an account (a) of those international agencies which have been formally constituted on the basis of an international charter or agreement, and (b) of the policies of the authorities responsible for the two national currencies in widespread inter-national use throughout the post-war period—sterling and the US dollar. Then in Part III, I give a brief chronological account of the post-war period, incorporating references to the various informal or ad hoc efforts at international cooperation which have taken place with increasing frequency, especially in the 1960s.

[1] Below, p. 255.

7

THE INTERNATIONAL MONETARY FUND

The IMF Agreement is much the most comprehensive inter-national monetary convention ever to be agreed on a world-wide basis, and the IMF itself is much more ambitious in its objectives than any other international monetary institution. In this and the three succeeding chapters, the Fund will be examined with special regard to each of the different fields which have already been noted as offering scope for international cooperation.

The Fund Agreement,[1] which provided for the setting up of the Fund and for its *modus operandi*, was one of two drafted at Bretton Woods in July 1944, the other agreement being concerned with the Fund's sister institution, the International Bank for Reconstruction and Development. The Fund Agreement had already been foreshadowed by the publication in 1943 of the British Keynes Plan[2] and the American White Plan.[3] Neither of these plans was nearly as detailed and comprehensive as the Fund Agreement, but the Keynes Plan made certain proposals, concerning the provision of additional liquidity, which went much beyond the provisions of the original Agreement and which will require special mention.

The Fund commenced operations in March 1947, a few months later than the Bank. The mid-1970 membership numbers 115, the larger members being listed in Table 4. The most important non-

[1] *United Nations Monetary and Financial Conference, held at Bretton Woods.* Cmnd. 6546, 1944.
[2] *Proposals for an International Clearing Union*, Cmnd. 6437, 1943.
[3] *United States Proposal for a United and Associated Nations Stabilisation Fund*, reprinted by HMSO, 1943.

members are the USSR, the European 'Peoples' Democracies' and Switzerland.

The objects of the Fund

The Fund is required by its Charter, the Fund Agreement, to appear in two roles. First, it has to provide its members with a code of international behaviour, and to ensure, so far as possible, that this code is respected. The two subjects with which this code is mainly concerned are *exchange rates*, which I shall treat later in the present chapter, and *the adjustment process* which I shall treat in Chapter 8. (Chapter 8 also includes a short section on *the international transmission of depressions*, dealing with the Fund's attitude to the issues raised in Chapter 5). The second role allotted to the Fund by its Charter is that of an international financial institution for the provision of additional liquidity to its members, for use at times of balance-of-payments difficulties. This financial role of the Fund will be treated in Chapters 9 and 10: the former chapter dealing with the 'General Account', as provided for in the original Charter, the latter dealing with the 'Special Drawing Account' as provided for by additional Articles in the revised Charter of 1969. In addition to playing the roles specifically assigned to it by its Charter, the Fund has also developed as a forum for consultation between members and a source of counsel and technical assistance to under-developed countries.

Structure and management

The Fund is run by a Board of Governors, on which all member countries are represented, a much smaller Executive Board, and an international staff. The Board of Governors, which in practice meets only once a year, in a joint Annual Meeting of the Fund and Bank, is the supreme authority in the Fund, but with the exception of several reserved subjects, for example the admission of members and changes in quotas,[1] it has delegated most of its powers to the Executive Board, and even in the case of the reserved subjects has always followed the latter Board's recommendations.

The Executive Board, whose membership was originally 12 but has now risen to 20, normally consists of five Appointed Directors appointed by the five members with the highest quotas,[2] and

---

[1] The significance of quotas is explained below, p. 107.
[2] Plus the two countries whose currencies have been most drawn in the preceding two years, unless they are already entitled to appoint. By virtue of this provision, Italy at present appoints a director, so that there are six appointed directors in total, and 14 elected directors.

Elected Directors each elected by a group of countries. The Managing Director, who is appointed by the Executive Directors, is Chairman of the Executive Board and chief of the Fund staff.

An important feature of the Fund is that it has to be staffed for the efficient transaction of large and complex financial deals, as well as for reporting on the performance of member countries in the observance of the various 'rules of the game' laid down in the Articles of Agreement and for drafting memoranda on general policy. Hence the secretariat has to include highly qualified specialists in the fields of economics, law, statistics, monetary and fiscal policy and economic forecasting.

Another feature which distinguishes the Fund from most other international organisations is the system of weighted voting. The voting strength wielded by each Governor or Executive Director is based primarily on the quotas of the member or members which appointed or elected him. More precisely, voting is not exactly proportional to quotas, since every member country has 250 votes in addition to one per $100,000 of its quota, and in addition the voting on certain questions is by a slightly different formula,[1] under which the weighting also varies inversely with the Fund's holding of the member's currency (which favours creditor members as against debtor members). But these refinements do not make a great deal of difference: for all practical purposes we may take it that the weighting of votes is approximately proportional to quotas—a system which strongly favours the great powers as against the smaller ones.

The procedures laid down in the Fund's Articles for making decisions allow large numbers of actions to be taken by a member on his own initiative without the requirement of a decision by the Fund. Moreover on two issues the Fund's decision depends *inter alia* on the view of the individual member: any alteration of individual currency parities or of quotas requires the approval of (and in some cases a proposal from) the members concerned. Otherwise, the Fund Articles provide, in almost every case, for decisions to be taken by voting and, except on certain subjects, voting is by majority of votes cast. These subjects are as follows:

(1) Special provisions, invoked for the first time in 1969, govern the procedure for the amendment of the Fund's Articles. A prerequisite to any amendment to the Articles is acceptance by at least three-fifths of the member countries commanding 80 per cent of the voting power.

[1] Article XII, Section 5(b).

(2) A uniform proportionate change in all parities in relation to gold (which affects the Fund's unit of account and may have important financial implications) requires a majority vote (amended in 1969 to a majority of 85 per cent *and* the specific approval of each member having more than 10 per cent of the voting power (which up to the present has meant the United States and Britain).

(3) Quota changes need to be supported by 80 per cent of the voting power (amended to 85 per cent in 1969) and the decision cannot take effect without the approval of the member.

(4) Alterations to the rates of charges under Article V Section 8(e) requires a three-quarters majority.

(5) Publication of a report to a member under Article XII Section 8 ('regarding its monetary or economic conditions and developments which directly tend to produce a serious disequilibrium') requires a two-thirds majority.

(6) Temporary suspension of certain provisions, under Article XVI Section 1(a), requires unanimity and the extension of the suspension under Section 1(c) of the same Article requires a four-fifths majority.

Though the special majorities required in the above circumstances may assume greater significance in the future, especially in view of the increase in 1969 in the majority required under (2) and (3) to 85 per cent (thereby giving the Common Market countries a collective veto) there has been so far 'no strong evidence to show that the requirement of a special majority for certain limited purposes has made any great difference to the work of the Fund'.[1] In fact, virtually all the decisions of the Executive Directors have since 1950 been taken by consensus without a vote, but the nature of the consensus is inevitably influenced to some extent by voting power.[2]

Exchange rates

Article I of the Fund Agreement specifies that one of the purposes of the Fund is 'to promote exchange stability, to maintain orderly exchange arrangements among members, and to avoid competitive exchange depreciation', and Article IV of the Agreement seeks to attain this end by requiring members to agree with the Fund suitable gold par values for their respective currencies, so as to create a system of stable exchange rates with orderly cross rates. The gold par values thus agreed must be observed (with a tolerance of only

[1] Allan G. B. Fisher, in *The Banker*, April 1968, p. 337.
[2] J. Marcus Fleming, *The International Monetary Fund, its Form and Functions*, published by the IMF, 1964, p. 4.

TABLE 4

MEMBERS OF THE IMF IN APRIL 1970, WITH THEIR
RESPECTIVE QUOTAS

(Expressed in millions of US dollars)

Member	Quota	Member	Quota
Algeria	75	Japan	725
Argentina	350	Malaysia	125
Australia	500	Mexico	270
Austria	175	Morocco	90
Belgium	422	Netherlands	520
Brazil	350	New Zealand	157
Canada	740	Nigeria	100
Ceylon	78	Norway	150
Chile	125	Pakistan	188
China	550	Peru	85
Colombia	125	Philippines	110
Congo	90	Portugal	75
Denmark	163	Saudi Arabia	90
Finland	125	Spain	250
France	985	Sweden	225
Germany	1,200	Thailand	95
Greece	100	Turkey	108
India	750	Union of South Africa	200
Indonesia	207	United Arab Republic	150
Iran	125	United Kingdom	2,440
Iraq	80	United States	5,160
Ireland	80	Venezuela	250
Israel	90	Yugoslavia	150
Italy	625	Smaller members[2]	1,526
		Total	21,349

one per cent upwards or downwards[1]) in all spot transactions involving the exchange of one member's currency against another's
or against gold. Countries which have not agreed par values with
the Fund may be denied access to the Fund's resources, and (apart
from a once-and-for-all change of 10 per cent allowed to each
member on his own initiative) all changes in par values require the
Fund's approval. There were, however, in January 1970, twenty-
four countries (of which seventeen were African members) for
whom par values had not yet been agreed, and a number of others
whose par values did not correspond to the exchange rates at which

[1] This provision had to be mildly reinterpreted, so as to facilitate the working of
foreign exchange markets. Below, p. 96.
[2] Members with quotas of under $75 million.

transactions actually take place;[1] while yet other members[2] observed their official parities in respect of certain transactions but also allowed non-parity rates as part of their multiple currency practices. However, the only *developed* member country which has since 1950 appreciably deviated from its obligation to maintain its spot exchange rate close to an agreed parity has been Canada, which has had a fluctuating exchange rate from October 1950 to May 1962 and again as from 1st June, 1970 (see below, pages 239–40).

The Fund does not take 'stability' to mean 'rigidity' of exchange rates, and (as we shall see below) is prepared to admit changes in par values as a means for curing persistent international disequilibria. On the other hand, since each member undertakes to keep the spot value of his currency very close to its par value, any appreciable change in the exchange rate of a currency requires, under the Fund Agreement, a change in its par value, which may be a hazardous operation, since it is difficult for a member to conduct the necessary negotiations without arousing the suspicions of speculators. It may well be argued that currencies should have greater freedom to fluctuate in value from day to day, provided they keep within a range of, say, 5 per cent on each side of their par value. In this way speculation in currencies would be made a more risky game to play.[3]

The question of modifying the Fund's Articles so as to permit a somewhat greater degree of variation in exchange rates was discussed at the Fund's Annual Meeting in 1969. At the beginning of the Meeting, the managing director observed that 'it has been questioned whether specific provision should be made for exchange rates to respond at an earlier stage to balance-of-payments disequilibria, by modifying in some degree the existing arrangements for exchange rate variation'. The Executive Directors, he pointed out, had already announced their intention to study the technical and policy issues involved, but he would look forward to hearing the views of Governors on the subject. Various Governors responded to this invitation, and in particular the UK Governor, Mr Roy Jenkins, devoted considerable attention to the exchange rate system. So far as the widening of the margin around parity was concerned, Mr Jenkins remarked that a 5 per cent margin

[1] Argentina, Bolivia, Brazil, Chile, Colombia, Lebanon, Paraguay, Peru, Uruguay and Venezuela.
[2] Afghanistan, Ecuador and Pakistan.
[3] As it is, the speculator can be almost certain that the value of a member's currency will either move in the direction he predicts, or not at all.

could quickly be dismissed as excessive; 2 per cent above and below par could, however, be useful in giving central banks greater ability to deal with speculation.[1]

Problems arising from exchange control

One of the purposes of the Fund is 'to assist in the establishment of a *multilateral* system of payments in respect of current transactions between members . . .'. How is this end to be achieved? The Fund's Charter was not enlightening on this point, and in fact it was not until the re-opening of the foreign exchange markets, made possible as from the early 1950s[2] by the progressive relaxation of exchange controls, that a suitable mechanism was discovered (or, rather, rediscovered) for arranging settlements on a multilateral basis. In the preceding years, many settlements continued to be made under the bilateral and regional arrangements, based on exchange control, which had been set up during the war or immediately following the liberation of Europe. Under these arrangements, the Fund's objectives in the field of exchange rates were frequently frustrated by the side effects of exchange controls. In this chapter I shall consider some of these difficulties under three headings, 'disorderly cross rates', 'multiple exchange rates' and 'retention quotas'. I begin with disorderly (or 'broken') cross rates.

Disorderly cross rates

'The Fund attaches great importance to the maintenance of orderly cross rates',[3] on the grounds that disorderly cross rates (arising through the use of certain forms of exchange control) must distort trade relationships in circumstances in which trade and payments are not already completely bilateral. If, for example, the official sterling-dollar rate ruling in Britain and the United States is £1 = $4, but the lira-sterling and lira-dollar direct rates are such that the sterling-dollar cross rate in Italy is £1 = $2.60,[4] then goods will be encouraged to flow from the Sterling Area to Italy and from Italy to America in preference to going from the Sterling Area direct to America, irrespective of the real merits of such roundabout trade.[5] 'Export and import restrictions may limit

[1] IMF's *Finance and Development*, no. 4, 1969, pp. 13 and 14.
[2] Below, p. 184.
[3] *Annual Report*, 1949, p. 22.
[4] This example is taken from an address by M. Gutt at Harvard on 13 February 1948, entitled 'The Practical Problem of Exchange Rates'. M. Gutt was then the managing director of the Fund.
[5] Suppose for the sake of argument that the direct exchange rates between the lira and the $ and £ are respectively $1 = 600 lire and £1 = 1,560 lire, giving a sterling-

the scope of such transactions, but it will be difficult to check them entirely when the goods diverted are raw materials which can be converted into manufactured goods for which the United States offers a market.'[1] In addition to any 'real' losses resulting from diverting trade unnecessarily into a roundabout course, there is the further consequence that the victim of the disorderly cross rate (the Sterling Area in this example) earns lire, a currency at one time unacceptable for settlements with the United States, instead of US dollars. Naturally the victims share the Fund's dislike of disorderly cross rates and in particular Britain disliked the disorderly sterling-dollar cross rates which prevailed in Italy prior to November 1948 and in France between February 1948 and September 1949, as the result of these countries each allowing a free market in dollars. Happily in these two cases the disputes were settled amicably: Italy agreed in November 1948 that the official lira-sterling rate should be henceforth determined by applying the direct sterling-dollar rate to the free lira-dollar rate, while France made important concessions to the British viewpoint at about the same time[2] and in the following year, soon after sterling was devalued, went over entirely to the Italian procedure.

The timing of the final French concession is significant, since it illuminates one of the motives for allowing disorderly cross rates. For both France and Italy argued that the harm they were doing Britain in allowing a disorderly sterling-dollar cross rate was mainly a means of compensating for the harm Britain was doing them in fixing an 'unfair' direct sterling-dollar rate. Britain, they argued in effect, had agreed with the IMF an excessively high par value which produced an official direct rate of £1 = $4, whereas the 'fair' value of the £ was considerably lower, say £1 = $3 or thereabouts. The alleged unfairness of the rate of £1 = $4 arose

dollar cross rate of £1 = $2.6, as in M. Gutt's example, compared with a direct sterling-dollar rate of £1 = $4. Now suppose further that the sterling cost price in England of a certain consignment of Sterling Area produce is £1,000. The equivalent dollar cost, if the consignment were sent direct to the United States, would be $4,000. If however the consignment were sent to Italy the equivalent lira cost would be 1,560,000 lire, and if the consignment were then re-exported to the United States its equivalent dollar cost would be only $2,600. Thus the roundabout shipment of the consignment would save the American purchaser $1,400, less the extra transport costs and the charges of the extra middlemen.

[1] IMF *Annual Report*, 1948, p. 27.
[2] After October 1948 the sterling-franc rate applicable to trade transactions was calculated by applying the direct sterling-dollar rate to the effective franc-dollar rate for trade transactions (this rate being the mean of the official and free franc-dollar rates). Thus between October 1948 and September 1949 the disorderly sterling-dollar cross rate in Paris applied only to non-trade transactions.

in part from the fact that a British importer with £1 to spend was (at this rate of exchange) no less attractive a customer to a French or Italian exporter than an American importer with $4 to spend, whereas the French and Italian authorities (who wanted their exporters to sell to the United States and earn dollars) would have preferred that £1 should be considerably less attractive than $4. If the £ had been worth only (say) $3, France and Italy would have obtained their 'fair' share of the American market. The other aspect of the alleged over-valuation of sterling in relation to the dollar was that it made British goods too expensive in relation to American goods, which gave French and Italian importers an inconvenient bias towards buying from the United States.

There seems to be no satisfactory way of striking a balance of blame as between the countries concerned. On the one hand both France and Italy could argue that, though short of dollars, they were continuously accumulating sterling. On the other hand Britain could argue that a devaluation of sterling would prove a mixed blessing to France and Italy, since it would increase Britain's competitive power in export markets,[1] and that if France and Italy were embarrassed by their sterling they should reduce their restrictions on imports from Britain. Happily these conflicting arguments did not lead to a prolonged deadlock, though in the case of France the final solution was reached only after the devaluation of sterling.

Other cases of disorderly cross rates have occurred in the post-war period, but none comparable in seriousness to the two we have already considered. There are, however, cases where disorderly cross rates, or arrangements very similar thereto, have arisen by virtue of the use of multiple exchange rates, a device which we must now consider.

Multiple exchange rates

Under Article VIII, Section 3 of the Fund Agreement, 'No member shall engage in . . . any discriminatory currency arrangements or multiple currency practices' without the approval of the Fund, except under Article XIV in the 'transitional period'.[2]

---

[1] It was indeed for this reason that France complained in September 1949 that the devaluation of sterling was excessive. See footnote 3, p. 237. It may be noted that neither France nor Italy suggested that the alleged over-valuation of sterling increased their *overall* deficits, and the presumption is of course that it would tend to reduce them.

[2] And possible relaxations under the Scarce Currency Clause. See below, p. 102.

However, though most of the major countries had emerged from this transitional period by February 1961,[1] and have not sought permission for multiple currency practices under Article VIII, many of the smaller members of the Fund, especially the Latin American members, still have recourse (whether under Article XIV or Article VIII) to such practices.

The Fund from its earliest days has worked 'to eliminate the more objectionable features of multiple rate systems, such as discrimination between countries of destination or of origin'.[2] Nevertheless, it may perhaps be inferred that in the Fund's view multiple currency practices may be the most readily workable type of currency restriction in a country lacking a bureaucracy adequate in size and efficiency, since the licensing of individual transactions represents a heavy administrative burden and can readily lead to widespread corruption. Multiple currency practices also have the advantage that the monopolistic profits arising from the restrictions go to the state, not to private traders who handle the imported goods.[3] In the words of one of the Fund's reports, 'certain countries, particularly in Latin America, have used them [multiple currency practices] as a means of restricting imports without resort to complicated administrative machinery and without giving the recipients of import licences opportunities for large windfall profits. They have also had fiscal significance in some countries. . . .'[4]

In 1949 eighteen Fund members had multiple exchange rates: of these twelve were Latin American countries. The number increased

[1] Before this date the position with regard to Article XIV was as set out in footnote 3 on page 100. The developments of February 1961 are explained below, page 101.
[2] *Annual Report*, 1949, p. 24. Multiple selling rates may discriminate either according to the categories of transactions for which the foreign currency is required (e.g. foreign currencies may be sold more dearly for luxury goods than for necessities) or according to the country to which the payment is to be made (e.g. payments to the United States may be penalised by making US dollars very dear). The latter type of discrimination inevitably corresponds very closely to a disorderly cross rate. Multiple buying rates can likewise discriminate either according to the type of transaction or according to the country from which the foreign currency has been obtained.
[3] Restrictions on trade and payments may be either *quantitative* restrictions (where certain kinds of transactions are prohibited except under licence) or *cost* restrictions (where the restrictions merely affect the cost of a commodity or currency). In the former case the traders who are fortunate enough to obtain licences cannot easily be prevented from exploiting for their own profit the scarcities which result from the restrictions. In the latter case traders cannot exploit the situation, since everybody who is prepared to pay the official levy (whether it be e.g. an import duty or an 'unfavourable' exchange rate) is quite free to trade, and traders' profits are thus kept down to the competitive rate.
[4] *Annual Report*, 1948, p. 27.

in the early fifties, partly through the admission of new members:
'by the end of 1955, the Fund had grown to 58 members, and 36 of
these had some kind of economic device which the Fund considered a multiple currency practice'.[1]

After 1955, however, there occurred a sudden and almost dramatic
breakthrough in the multiple exchange rate war. In its *Annual Report
on Exchange Restrictions* for 1956, the Fund was able to report great
progress within a single year. A marked general improvement in the
international payments situation was at its roots . . . . Increased supplies
of goods, together with the improved domestic financial and monetary
positions of Western European countries and the realigned exchange
rates of 1949, brought the world dollar shortage to an end.

Within the next few years, the major industrial countries lowered or
abolished many barriers to trade and payments and established the
convertibility of their currencies. Multiple currency practices which
distinguished between 'hard' and 'soft' currencies could be, and were,
quickly removed. By 1958 the partial free markets and other special
devices of a number of Western European countries had all been
discontinued . . . .

The experience of the Fund had shown that it was very much easier
for a country to simplify its rate structure than to unify entirely . . . .
In addition, Fund experience had shown that it was the complexity of
multiple rates that had led to difficulties.

For these reasons, in June 1957 the Fund worked out a new decision
on multiple currency practices. (This was reproduced as Appendix VI
to the Fund's 1957 *Annual Report*, pp. 161–2.) It urged countries to
simplify their existing rate structures and offered to help them map out
specific exchange systems. Simplification meant more than merely a
reduction in the number of existing rates: emphasis was placed on a
total of two or three rates which should be sufficiently realistic to
maintain a satisfactory balance of payments with only a minimum of
restrictions.

Following this new announcement, and with other countries encouraged by the success of those that had already unified their exchange
systems, the next several years were to witness a further series of elimi-
nations of multiple rates . . . . By the end of 1962, only 15 Fund members
out of a total of 82 had multiple rates.[2]

A survey of the position in 1969 showed that multiple rates were
then imposed by only a very small minority of Fund members,

[1] Margaret G. de Vires, 'The Decline of Multiple Exchange Rates, 1947–76', in
Finance and Development, December 1967, p. 300.
[2] op. cit., pp. 301–2.

whose total imports were less than one tenth of all members' imports.[1]

Retention quotas

A currency arrangement which has much in common with the more objectionable features of multiple rate systems, is the so-called 'retention quota'.[2] In its *Fourth Annual Report on Exchange Restrictions*, 1953, the Fund describes such arrangements, which 'existed in a number of countries', in the following terms:

> In the consultations with certain European countries, the Fund also discussed their practices under which part of the exchange earnings or their equivalent are allowed to be retained by exporters, or where rights to import certain commodities are granted in connection with exports, particularly those to the dollar area. Most of these practices have discriminatory currency features; some are clearly multiple currency practices.

The Fund subsequently issued a statement[3] disapproving such arrangements and in view of this, and in view also of the diminishing severity of the dollar shortage, the practice thereafter rapidly went out of fashion.[4]

Multilateral settlement

In the early years of the Fund, it was not at all apparent how (or even whether) multilateral settlement would be achieved. By the early 1950s however it had become clear that the line of advance was to be through the re-opening of the foreign exchange markets in London and other European centres (below, page 184) and the authorisation of arbitrage initially between these centres and subsequently (with the adoption in December 1958 of almost complete non-resident convertibility by Britain and twelve other Western European countries[5]) between them and the New York markets. These inter-connected markets automatically provided for fully multilateral settlement: what had to be assured was that the rates of exchange ruling in them should not deviate by more

---

[1] Josef Swidrowski, 'Exchange Restrictions in 1969', in the IMF's *Finance and Development*, no. 4, 1969, p. 28. This survey embraced Switzerland and seven other non-member countries (all very small) as well as all IMF members.
[2] The consequences of a retention quota are illustrated by a hypothetical example, below, p. 194.
[3] Reported in the IMF's *International News Survey*, 15 May 1953.
[4] According to the IMF's *Fifth Annual Report on Exchange Restrictions*, p. 16.
[5] Below, pp. 187–8.

than a small margin from their relative gold parities as agreed with the IMF. This second objective was in practice achieved by the central banks in the Western European countries (or the Exchange Equalisation Account in the case of the UK) intervening in the market by buying (or selling) US dollars against the domestic currency whenever the market value of the domestic currency would otherwise have gone to an undue premium (or discount) in relation to the official parity. Hence the US dollar was used by the UK and other European countries as an 'intervention currency', in much the same way as sterling has always been used by the countries of the Outer Sterling Area. Thus the re-opening of the European foreign exchange markets and the use of the dollar and sterling as intervention currencies were the devices by which the Fund's objectives of multilateral settlement with a stable pattern of exchange rates were in due course achieved. The only problem which arose for the IMF was to ensure that the permitted margin in exchange rates (i.e., the degree of fluctuation in an actual exchange rate above or below the official parity) was wide enough for a free market to operate efficiently on a commercial basis. The margin permitted in the Charter under Article IV, Section 3(ii) was one per cent above or below the parity rate as between any currency and any other, which is slightly more than the margin (about $\pm \frac{3}{4}$ per cent) required for an efficient market. However if an Outer Sterling Area country kept its exchange rate with sterling within $\frac{3}{4}$ per cent parity, and sterling in turn was kept within $\frac{3}{4}$ per cent of its dollar parity, the maximum variation as between the Outer Sterling Area currency and the dollar would be as much as $\pm 1\frac{1}{2}$ per cent, thus violating the letter of the Fund's margin requirements. However the Fund was able to legitimise this arrangement by regarding it as a multiple currency practice, which as such the Fund could permit. It thereby widened to ± 2 per cent the margin between any two member currencies.[1]

The price of gold

Gold has operational significance in the Fund mainly as the measuring rod by which the values of national currencies are determined: this measuring rod may be changed, but so far it has not been and a decision to do so (i.e. to revalue all members' currencies in terms of gold) has (under Article IV Section 7 of the Charter) to run the gauntlet of a deliberately complicated voting

[1] Fleming, op. cit., p. 13.

procedure (above, page 87). The Fund's use of gold as a measuring rod accounts for its apprehension about transactions in gold at prices appreciably different from the gold par value of the currency against which the gold is exchanged. The Fund has always made an uncompromising stand, so far with almost complete success, on the observance of the parity price of gold ($35 an ounce, or its equivalent in other currencies) in all *official* transactions, but it has been less consistent in its attitude to gold markets, open to non-official transactors, in which the price is settled by supply and demand. The Fund began by deprecating all 'international transactions in gold at premium prices'[1] but its efforts to suppress free markets (in which premium prices prevailed from time to time) proved unavailing, and eventually had to be abandoned. The Fund's retreat on this issue made possible the re-opening of the London gold market, which occurred (see below, page 185) in March 1954.

In the London market the price of gold has never fallen appreciably below $35 an ounce but has from time to time risen above that price, as will be explained in Chapter 21.

---

[1] *Annual Report*, 1950, p. 70.

8

THE INTERNATIONAL MONETARY FUND

(CONTINUED)

The roles of the IMF and GATT

The Fund's jurisdiction over international restrictions is limited to those affecting international payments. Restrictions on international *trade*, for instance tariffs and import quotas, fall within the province of another international institution, the GATT,[1] the successor of the stillborn International Trade Organisation.[2] The GATT is an international agreement, with a very extensive membership, laying down various principles of trade policy to which members must adhere and setting out the procedure to be followed in arranging tariff reductions on a reciprocal basis. It has therefore rested with the contracting parties of the GATT, assisted by a small but highly expert staff at Geneva, to lead the attack on restrictions falling on trade rather than on payments. Nevertheless the IMF has inevitably been interested in the progress made under the GATT, since, as we saw in Chapter 2, restrictions on payments and on trade are to a large extent similar in their consequences.

The restrictions which the IMF and GATT have been called upon to deal with have in practice mainly taken the form of the exchange control practices described in Chapter 7 and of tariffs

---

[1] The General Agreement on Tariffs and Trade. The text is available in *Basic Instruments and Selected Documents, Volume III*, published by the Contracting Parties to GATT, Geneva, November 1958.

[2] The form of the ITO agreement, unlike that of the General Agreement, was such that adherence by the USA would have required Congressional approval, which the US government was not prepared to seek.

and import quotas, both of which come, strictly speaking, within the purview of GATT, though the widespread practice of basing exchange control on the issuance of import licences has made import quotas of great interest to the IMF too.

Now the GATT agreement tackles tariffs and quotas by completely different procedures: tariffs are to be reduced by a process of bargaining, quotas (on the other hand) are simply prescribed, except for certain specified loopholes. As regards tariffs, GATT has organised six rounds of bargaining, of which the first was at Geneva in 1947, the second at Annecy in 1949, the third at Torquay in 1950–1 and the fourth at Geneva in 1956, and these resulted in very widespread tariff reductions and in numerous undertakings not to raise the existing level of duties.[1] Then in 1960–1 there has been the 'Dillon round' (named after Mr Douglas Dillon, the US Under Secretary of State) and more recently the highly successful 'Kennedy round'.

As regards quotas, a weakness of GATT has been that there is no provision for bargaining one quota against another or a quota against a tariff, while the general prescription of quotas (Article XI) is robbed of some of its force by the wide scope of the permitted loopholes.[2] For besides the loopholes with which we shall be mainly concerned (namely the authorisation of 'restrictions to safeguard the balance of payments') there are others which permit the protection of agriculture and give almost complete freedom of action to under-developed countries.

The treatment of disequilibria

As we shall see in the next chapter, the Fund is intended to provide additional liquidity only for purposes of accommodating temporary disequilibria. Disequilibria which cannot be expected to be self-correcting are not therefore intended to be accommodated in this way except for limited periods and on the understanding that suitable action will be taken to cure or (failing that) to suppress them. We must now consider what in the Fund's view would constitute suitable action.

In general, the Fund's bias is very strongly in favour of curing in preference to merely suppressing disequilibria. Unfortunately,

[1] See *The Attack on Trade Barriers*, published by the Interim Commission for the ITO, the *Report on the Torquay Tariff Negotiations*, published in May 1951 by HMSO, Cmnd. 8228, and *International Trade* published annually, in 1952 and subsequently, by the GATT secretariat.
[2] The OEEC was more successful than GATT in eliminating quotas. Below, p. 157.

however, the available cures[1] may not be adequate for all circumstances. For, first, there is nothing in either the GATT or the IMF Agreement to prevent surplus countries from retaining protective tariffs, however much they may be warned off other types of restrictions. (Such countries are of course encouraged to participate in the rounds of tariff bargaining organised under the GATT, along with all other parties to the Agreement, but *reciprocal* tariff deductions are likely to increase both the exports and the imports of a surplus country, and thus leave its surplus substantially unaffected.) Second, though a curtailment of home demand is an appropriate cure for the deficit of a country where demand is excessive in relation to the amount of labour and equipment available for employment, it cannot be considered suitable for a country whose labour force and capital equipment are less than fully occupied. Third, as we saw in Chapter 4, the restoration of equilibrium by means of adjusting exchange rates is in certain circumstances subject to serious difficulties, arising (for example) from an inelastic demand for exports;[2] moreover (as we shall see in subsequent chapters) the adjustment of exchange rates, or even the possibility of adjustment, may have the undesirable consequence of provoking speculative movements of capital. Finally, as we also saw in Chapter 4, there have in the post-war period been special difficulties in the way of correcting disequilibria by inducing compensatory movements of private capital (an issue to which we shall return later in the present chapter).

Restrictions on trade and payments

Due for the most part to such genuine difficulties in applying 'curative' treatments to balance of payments disequilibria, there has been a tendency, which was particularly strong in the first ten years or so after the war, for countries to deal with external deficits *inter alia* by imposing restrictions on payments and trade. Hence it is important to understand the provisions in the IMF Charter and the GATT, under which such restrictions may be permitted.

In the case of the Fund, many members began by retaining payments restrictions under the 'transitional provisions' of Article XIV[3] and until 1961 this was also in practice the Article invoked by

---

[1] Above, pages 65–6. For a statement on the Fund's attitude to these 'cures', see its *Annual Report* for 1964, pp. 28 and 29.

[2] See pages 58 et seq.

[3] The only countries not in 1960 appealing to the 'transitional period' of Article XIV were the United States, Canada, Venezuela and most of the Central American states.

members wishing to impose such restrictions for balance-of-payments reasons. According to this Article,

> In the post-war transitional period members may, notwithstanding the provisions of any other articles of this Agreement, maintain and adapt to changing circumstances (and, in the case of members whose territories have been occupied by the enemy, introduce where necessary) restrictions on payments and transfers for current international transactions. Members shall, however, have continuous regard in their foreign exchange policies to the purposes of the Fund. . . . In particular, members shall withdraw restrictions maintained or imposed under this Section as soon as they are satisfied that they will be able, in the absence of such restrictions, to settle their balance of payments in a manner which will not unduly encumber their access to the resources of the Fund.

Under Section 4 of the same Article the transitional period is of indefinite duration, but 'five years after the date on which the Fund begins operations' (i.e. as from April 1952), any member still retaining any restrictions inconsistent with the full obligations of membership,

> . . . shall consult the Fund as to their further retention. The Fund may, if it deems such action necessary in exceptional circumstances, make representations to any member that conditions are favourable for the withdrawal of any particular restriction, or for the general abandonment of restrictions, inconsistent with the provisions of any other articles of this Agreement. The member shall be given a suitable time to reply to such representations. If the Fund finds that the member persists in maintaining restrictions which are inconsistent with the purposes of the Fund . . . [the Fund] may declare the member ineligible to use the resources of the Fund.[1]

The results of the Fund's first round of consultations were presented in its *Fourth Annual Report on Exchange Restrictions*, 1953. In this Report the Fund made it clear that the use of restrictions was still widespread, but subsequent Reports recorded considerable progress in the removal both of payments restrictions and of trade restrictions imposed for balance-of-payments reasons. Finally, in February 1961, ten countries which had hitherto availed themselves of Article XIV (Belgium, France, Germany, Ireland, Italy, Luxembourg, Holland, Peru, Sweden and the United Kingdom) all agreed to emerge from the shelter of this Article, a step which put most of the major 'western' powers out-

[1] The quotations are from Article XIV and Article XV, Section 2(*a*).

side the ambit of the transitional provisions, though even in April 1970 only 34 of the Fund members had accepted Article VIII status.

Once a member abandons Article XIV status he assumes the 'General Obligations of Members' set out in Article VIII, and the step once taken is an irreversible one, since once a member ceases to appeal to Article XIV he has no right to invoke it again. However he can still seek a special dispensation from the Fund under Article VIII, as many members have in fact done from time to time,[2] and there is also in theory (if not in practice) the possibility of invoking the so-called Scarce Currency Clause of Article VII. The main provisions of this Article are as follows:

(a) If it becomes evident to the Fund that the demand for a member's currency seriously threatens the Fund's ability to supply that currency, the Fund, whether or not it has issued a report under Section 1 of this Article, shall formally declare such currency scarce and shall thenceforth apportion its existing and accruing supply of the scarce currency with due regard to the relative needs of members, the general international economic situation, and any other pertinent considerations. The Fund shall also issue a report concerning its action.

(b) A formal declaration under (a) above shall operate as an authorisation to any member, after consultation with the Fund, temporarily to impose limitations on the freedom of exchange operations in the scarce currency.

Thus the formal declaration by the Fund that a member's currency is scarce allows all other members to introduce restrictions directed solely against that member, this discrimination being wisely conceived to prevent the deficit countries from having, quite pointlessly, to impose restrictions against each other.

The main weakness of the Clause is that it cannot be invoked unless a currency seriously threatens to become scarce *in the Fund*, which would not occur, even though the currency were scarce outside the Fund, if for any reason the Fund had decided that the deficit countries were largely ineligible to use its resources. For instance, the US dollar was de facto scarce outside the Fund for a number of years after the Fund commenced business, but this currency never became formally scarce.

Let us now turn from the Fund to the GATT. The GATT

[1] Austria, Australia, Denmark and Japan also came into line in due course.
[2] For a survey of exchange restrictions, whether under Article XIV or Article VIII, in force in 1969, see Jozef Swidrowski, 'Exchange Restrictions in 1969', in the IMF's *Finance and Development*, no. 4, 1969, p. 27.

contains important provisions which permit of the use of *trade* restrictions to deal with balance-of-payments disequilibria.[1] Trade restrictions *of a non-discriminatory nature* may be imposed for balance-of-payments reasons even by a country which has emerged from the transitional period provided for in Article XIV of the Fund Charter, provided that such measures are necessary:

(1) to forestall the imminent threat of, or to stop, a serious decline in its monetary reserves, or

(2) in the case of a country with very low monetary reserves, to achieve a reasonable rate of increase in its reserves,

where the interpretation of the key words 'serious', 'very low' and 'reasonable' rests with the Fund. The GATT Charter is however much stricter about discriminatory trade restrictions than about non-discriminatory ones. The former are indeed permissible for balance-of-payments reasons (GATT Article XIV), but only for countries able to claim the privileges of the transitional provisions or the Scarce Currency Clause of the Fund Agreement, and for those whose need to discriminate arises from the unwillingness of their trading partners to adopt any form of multilateral settlement. Otherwise the GATT Charter condemns discrimination in trade restrictions imposed for balance-of-payments reasons.

In the light of the discussion in Chapter 4 above, it may reasonably be argued that both the IMF and GATT have been inclined to shirk the question: in so far as the world does use restrictions to deal with international disequilibria, what kind of restrictions are best (or least objectionable) for this purpose, and by what machinery can they best be imposed? In particular:

(1) Should deficit countries impose *discriminating* restrictions, so as to avoid needlessly imposing restrictions against each other?

(2) Should trade restrictions imposed to deal with balance-of-payments difficulties take the form of quotas (as has been usual in the post-war period) or of tariffs?

As regards (1) the Fund has been firm in its opposition to any form of discrimination in restrictions on either payments or trade. This was so even before the major European countries emerged (in February 1961) from the shelter of the transitional provisions of Article XIV: in October 1959 (one year after the adoption of non-resident convertibility by Britain and twelve other European

---

[1] Articles XII, XIII and XIV of GATT.

powers[1]) 'the Executive Board expressed its view that there was no longer any balance-of-payments justification for discrimination by members whose current receipts were largely in convertible currencies'[2]—a view which in the circumstances of the time (and subsequently) really amounts to a clear condemnation of discrimination. Nor has the Fund ever retreated from the position it adopted in 1959: in particular no attempt has ever been made to invoke the Scarce Currency Clause.

As regards (2) the GATT Charter implies that quotas, and not tariffs, are the appropriate restrictions to be used for this purpose, since tariffs which have been reduced or bound at any of the rounds of GATT tariff negotiations (as most tariffs have come to be) cannot thereafter be increased for balance-of-payments reasons. There is however no apparent economic justification for preferring quotas to tariffs in this connection (rather the contrary[3]) and recently several members (Canada in the period June 1962 to April 1963[4] and the UK in the two years beginning October 1964) have in fact chosen to impose tariffs (*alias* import surcharges), rather than quotas, in defiance of the GATT rules.

Capital movements

When the Fund's Charter was drafted, it was thought that most members would retain the power to impose exchange control on capital movements, and indeed that they *ought* to retain such powers and make use of them, rather than draw on the Fund to finance a deficit on capital account.[5] However by the time of its *Annual Report* for 1964 the Fund had become less favourably disposed towards restrictions on capital movements and merely conceded that they 'may be less objectionable' than other exchange restrictions, 'particularly where they are intended to deal with speculative movements'. But 'because of the difficulties and drawbacks attached to such restrictions, it is . . . preferable to follow, wherever possible, policies aimed at attracting appropriate equilibrating movements of private capital through international coordination of interest rates or similar international action, or to offset undue movements of short-term capital through the use of

[1] Below, p. 187.
[2] Fleming, op. cit., p. 19.
[3] See my article, 'The Use of Restrictions to Suppress External Deficits', in *The Manchester School*, September 1960.
[4] The IMF's *Fourteenth Annual Report on Exchange Restrictions*, 1963, p. 62.
[5] The Executive Board did not in practice follow this strict line on drawings by members in deficit on capital account. See below, p. 117.

international liquidity'.[1] Unfortunately however 'difficulties and drawbacks' may (as we saw in Chapter 4) also be encountered in attempting to influence the flow of international capital by the manipulation of interest rates, even when supported by official intervention in the forward exchange markets. Thus the position seems to be that though there are various ways (including exchange control) by which countries may attempt to cure international disequilibria by influencing capital transactions, none of them can be relied upon to work very satisfactorily in the conditions of the post-war period so that (a) cures must also be sought in devices which influence *current* transactions and (b) international liquidity must be on a scale large enough to accommodate substantial temporary disequilibria, including those which arise from substantial movements of short-term capital.

The international transmission of depressions[2]

Neither the Fund Agreement nor the Fund's pronouncements since it began business accept that restrictions on payments and trade should ever be imposed for purposes of exporting, or even preventing the import of, business depressions. However, the Fund lays upon its members no obligation to take steps to prevent depression in their respective countries, and therefore offers no assurance that one member may not suffer as the result of another's failure to take such steps.[3] The Australian delegation to the Bretton Woods conference wanted

to see Governments specifically accept the obligation to maintain employment. . . . An *agreement* to maintain employment is, of course, only a first step. . . . Nevertheless, acceptance by nations of an obligation to maintain employment would do much to mobilise public opinion to see that the obligation was carried out, and it would give smaller nations, so dependent on the employment levels of others, sufficient confidence to accept obligations that would not otherwise be easy for them.

Perhaps as the result of this protest, the Charter of the still-born ITO made concessions to the Australian point of view. These

[1] op. cit., p. 28.
[2] See Chapter 5, above.
[3] The only reference in the Fund Agreement to the level of employment is in Article I, where 'the expansion and balanced growth of international trade' is recommended as a means of promoting and maintaining 'high levels of employment and real income'.

appear in Articles 2, 3 and 6, from which the following are extracts:

The Members recognise that the avoidance of unemployment or underemployment . . . is not of domestic concern alone, but is also a necessary condition for the achievement of the general purpose and the objectives set forth in Article 1, including the expansion of international trade, and thus for the well-being of all other countries.

The Members recognise that, while the avoidance of unemployment or underemployment must depend primarily on internal measures taken by individual countries, such measures should be supplemented by concerted action under the sponsorship of the Economic and Social Council of the United Nations in collaboration with the appropriate inter-governmental organisations, each of these bodies acting within its respective sphere and consistently with the terms and purposes of its basic instrument.

Measures to sustain employment, production and demand shall be consistent with the other objectives and provisions of this Charter. Members shall seek to avoid measures which would have the effect of creating balance-of-payments difficulties for other countries.

The Organisation shall have regard, in the exercise of its functions under other Articles of this Charter, to the need of Members to take action within the provisions of this Charter to safeguard their economies against inflationary or deflationary pressure from abroad. In case of deflationary pressure special consideration shall be given to the consequences for any Member of a serious or abrupt decline in the effective demand of other countries.

These provisions in the ITO Charter included virtually the whole field which was marked out in Chapter 5 as suitable for international cooperation in anti-depression policies, and even cover the possibility of action to counter the opposite evil of inflation. However, the relevant provisions have not been incorporated in the GATT.[1]

---

[1] At the sixth session of GATT (in 1953) several countries suggested that the Articles in question be written into the GATT. However this suggestion did not lead to any formal decision.

9

THE IMF'S FINANCIAL TRANSACTIONS[1]

Under the original Bretton Woods Charter, which remained unamended until 1969, all the Fund's financial transactions were in what has come to be called its General Account. It is with this Account that the present chapter deals. The Special Drawing Account, provided for in Articles introduced into the amended Charter of 1969, is left for consideration in Chapter 10.

Subscriptions

The resources which the Fund's General Account has at its disposal for financing members in balance-of-payments difficulties are obtained (a) by members' subscriptions in their own national currencies and in gold and (b) by borrowing national currencies. Since the finance supplied by the Fund to members in balance-of-payments difficulties is always in the form of other countries' national currencies the Fund makes use of its gold by selling it against national currencies of which its holdings have become low. No borrowing was undertaken until 1964, with the first activation of the General Arrangements to Borrow, which is described below.

As regards subscriptions, Article III of the Fund Agreement provides that each member country shall have a *quota*, and must make a subscription to the Fund, normally 25 per cent in gold and 75 per cent in its domestic currency, equal in value to its quota. For this purpose, all currencies are valued at their official gold

[1] For a more detailed exposition, see 'The International Monetary Fund: use and supply of resources', in the Bank of England's *Quarterly Bulletin*, March 1969.

par values, as determined under Article IV. The size of each of the larger quotas (and of the sum total of the smaller ones) as at April 1970 is shown in Table 4 on page 88. Before September 1959, when a scheme was adopted to increase all quotas by 50 per cent, and in some cases by rather more, the grand total had been only $9.2 billion. By the beginning of 1960, thanks to this scheme, the total of quotas had risen to $14.7 billion. A further increase in quotas by 25 per cent (and in some cases rather more) was agreed in 1965, and this (together with the admission of additional members) had by the end of 1969 brought the grand total of all quotas up to over $21 billion, as shown in Table 4. The next review of quotas is due in 1970, and the Executive Board has proposed that there should be a further general increase of about one third, thus bringing the grand total to about $28 billion.[1]

The General Arrangements to Borrow

An important turning point in the history of the Fund was the recognition by the United States that her balance-of-payments deficit had become a major problem. This turning point may be taken as occurring in 1960 or thereabouts. The many initiatives which were taken by the US administration to cope with the US deficit have been described by Mr Roosa,[2] who was the Under Secretary at the Treasury for Monetary Affairs from the end of 1960 until he was succeeded by Mr Deming in 1965.

One such initiative was to propose that arrangements should be made so that the Fund's resources could (if the need arose) be increased to provide *inter alia* for the possibility of a large drawing by the United States (a possibility which had previously not been taken seriously). The proposal took the form of a recommendation that a group of the larger and richer members should agree to lend their currencies to the Fund, whose Charter conveniently permits it to borrow from members.[3] In the event the United States has used other means to finance her deficit, so that the large US drawing which was considered a possibility in 1961 has not in fact been made, and so far the arrangements made as the result of the US initiative have been activated solely for the benefit of the UK (in 1964 and subsequently) and France (in 1969).

---

[1] IMF Press Release, 30 December 1969.

[2] Roosa, *The Dollar and the World Economy.*

[3] The legal basis for the GAB is in Article VII, but its scope is narrower than that of the Article in that the GAB is to be used only when the Fund needs 'supplementary resources to forestall or cope with an impairment of the international monetary system'.

The arrangements in question, which became known as the GAB (General Arrangements to Borrow) were discussed at the annual meeting of the Fund in September 1961 and settled by the end of the year. They provided for ten industrial countries to make, if necessity arose, supplementary resources available to the Fund to meet drawings by the US or the UK (and since 1968 also by the rest of the Ten). The lending commitments of the ten countries were arranged as follows:[1]

	$ *million*
United States	2,000
United Kingdom[2]	1,000
West Germany[2]	1,000
France[2]	550
Italy	550
Japan	250
Netherlands	200
Canada	200
Belgium	150
Sweden	100
Total	6,000

These supplementary resources are not available automatically, since use of them requires the approval of the 'Group of Ten'. Broadly speaking, following a request to the Fund for a drawing or stand-by facility, made by one of the participants in the arrangements, the Fund may make a call on the supplementary resources. The participating countries, however, undertake to meet the call only if they agree, after consultation, as to the need for it. Then contributions are made by individual countries, possibly up to the maximum of their commitments, but only to the extent that their reserves and balances-of-payments positions permit. In this way any request for a drawing which may require the activation of the GAB is dealt with in accordance with the Fund's established policies and practices, though the agreement of the countries providing supplementary aid is necessary. Repayment of the Fund's borrowing is subject to a 'gold-value clause', guaranteeing reimbursement in terms of the equivalent in gold of the amount lent.

[1] In March 1963 the ten countries were joined by Switzerland, with a contribution of the equivalent of $200 millions, as provided for in an exchange of letters with the Managing Director in June 1964. Suitable arrangements were made to deal with the difficulty that Switzerland is not a member of the IMF.
[2] As the result of subsequent changes in exchange rates, the UK's commitment (in $ million) is now 857, West Germany's is 1,093 and France's is 489.

Should a country that has provided supplementary resources subsequently suffer from a deterioration in its balance-of-payments position, it can request the Fund to repay the sums advanced. Interest payable on such resources lent to the Fund is based on a formula that, at present, represents a rate of $1\frac{1}{2}$ per cent per annum. The Fund, in addition, pays a charge of $\frac{1}{2}$ per cent on the amount of each borrowing transaction.

These arrangements were to come into effect when certain of the participating countries formally indicated their adherence to the scheme: in the event the participants had performed this formality before the end of 1962. However, it was not until the end of 1964 that the scheme was first activated—in order to make possible a massive drawing by the UK in December of that year (see below, page 262).

Borrowing by the Fund under the relevant Article of its Charter is not necessarily confined to transactions within the framework of the GAB. The Fund can also borrow from an individual member, and indeed did so in 1966, when it negotiated a loan of $250 millions of lire from Italy.

Drawings

Having obtained resources from subscriptions and (more recently) from borrowings, the IMF is in a position to honour the *purchase rights* which its members enjoy against the pool of currencies thus formed. These purchase rights are governed by Article V, Section 3, which, in the version in the original Charter, gives a member access to the Fund's resources only if:

The proposed purchase would not cause the Fund's holdings of the purchasing member's currency to increase by more than 25 per cent of its quota during the period of twelve months ending on the date of the purchase nor to exceed 200 per cent of its quota, but the 25 per cent limitation shall apply only to the extent that the Fund's holdings of the member's currency have been brought above 75 per cent of its quota if they had been below that amount. [Section 3 (a)(iii)]

This clause is subject to a waiver clause, Article V, Section 4, giving the Fund discretionary power to waive the limitation, 'especially in the case of members with a record of avoiding large or continuous use of the Fund's resources', and there were since August 1953 frequent waivers of the 25 per cent limitation, which was abolished altogether when the Charter was amended in 1969. So far only very few countries have been granted a waiver that would increase the Fund's holding of their currencies beyond the limit of 200 per cent of their quotas, these waivers having arisen under an arrangement adopted by the Fund early in 1963 (and extended in 1966) to alleviate the adverse impact of a sudden fall in primary product prices on the balance of payments of countries highly dependent on the export of the products concerned.[1]

The IMF Agreement, in its financing provisions, follows more closely the White Plan than the Keynes Plan, which suggested different machinery and proposed a much greater amount of additional means of settlement. The Keynes Plan gave the international body, which was to be called the 'Clearing Union', the authority to create an entirely new paper currency, *Bancor*, which all members would undertake to accept as a means of settlement and against which each member had a limited overdraft right. The overdraft rights enjoyed by the various countries would however have been several times greater in amount than their original purchase rights as members of the Fund. Another, and even more important, difference between the Keynes Scheme and the IMF is that under the latter the maximum contribution that a surplus country can be called upon to make is its total initial subscription (equal to its quota), whereas the Keynes Scheme required a surplus country to accept Bancor from all deficit countries up to the limit of their aggregate overdraft facilities. Admittedly the facilities of the Fund are supplemented by those of the International Bank, but the Bank's resources are available solely to provide members with foreign currency requirements for investment projects.

The Keynes Plan and the IMF also differ very considerably as regards the conditions on which members are eligible to exercise their drawing rights. Under the former scheme, the only conditions attaching to a member country's use of overdraft rights at an annual rate of one quarter of its quota up to a total of three-quarters of its quota are set out in paragraph (8) (*b*) of the published text, as follows:

The Governing Board may require from a member State having a debit balance reaching a *half* of its quota the deposit of suitable collateral against its debit balance. Such collateral shall, at the discretion

---

[1] This arrangement, the so-called *compensatory financing scheme*, provides assistance, on more liberal terms than regular drawings, for up to 50 per cent of a country's quota. In permitting such drawings, the Fund may be willing to hold a member's currency up to 250 per cent of his quota. See Horsefield, 'The Fund's Compensatory Financing', in the IMF's *Finance and Development*, no. 4, 1969, p. 34.

of the Governing Board, take the form of gold, foreign or domestic currency or Government bonds, within the capacity of the member State. As a condition of allowing a member State to increase its debit balance to a figure in excess of a half of its quota, the Governing Board may require all or any of the following measures:—

(i) a stated reduction in the value of the member's currency, if it deems that to be the suitable remedy;

(ii) the control of outward capital transactions if not already in force; and

(iii) the outright surrender of a suitable proportion of any separate gold or other liquid reserve in reduction of its debit balance.

Furthermore, the Governing Board may recommend to the Government of the member State any internal measures affecting its domestic economy which may appear to be appropriate to restore the equilibrium of its international balance.

These are clearly conditions which any member country could fulfil if it wished to, so that in spite of them the drawing rights remain irrevocable or automatic. However, in the case of the Fund, the relevant Articles of Agreement are anything but clear, so much so that the Executive Board took some five years to clarify the position, as I shall shortly explain.

First however it should be emphasised that what is at issue here is a member's access to other members' currencies from the Fund in exchange for his own, *supposing the Fund already to hold an amount of his currency equal to, or exceeding, that portion of his initial subscription (75 per cent of his quota) which Article III states shall normally be payable in a member's own currency*. So long as the Fund's holding of a member's currency is *less* than 75 per cent of his quota (a state of affairs which can arise only through other members having previously drawn his currency[1]) then he enjoys an unquestionable right to draw and need never repay his drawing, since the Fund is always willing to restore its holding of his currency to the 'normal' level of 75 per cent of his quota. Such a drawing is known, in the jargon of the Fund, as a 'super-gold-tranche drawing'.

We may now proceed to consider the position of a member the Fund's holding of whose currency is at present 75 per cent of his quota, but who now wants to draw one or more of the five 'tranches' (each equal to 25 per cent of his quota) which in total would bring the Fund's holding of his currency to 200 per cent of his quota—the presumptive ceiling laid down in Article V,

---

[1] Or through the member repurchasing his currency with gold.

Section 3(a)(iii). Members in this position are, according to the Fund's Articles, denied access to the Fund's resources either to meet a large or sustained outflow of capital[1] (except to make gold tranche purchases[2]) or again if they make an unauthorised change of their par values,[3] and are in addition subject to a number of other 'ineligibility provisions', most of which appear under Article V. Taken together, these provisions imply that, subject usually to any waiver which the Executive Board is entitled to give, certain kinds of *transactions* are illegal and certain actions make *members* ineligible: otherwise a member may draw subject to the presumptive constraints specified in Article V, Section 3(a)(iii). But is a member's right to make such a drawing automatic, as was intended under the Keynes Plan, or must all drawings receive the approval of the Executive Board? Several countries including the UK and France (significantly both then in balance-of-payments difficulties) initially interpreted the Articles as giving all members an automatic right to draw within the specified constraints at their own discretion: on the other hand the US (at that time in balance-of-payments surplus) took the contrary view, namely that *all* drawings beyond the super-gold-tranche were at the discretion of the Executive Board. After many debates on the Executive Board, the US interpretation was conceded at least by the early 1950s, though later on (as I shall explain) automaticity was introduced for drawings within the so-called 'gold tranche' (the tranche the use of which by a member would bring the Fund's holding of his currency up to 100 per cent of his quota).

Another problem of interpretation which presented grave difficulties concerned the conditions of repayment. It was generally accepted that, with its limited resources, the Fund can enjoy a continuous useful existence only if countries exercising purchase rights in due course restore the status quo by repurchasing their own currencies from the Fund. It therefore follows that the main purpose of the Fund's resources is to provide 'temporary' assistance, which means that members making drawings must be put under some obligation to repay. But (as I shall shortly explain) the repayment conditions specified in the Charter (Article V, Section 7) were *de facto* inoperative for the UK and *so long as the UK retained its Article XIV status* were moreover also inoperative for the other members of the Sterling Area. Nor did the repayment

[1] Article VI, Section 1.
[2] Article VI, Section 2. The 'gold tranche' is defined at the end of this paragraph.
[3] Article IV, Section 6.

provisions operate at all reliably in the case of many other countries. Such a state of affairs was viewed with alarm by the US, whose reaction was as one might have expected: 'During 1950 the United States, concerned over the tendency of the Fund's currency sales to become long-term loans, urged a most careful husbanding of its resources'.[1] In order to avoid an impasse, the US Executive Director proposed in 1949 that all drawings should be due for repayment within a period of five years. This the other Executive Directors were not prepared to concede without a quid pro quo in the form of a concession which would go some way to meet their view that drawings should be automatic.

To understand the basis of the trouble, we need to look into the details of the repurchase provisions of Article V, Section 7. These 'are such that any member that has drawn more than half of its balance-of-payments deficit in any year has to pay back the excess; and thereafter half of any payments surplus, or rise in reserves, has to be paid back to the Fund. Such repurchases, however, are not required of a member whose reserves are less than its quota . . . These repayment provisions are comparatively painless to the member, but have the disadvantage that if the member so acts as never to reconstitute its reserves the Fund might never be repaid at all':[2] moreover the definition of 'reserves':

(1) permitted the UK to take her official reserves *net of sterling liabilities*,[3] thereby ensuring that her reserves, for purposes of Article V, Section 7, would be negative, thus exempting her from her repayment obligation

(2) excluded official holdings of the currencies of countries which (like the UK prior to 1961) were still appealing to the transitional provisions of Article XIV, thereby reducing the reserves (thus defined) of the outer sterling area countries to very small proportions.

Partly in consequence of the difficulty of interpreting the drawing and repayment provisions of the Articles, partly because of the unusual circumstances of the early post-war years, the Fund began by adopting a moderately cautious attitude:

---

[1] International Finance Section, Princeton University, *Survey of United States International Finance 1950*, pp. 149–50.

[2] J. Marcus Fleming, *The International Monetary Fund, its Form and Functions*, pp. 29–30.

[3] When the original charter was for the first time amended in 1969, this definition of reserves was changed. Under the amended charter, reserves are defined as *gross* reserves.

The Executive Board recognised that in starting operations in a war-devastated world before relief and reconstruction requirements had been fully met, the Fund was running the risk that some of its resources might be used for other than temporary assistance and this was pointed out in the first Annual Report of the Executive Directors . . . . In considering applications for the use of the Fund's resources during this period, the Executive Board has endeavoured to limit the risk involved to a minimum.[1]

Then in 1949 the Fund took the view that countries receiving Marshall Aid should request the purchase of US dollars from the Fund only in exceptional or unforeseen cases,[2] and in consequence the flow of transactions almost dried up.

The resulting growth of general dissatisfaction with the level of the Fund's activity made it increasingly urgent to break the logjam and to demonstrate that the Fund was effectively able to fulfil the purposes for which it was founded. A first move in this direction was made in May 1951, when the Board adopted a proposal under which members wishing to draw would consult with the Fund so as to ensure that the use of its resources would be temporary. Later that year, the Board also agreed to changes in the scale of charges for drawings, so as to encourage the shorter-term use, and discourage the longer-term use, of Fund resources. (At the same time, the rate of charge at which consultations between member and Fund became obligatory was reduced from 4 per cent to $3\frac{1}{2}$ per cent which would be reached after a period varying between eighteen months and three years.) The changes in the provisions for charges were not however a very effective way of influencing the behaviour of members.[3]

The way was opened for a resumption of business only as the result of decisions (or clarifications) reached by the Executive Board after the appointment in 1952 of Mr Ivor Rooth as managing director. Under the first of these, taken in February 1952, the inadequate repurchase provisions of Article V, Section 7, were reinforced by a new rule 'that a member drawing on the Fund should repay the Fund within a period of three to five years'.[4] There followed three decisions, or clarifications, the first two in 1952 and the third in 1955, all serving to liberalise the terms on which the Fund is prepared to do business. The *first* of these is

[1] *Annual Report*, 1948, p. 46.
[2] *Annual Report*, 1949, p. 43.
[3] Bank of England, *Quarterly Bulletin*, March 1969, p. 40.
[4] Mr Ivar Rooth (M. Gutt's successor as managing director of the Fund), quoted in the IMF's *Financial News Survey*, 29 May 1953.

with respect to what are sometimes called drawings within the 'gold tranche'. This term refers to drawings by a member which do not increase the Fund's holdings of its currency beyond an amount equal to its quota. Where the Fund holds less than this amount of the currency of a member, this is because the amount below the quota represents the member's original gold subscription to the Fund, or repurchases of its currency with gold or convertible currencies which it has made, or purchases of its currency by other members. The Board has stated that for drawings within the so-called 'gold tranche' members can expect to receive 'the overwhelming benefit of any doubt' which might arise in connection with requests to make such drawings.[1]

Under the amendment to the Charter carried out in 1969, this provision is reflected in Article V, which now establishes the legal automaticity of drawings in the gold tranche, while at the same time—and in the spirit of the February 1952 Decision—terminates the Fund's power to create new facilities for the unconditional use of its resources.[2]

Under the *second* decision, the Fund is

prepared, in appropriate cases, to enter into stand-by arrangements with members. Under a stand-by arrangement, a member is assured the right to purchase a stated amount of foreign exchange for a fixed period of time. The time announced for stand-by arrangements is six months, with the possibility of renewal.[3]

In fact, only one stand-by had been granted under this decision by the time it came to be reviewed by the Board at the end of 1953. One of the reasons for this was that the limitation of arrangements to six months had proved too restrictive. Fund policy on this point was, therefore, reformulated and the Fund undertook to '. . . give sympathetic consideration to a request for a longer stand-by arrangement in the light of the problems facing the member and the measures being taken to deal with them.' However: 'With respect to stand-by arrangements for periods of more than six months, the Fund and the member might find it appropriate to reach understandings additional to those set forth in this decision'. Since 1953, the stand-by procedure has developed to the point where it has come to represent the usual means of access to Fund resources (as opposed to the immediate drawing). The history of this development is very largely one of the gradual elaboration of more or less standard types of '. . . understandings additional to those set forth in this decision. . . .'

A prerequisite of a stand-by arrangement is the preparation by the member of a programme designed to correct the imbalance which is the

[1] The IMF's *Annual Report* for 1952, p. 42.
[2] Bank of England, op. cit., p. 41.
[3] Mr Rooth, op. cit.

occasion for the stand-by. The policies to be pursued under the programme, usually with specific commitments known as performance
criteria, are set out in a Letter of Intent by the member concerned.
Failure to meet such criteria (which may cover the level of bank credit,
public sector borrowing, net foreign exchange position, and so on) can
lead to automatic interruption of the member's right to draw under the
stand-by until further consultations have been held. As a corollary to
this, access to resources under the stand-by is normally made available
at periodic intervals over the one-year life of the arrangement. Finally,
members are required to remain in close consultation with the Fund
during the stand-by period. More recently, this safeguard has been
extended to provide for a continuation of close consultation, beyond
the life of the stand-by, so long as the Fund's holdings of the member's
currency remain above 125 per cent of its quota.[1]

Under the *third* decision, or rather 'clarification', it was
announced that

in practice the Fund's attitude towards applications for drawings within
the first credit tranche (i.e. drawings that raise the Fund's holdings of
a member's currency above 100 per cent but not over 125 per cent of
its quota) is a liberal one.[2]

None of these decisions clarified the significance of the provision
(noted above) that a member may not use the Fund's resources
'to meet a large or sustained outflow of capital': nevertheless the
Fund always avoided drawing any sharp distinction between the
financing of capital and of current transactions. Formal
clarification followed later on: a decision of the Executive Board
in July 1961 finally eliminated any doubt which had not already
been dissipated by the practices of the Fund, that the Fund's
resources can be used to alleviate pressures brought about by
capital transfers.

The 1961 Decision, however, cannot be said to have removed all
uncertainties about the role of the Fund in relation to capital flows.
There remains an area of difficulty which arises from a fundamental
lack of congruence between the provisions of the Articles on the one
hand and the international payments system as it has developed on the
other. This is because the Articles were drawn up on the basis of
assumptions about capital movements which have not proved generally
valid. For example, the limitation on the use of the Fund's resources
for meeting a capital outflow presupposes that it is always possible, at
a time when a country's reserves are declining, to distinguish clearly
between the parts played by current and capital transfers. It seems also

[1] Bank of England, *Quarterly Bulletin*, March 1969, pp. 42–3
[2] *Annual Report*, 1955, p. 85. See also the *Annual Report*, 1957, p .119.

to have been assumed that capital transfers would normally be subject to control and hence unlikely to give rise to large or sustained outflows; in practice, however, members have preferred since the advent of convertibility to allow a significant degree of freedom for capital transfers.[1]

Despite the clarifications and innovations adopted by the Executive Board after Mr Rooth's assumption of the managing directorship, the Fund's transactions continued for a number of years to be on a very modest scale, as will be seen from Table 5A. Then in 1956 came the Suez crisis, the financial aftermath of which led both Britain and France to seek, and obtain, large-scale accommodation from the Fund. From then onwards, none could doubt the importance of the role which member countries wished the Fund to play in contributing to world liquidity. A symptom of this change in the Fund's standing are the general increases in quotas agreed in 1959 and again in 1965 (above p. 108).

The total of drawings shown in Table 5A are, in Table 5B, analysed by country. It will be seen that 67 members had on some occasion before the end of 1969 purchased other members' currencies from the Fund.

Choice of currencies for drawing and repayment

The provisions of the Fund Charter governing the choice of currencies to be drawn by a member, and the choice of those which he may use for repayment, are to say the least rather complicated[2]. The most important provisions are, however, that no currency may be used for repayment unless:

(1) the Fund's holding of it is not in excess of the original subscription: thus sterling might not be used for repayment if the Fund's holding of sterling had (by virtue of prior drawings of other currencies by the UK) increased to more than 75 per cent of the UK quota; and

(2) the country whose currency it is has emerged from the transitional provisions of Article XIV: hence sterling, and indeed the currencies of all the major powers except the US and Canada, might not be so used prior to the concerted move in February 1961 from Article XIV status to Article VIII status (above, page 101).

Prior to February 1961 the effect of these two conditions was to make the two dollars virtually the only currencies suitable for repurchases, and in practice no other currency was so used. As a

[1] Bank of England, op. cit., pp. 43–4.
[2] For a full explanation, see Horsefield, 'Drawings, Repurchases and Currencies', in *Finance and Development*, no. 4, 1968, p. 20.

result (and also because in the early post-war years many essential goods were readily obtainable only for dollars)

Fund members were most reluctant to draw any currency except dollars, since they would have to repurchase with dollars . . . .

But then things changed, as the main European currencies gradually became more useful to buy commodities with, and therefore more desirable. And in February 1961 the situation was transformed by the acceptance of the obligations of convertibility by nearly every country in Western Europe. Thereafter their currencies, as well as US dollars, could be used in repurchases. Consequently their currencies, as well as US dollars, became acceptable in drawings.

The acceptance by these countries of convertibility also did away

TABLE 5A

IMF DRAWINGS AND STANDBYS 1947–69

(*In millions of US dollars*)

| | Gross Drawings by Members | | | Standbys in force at year-end |
	In US dollars	In other currencies	Total	
1947	461	7	468	
1948	197	11	208	
1949	101	—	101	
1950	—	—	—	
1951	7	28	35	
1952	85	—	85	55
1953	68	162	230	50
1954	62	—	62	90
1955	28	—	28	62
1956	678	14	692	1,117
1957	977	—	977	870
1958	252	86	338	911
1959	139	41	180	208
1960	148	132	280	383
1961	822	1,656	2,478	1,415
1962	109	475	584	1,567
1963	194	139	333	1,743
1964	282	1,668	1,950	685
1965	282	2,151	2,433	280
1966	159	1,289	1,448	365
1967	114	721	835	1,804
1968	806	2,746	3,552	339
1969	1,341	1,530	2,871	849
	7,312	12,857	20,169	

TABLE 5B

DRAWINGS FROM THE IMF: TOTALS FROM THE BEGINNING
OF OPERATIONS TO THE END OF 1969

(In millions of US dollars)

Afghanistan	43.8	Japan	249.0
Argentina	425.0	Korea	12.5
Australia	225.0	Liberia	25.5
Belgium	199.5	Mali	20.4
Bolivia	45.4	Mauritius	4.0
Brazil	578.4	Mexico	112.5
Burma	34.5	Morocco	73.1
Burundi	19.4	Netherlands	144.1
Canada	726.0	New Zealand	159.2
Ceylon	150.3	Nicaragua	70.5
Chile	348.0	Nigeria	9.2
Colombia	345.6	Norway	9.6
Costa Rica	40.8	Pakistan	150.5
Cyprus	2.9	Panama	12.1
Denmark	89.2	Paraguay	8.1
Dominican Republic	49.6	Peru	112.0
Ecuador	58.2	Philippines	140.8
El Salvador	69.5	Rwanda	12.0
Ethiopia	0.6	Sierra Leone	6.9
Finland	103.2	Somalia	18.9
France	1,764.6	South Africa	211.9
Germany	880.0	Spain	216.0
Ghana	106.4	Sudan	79.4
Guatemala	36.0	Syria	61.4
Guinea	4.8	Trinidad & Tobago	4.8
Haiti	29.1	Tunisia	44.2
Honduras	32.5	Turkey	230.5
Iceland	21.8	United Arab Republic	276.7
India	1,090.0	United Kingdom	7,134.0
Indonesia	283.2	United States	1,840.0
Iran	167.5	Uruguay	51.3
Iraq	40.0	Yugoslavia	269.4
Ireland	22.5	Former members	78.8
Israel	61.2		
Italy	225.0	Total	20,168.8

with almost the last remnants of the bilateralism which the founding fathers had regarded as the natural way to trade. Once a country's currency is exchangeable for gold, and therefore, through gold, for any other currency, it becomes natural to regard balance of payments deficits as incurred against the world at large, and not against one particular country. Thus there was no longer any need to pick one particular currency with which to settle one's deficits.

By 1961, therefore, there was a wide range of currencies in which a drawing would be perfectly acceptable to the drawer, and a wide range of currencies in which repurchases would be perfectly acceptable to the Fund. . . .

In these circumstances something had to be done to decide which currencies countries should draw, and in which they should repurchase. Otherwise there would be no way of influencing drawings and repurchases toward the ideal situation in which the Fund's holdings of each member's currency equalled 75 per cent of the member's quota. This problem . . . took a long time to solve, but in July 1962 the Board of the Fund took a comprehensive decision. This recounted that since February 1961 member countries had been consulting the Managing Director about which currencies it would be best for them to draw, and went on to prescribe that such consultations should in future take place both for drawings and for repurchases. It then set out the principles which the Managing Director would adopt in making recommendations as to the currencies to be used.

As regards drawings, three factors were to be taken into account: the balance of payments of the countries whose currencies would be considered for drawing, their reserves, and the Fund's holdings of their currencies. Accordingly, drawings would be directed toward the currencies of countries whose balance of payments was good, and whose reserves were in good shape, provided that the Fund's holdings of the currency of that country were not being depleted too much. As regards repurchases, what would be watched would be the Fund's holdings of each currency compared with that country's quota, although some consideration would also be given to the country's balance of payments. . . . The Fund could not accept in repurchases any currency of which its holdings were at or above 75 per cent of that country's quota, nor the currency of any country that had not accepted the obligations of convertibility.

From these general principles a regular procedure has been evolved, based on a quarterly forecast of the drawings that may be made in the ensuing quarter, and of the repurchases that may be expected during the quarter. A list is drawn up of countries whose balances of payments and reserves would permit them to provide assistance to other members. . . . If, however, the Fund's holdings of a particular currency in the list should fall very low, its use in drawings will be limited unless the Fund can borrow more of that currency under the General Arrangements to Borrow or otherwise.

The budget thus worked out is discussed in advance by the Managing Director with the Executive Directors appointed or elected by the countries whose names are on the list and, subject to any modification introduced as a result of this consultation, the list is used as a guide when advising members what currencies to draw.[1]

[1] Horsefield, op. cit., pp. 22 and 23. There are various additional complications to which I have not referred: for these the reader is referred to Mr Horsefield's article.

The main consequence of these new arrangements of 1961–2 was a marked swing away from drawing in US dollars in favour of other currencies (see Table 5A). This great change in the position of the dollar in the Fund's operations is a symptom of the swing in the US balance of payments from surplus to deficit (see Chapter 16) but it also conforms to a deliberate policy of broadening the range of currencies in use for drawings. The currencies drawn in addition to dollars may be seen from Table 5C.

TABLE 5C

IMF: CURRENCIES DRAWN FROM THE BEGINNING OF
OPERATIONS TO THE END OF 1969

(In millions of US dollars)

Argentine pesos	107.0	Malaysian dollars	5.0
Australian dollars	277.0	Mexican pesos	96.5
Austrian schillings	191.5	Netherlands guilders	927.2
Belgian francs	728.6	Norwegian kroner	65.8
Brazilian cruzeiros	25.0	Pounds sterling	984.7
Canadian dollars	1,411.2	S. African rand	182.0
Danish kroner	66.8	Spanish pesetas	128.5
Deutsche mark	3,390.2	Swedish kronor	262.5
Finnish markaa	14.0	US dollars	7,311.9
French francs	1,454.0	Venezuelan bolivares	28.5
Irish pounds	53.0		
Italian lire	1,786.1	Total	20,168.8
Japanese yen	671.8		

As regards the selection of currencies for repurchases:

The budget for repurchases allocates those that are expected to fall due during the quarter among the currencies which the Fund can accept (i.e. convertible currencies of which its holdings do not exceed 75 per cent of the members' quotas) roughly in proportion to each member's 'reserve position in the Fund'. By this is meant (a) the excess of a member's quota over the Fund's holdings of its currency, plus (b) any loans which it has made to the Fund (for example, under the General Arrangements to Borrow). . . .

Special considerations led to the use of different technique for effecting most repurchases during 1964–6. Fund holdings of US dollars had risen to 75 per cent of the US quota about the end of 1963, so that no more US dollars could be accepted in repurchases. Many countries, however, were accustomed to using that currency in making their repurchases from the Fund, since it was the main currency in which they held their foreign exchange reserves. To allow the repurchase procedure to continue to function smoothly, the Executive Board accepted a US offer of a 'conversion facility'. Under this technique, the United States drew from the Fund currencies that the Fund was able to accept in repurchase. The United States then sold the currencies it had drawn to countries wishing to make repurchases; these sales were made at par against US dollars. Since the currencies drawn in this way by the United States were promptly paid back into the Fund by the country making the repurchase, the position of the country whose currency was drawn was unaffected by the procedure, and it did not therefore matter which currency the United States drew. In fact, it drew a number of different currencies at various times. This technique was last used late in 1966, and currencies for subsequent repurchases have been chosen in accordance with the budget method described above.[1]

Fund missions

As we have seen, the Fund's resources are available only for providing members with *temporary* assistance, so that except where a member is drawing within his gold tranche, and hence enjoys (at any rate since 1952) 'the overwhelming benefit of any doubt', the Fund has to decide in advance whether the prospective drawer's balance of payments difficulties are going to be temporary—a task which is liable to be difficult and even delicate.

In some cases, no doubt, a disequilibrium could be judged temporary simply on the ground that it would correct itself, without any official action being required by the country concerned. Thus, for instance, a country might require abnormally large imports in a particular year, due to having an exceptionally bad harvest: this would give rise to a disequilibrium lasting for one year and no longer. In other cases, however, a disequilibrium could be expected to be temporary only if the authorities in the countries concerned seemed able and willing to take effective remedial action. In such cases the Fund would have to decide first, what kind of remedial action, if any, was possible, and second, whether the authorities in the country concerned could be trusted to carry it out. The administrative arrangements which have been evolved by the Fund for taking the required decisions are based on the Fund's *missions*.

The only provision in the Articles of Agreement which seems to envisage Fund missions to member countries was that which calls for 'Article XIV consultations' with any member country continuing (after the Fund's first five years, i.e., as from 1952) to impose restrictions under the 'transitional provisions' of Article

[1] Horsefield, op. cit., p. 24.

XIV. Nevertheless a consultation does not *require* a mission, and in the case of the earliest consultations (undertaken by 1954), only half took the form of a mission to the countries concerned (the remaining consultations taking place in Washington or by correspondence). Only later did missions become normal for Article XIV consultations; and only later still (1961) did members accept that Article VIII countries should voluntarily undertake substantially the same consultation procedure as required under Article XIV.

Another crucial development, dating from the mid-1950s, was the acceptance that the Fund's missions should undertake negotiations for drawings and standbys, with the associated provisions for programmes, performance criteria, letters of intent and continued consultations.[1] Up till then the US authorities are believed to have been consulted about all requests for drawings on the Fund and (as was not unreasonable, given that up till then virtually all drawings were of US dollars) no drawing was approved by the Executive Board without it being clear in advance that the US authorities were in agreement. Hence up to the mid-1950s the Fund's staff obviously could not negotiate on financial transactions, since the effective decision-making authority lay in the US administration. But thereafter for small drawings, and as from a somewhat later date for large ones, the Executive Board came to accept as the normal procedure that decisions about financial transactions with particular members should effectively be taken by the Staff (on the basis of broad policies laid down by the Board and subject to informal guidance from Executive Directors) and be ratified as a matter of course by the Board.

An equally important development in the Fund's mission technique was the realisation that the good doctor does not treat individual symptoms; an essential preliminary to any action is a diagnosis of the general state of the country's economy: the rate of growth, the pace of inflation, the balance of payments, the financial deficit or surplus of the public sector, and so on—the survey embracing both what has already happened in the past and what (on stated hypotheses about official policy) might reasonably be expected to happen in the future. Only after this extensive preliminary has been completed should the mission tackle the items in its brief which arise out of the possible need for financial or other action on the part of the Fund.

[1] Above, pp. 116–17.

10

SPECIAL DRAWING RIGHTS

A new reserve asset

Except where the Fund's holding of a member's currency is less than his initial currency subscription of three-quarters of his quota (a state of affairs which arises through other Fund members having previously drawn his currency) the Fund's original Charter as drafted at Bretton Woods requires that a member may draw only temporarily, and since 1952 'temporarily' has been interpreted to mean 'at all events for less than five years'. Moreover, all drawings which take a member beyond his gold tranche are at the discretion of the Fund. Hence the liquidity made available by the Fund under its original Charter, which was not amended until 1969, is open to the possible objection of being inferior to liquidity in the form of owned reserves and particularly of owned gold reserves.

For this reason there have been proposals put forward from time to time for the creation of some new kind of reserve asset, a kind of 'paper gold', to supplement (and possibly also to replace) owned reserves in the traditional form of gold and foreign exchange. The first proposal I need refer to is that of Sir Hubert Henderson, whose *Monetary Proposals for Lausanne*, originally published on the eve of the Lausanne Conference in 1932, have subsequently been made more widely available in his collected works, *The Inter-War Years*. The next important scheme was Keynes's *Proposals for an International Clearing Union*, published as a British white paper in 1943. This scheme, which would have introduced Bancor (a completely new reserve asset), was put forward as a basis for the institution which was later to emerge as the IMF. However, in the negotiations preceding the Bretton Woods conference the proposals in the White Plan prevailed, with the result that Keynesian Bancor did not see the light of day. After Keynes' Clearing Union came another scheme with some family resemblance: the Triffin Plan, originally put forward in 1959, and described below in Chapter 20. Following Triffin, many other eminent economists, including Edward Bernstein, came forward with a variety of suggestions for a new kind of reserve asset.

A classification of proposals

In order to clarify the different kinds of new reserve media which have been suggested by such reformers, I suggest the following fourfold grouping, according as to whether the proposed new asset most closely resembles:

(1) inconvertible bank notes (e.g. Keynes' Bancor)
(2) bank deposits (as in the Triffin Plan)
(3) unit trust units (e.g. Bernstein's Composite Reserve Unit)
(4) IMF super-gold-tranche General Account drawing rights.

Such a fourfold grouping gives us four convenient labels by which to distinguish the various kinds of new assets which have been proposed:

(1) Bancor-type
(2) deposit-type
(3) CRU-type
(4) drawing-right-type.

(1) The characteristic of a Bancor-type reserve asset is that it would not rely in any meaningful sense on having any *backing*: hence it could never in practice achieve widespread acceptability except thanks to a prior agreement between the major powers to accumulate it either without limit or at any rate up to a certain ceiling.

(2) The characteristic of a deposit-type reserve asset is that it is convertible on demand into some other valuable asset (gold in the case of the Triffin Plan) and hence needs a prudent minimum of backing, which however need not of course be 100 per cent. By virtue of its convertibility, such a reserve asset would be an attractive investment in the eyes of a holder: hence there is in this case less need for prior agreement on minimum holdings (though under the Triffin Plan, as we shall see in Chapter 20, there would be a minimum holding set initially at 20 per cent of reserves).

(3) The characteristic of a CRU-type reserve asset, as initially pro-

posed by Mr Bernstein, is that it would be in some sense a legal claim on a portfolio constituted according to prescribed rules—the portfolio in this case comprising a collection of national currencies. Here also the new reserve asset could be made attractive as an investment, so that prior agreement on minimum holdings might well not be necessary.

(4) The characteristic of a drawing-right-type reserve asset is that it must be unconditional and with no irksome rules about repayment, i.e., it would have to be like the drawing right on the IMF General Account enjoyed by a member, the Fund's holding of whose currency is less than three-quarters of his quota.

The Group of Ten's initiative

For a long time the statesmen and officials in the economically advanced countries appeared to turn a deaf ear to the chorus of reformers. As a senior Fund official, Dr J. J. Polak, put it in 1967:

Until a few years ago there was a tendency to speak of international liquidity in general, without a sharp distinction between its two main categories, unconditionally available reserves, i.e., the kind of liquidity that countries can use without being subject to any commitments or discussion as to policy; and 'conditional liquidity' such as the Fund provides in the credit tranches.[1]

Then, in September 1963, following an American initiative at the Fund's annual meeting that year, the Ministers and Governors of the Group of Ten (the ten IMF members participating in the General Arrangements to Borrow) decided to entrust a committee of officials, the so-called Group of Deputies, with the task of undertaking 'a thorough examination of the outlook for the functioning of the international monetary system and of its probable future needs for liquidity'. The Deputies were given wide terms of reference, except that they were not required to reconsider what was taken to be the proven value of a monetary system 'based on fixed exchange rates and the established price of gold'.

The Deputies duly reported back to the Ministers and Governors in June 1964, and on the basis of the report the latter agreed to sponsor two proposals for action and two for further studies. The first of the proposals for action was to support an increase in IMF quotas—an increase which (as we saw in Chapter 9) was successfully negotiated in the course of 1964 and came into operation in 1966. The second proposal for action was to invite

[1] J. J. Polak, in article on Special Drawing Rights, in *Finance and Development,* December 1967, p. 277.

Working Party No. 3 of the OECD[1] to engage in the 'multilateral surveillance' of the ways and means of financing balance of payments disequilibria, based on much improved statistical data to be collected from the member countries through the agency of the Bank for International Settlements at Basle. This 'multilateral surveillance' was duly brought into operation by W.P.3 before the end of 1964.

To turn now to the two studies sponsored by the Ten, the first was for a study by W.P.3 of the 'balance of payments adjustment process'. In the words of the ministerial statement covering the Deputies' Report:

The smooth functioning of the international monetary system depends on the avoidance of major and persistent international imbalances and on the effective use of appropriate policies by national governments to correct them when they occur. The Ministers and Governors have therefore decided to initiate a thorough study of the measures and instruments best suited for achieving this purpose compatibly with the pursuit of essential internal objectives. In view of the experience it has already acquired in this field, Working Party 3 of the OECD is being invited to take charge of this study.

The study thus requested duly appeared as an OECD publication in August 1966, under the heading of *The Balance of Payments Adjustment Process, a Report by Working Party No. 3 of the Economic Policy Committee.*

The other study proposed by the Deputies in their Report of June 1964 arose out of their discussions 'concerning two types of proposal: one for the introduction, through an agreement among the member countries of the Group, of a new reserve asset, which would be created according to appraised overall needs for reserves; and the other based on the acceptance of gold tranche or similar claims on the Fund as a form of international asset, the volume of which could, if necessary, be enlarged to meet an

[1] The Working Party was instituted in 1961. Its purpose is 'the promotion of better international payments equilibrium'; and its terms of reference state that it 'will analyse the effect on international payments of monetary, fiscal and other policy measures, and will consult together on policy measures, both national and international, as they relate to international payments equilibrium'. The countries directly represented on Working Party No. 3 are: Canada, France, Germany, Italy, Japan, the Netherlands, Sweden, Switzerland, the United Kingdom and the United States (i.e. the 'Ten' minus Belgium plus Switzerland). The Working Party consists of senior officials (from Ministries of Finance and other key government agencies and Central Banks) concerned with balance of payments questions within their own administrations; and has established the practice of holding its meetings at six- to eight-week intervals.

agreed need'. The task of exploring these two types of proposals was entrusted to an ad hoc committee of officials, reporting to the Group of Ten, under the chairmanship of the Italian member, Rinaldo Ossola. The Ossola Report was prepared in 1965 and published in May of that year as the *Report of the Study Group on the Creation of Reserve Assets*. On receipt of the Ossola Report, the Ministers and Governors instructed their Deputies (who were at that time presided over by Dr Emminger of the Bundesbank) to 'determine and report to Ministers what basis can be reached on improvements needed in the international monetary system, including arrangements for the future creation of reserve assets, as and when needed, so as to permit adequate provision for the reserve needs of the world economy'. Thus the Ossola Report was followed by the Emminger Report, which was published in July 1966.

It is important to bear in mind that the two studies initiated by the Group of Ten (the study of the Adjustment Process by W.P.3 and of international liquidity by Ossola) were closely inter-related, especially in the minds of the Ministers and Governors from Continental Europe, in the sense that the introduction of any new kind of international asset far from being allowed to absolve deficit countries from the need to balance their accounts with the rest of the world, was intended to be matched by a firm resolve by all countries in deficit or surplus (but especially the former) to adopt, with greater alacrity than before, remedial policies appropriate to the treatment of the prevailing inter-national disequilibria. At one time, indeed, it seemed that some of the Continental members of the Group of Ten would be prepared to consider the possibility of a new kind of liquidity only as part of a package deal which would also prescribe certain unconditionally binding rules for remedial policies to be adopted by countries in balance-of-payments deficit. In due course, however, the view which prevailed was that remedies appropriate to all circumstances could not be prescribed in advance, and hence that prior agreement could reasonably be sought only for the acceptance of rather general guidelines. Thus the W.P.3 Report, as it appeared in August 1966, turned out to be a mild and rather academic document, analysing (in greater detail and with more attention to immediate problems) much the same kind of issues as were considered above in Chapter 4.

Ossola, Emminger and Rio

The work of the Ossola Group was by intention only explor-atory. The resulting report described and analysed the various proposals for new kinds of liquidity which were submitted for consideration by members of the Ten and by the IMF. The Emminger Group was intended to proceed to the next stage, that of making positive recommendations, but though it can claim to have made some progress, it was not able, in its 1966 Report, to produce any generally acceptable scheme, and indeed one member (France) did not in the end accept that any scheme was necessary, even as a basis for 'contingency planning'. Hence the Ossola and Emminger reports have to be regarded as only the first stages of a long process of international negotiation, which until September 1966 was conducted almost entirely within the Group of Ten, though with the Fund's managing director in attendance and with the assistance of experts from the staff of the IMF, the BIS, and the OECD. However, at the IMF Annual Meeting in September 1966 it was agreed to build on the foundations laid by the Emmin-ger Report in a new forum, a joint group of the Deputies of the Ten and the Executive Directors of the Fund. This new body met for the first time in Washington in November 1966, and on three occasions in 1967. The Ten also continued to meet separately as did also the Common Market countries, so that in the twelve months between the IMF annual meetings of 1966 and 1967 three separate bodies were engaged in the same exercise. The result of all these deliberations was the 'Rio draft', an outline for a scheme for Special Drawing Rights, put before the IMF Annual Meeting at Rio de Janeiro in September 1967. The Rio draft was translated into draft Articles and then further amended at a Ministerial meeting of the Ten in Stockholm in March 1968, whereupon it was accepted by the Executive Board of the Fund as the basis for a proposal for an extensive amendment to the Articles of Agreement, to be submitted to the member countries for ratification.

The amendment to the Articles, which was submitted to member countries in 1968 and duly ratified in 1969 by the appropriate voting procedure, was the first amendment to the Fund's Charter, as originally settled at Bretton Woods. The main purpose of the amendment was to entrust the IMF with the operation of a new 'Special Drawing Account', in addition to operating the 'General Account', the label now given to the financial arrangements (described in Chapter 9) provided for in the original Charter.

At the same time, however, as a kind of package deal, various other amendments were introduced into the Bretton Woods Charter, notably concerning voting procedures, the procedure for interpreting the Articles, and some of the drawing and repayment provisions of the General Account: the more important of these changes have already been noted, so they need not detain us here. Hence I propose now to proceed to a description of the Special Drawing Rights Scheme, as provided for in the amended Charter, with a brief explanation of how its main provisions came to be negotiated.

Membership

It was not until towards the end of 1966 that it was accepted that contingency planning for a new reserve asset should be on the basis that membership of any new scheme would be open to all members of the IMF on an equal footing. Previously there had been considerable support within the Group of Ten for a much more restricted membership, comprising the Ten with the addition of other rich countries, such as Austria and Australia, should they wish to join. On this basis the developing countries would have been excluded from membership, though as a quid pro quo they might have been offered more favourable treatment in the IMF General Account, for example by an increase in their quotas (and hence in their drawing rights). At the earliest stages in the negotiations among their Ten it had even been envisaged as a possibility that the scheme should be wholly divorced from the IMF and operated instead under the auspices of the BIS. However in the end it was unanimously accepted that the scheme should be under the IMF's purview and open to membership by all IMF members on an equal footing, and the Rio draft took this for granted.

The case for reform

The first issue which inevitably arises in any proposal for a new reserve asset is whether this is allegedly needed to supplement existing reserve media, to replace them, or to do both (as in the Triffin Plan). On this issue all the Ten had by 1965 come to accept that for the time being it is not practical politics to replace the dollar and the pound as reserve currencies. 'Certain radical proposals for the elimination of this potential instability inherent in the present reserve system, such as the total exclusion of the foreign exchange component by transition to a pure gold reserve standard or the transfer of today's foreign exchange reserves to the IMF, accompanied by the transformation of the latter into a sort of world central bank, were rejected by the leading countries from the outset as being impracticable under the present circumstances.'[1]

The alternative case for introducing a new reserve asset (namely to *supplement* existing reserve media) is the one which is seriously canvassed in the Ossola and Emminger Reports. All the Ten except France agreed that (though there might be no immediate need for a new kind of liquidity) contingency planning should go ahead lest the need should arise in the not-too-distant future. When, then, should the creation of any kind of liquidity begin, and at what pace should it proceed? The Ossola Report stressed that the need for additional reserves could not be assessed by any simple formula. Instead, many symptoms would have to be taken into account:

An indication that reserves are inadequate might be found in a reluctance to extend inter-governmental credit, or in an increasing propensity to seek credit, in preference to parting with reserve assets. Clearer evidence of a general scarcity might be found in a marked tendency to make maintenance, increase or restoration of reserves an overriding objective of economic policy, taking priority over other fundamental objectives, such as economic growth, a high level of employment and freedom of international trade . . . . Significant symptoms of strain would be a generalisation of trade and payments' restrictions, instability of exchange rates, rising unemployment and falling international prices.[2]

When would any of these 'symptoms of strain' appear? At the time of the Emminger Report the majority of opinion among the Ten was that they had not yet appeared. As the Bundesbank puts it, in its *Report* for the year 1965,[3]

It is true that the total holdings of monetary reserves have increased only slightly in 1965, especially when the statistics are adjusted for the influence of some temporary special circumstances. It is also true that new accruals of monetary gold in the western world have, especially owing to persistent hoarding of gold, since the beginning of 1965 dwindled to very small proportions, which alone would never suffice to meet the world's demand for reserves in the longer run. On the other hand, however, this slow expansion of the world's monetary reserves has by no means prevented world trade from developing vigorously.

[1] *Report* of the Deutsche Bundesbank for the year 1965, pp. 39 and 40.
[2] Ossola Report, para. 10.
[3] Bundesbank *Report*, 1965, pp. 40–1.

Nevertheless, the Group of Ten (except for France, who had not so far accepted the need for contingency planning) thought it prudent to work on the basis that the stagnation of world reserves in 1965 (a phenomenon which was repeated in subsequent years) might betoken the end of the upward trend in total reserves of the traditional kinds, and that (even if this evidence was inconclusive) the upward trend would anyway 'come to a natural end since the creation of additional reserves by US balance-of-payments deficits, which in the past seven years accounted for more than half of the new gold and exchange reserves, would in the long run be neither desirable nor indeed possible.'[1] Hence prudence required, in the opinion of all the Ten except France, that contingency planning should go ahead for the introduction of some new kind of reserve asset. What kind, then, should it be?

What kind of reserve asset?

In the early stages of the discussions in the Group of Ten, i.e., at least up to the time of the Emminger Report, the choice was taken to lie between a CRU-type asset, which seems to have made the running up to 1967, and a drawing-right-type scheme, which came more to the fore in the course of 1967, thanks to French support.

As regards the former, Dr Polak, looking back at the end of 1967, wrote:

Three or four years ago, there was some groping for the creation of additional reserve assets by a further extension of the reserve currency concept. It was suggested, in particular, that half a dozen or so currencies other than dollars or sterling should also perform the functions of reserve currencies. Traces of this approach can also be found in the early suggestions for a composite reserve unit, which would make the value of this unit to some extent derive from the market value of the underlying currency balances . . . .

Although the discussions continued for a while in terms of a reserve asset 'backed' by currency balances, it became increasingly clear that the essential value of the new asset derived from the obligation of participants to accept it, in much the same way as the value of domestic fiduciary money derives from its status as legal tender. The acceptance obligation was gradually made more precise, and the balances of their own currency by which countries were originally supposed to acquire the new asset were increasingly seen as immaterial to the plan, and in fact they were dropped when we drafted the Outline.[2]

[1] Bundesbank, ibid.
[2] Polak, op. cit., pp. 277–8.

Thus by the time of the Outline, or the 'Rio draft' as I have called it, the negotiating statesmen and officials of the Group of Ten had settled for contingency planning on the basis of a Bancor-type reserve asset. The only hesitant member of the Group was France: she had agreed, at an important meeting of the Common Market countries at Munich in April 1967, to join the rest of the Ten in contingency planning only on the understanding that this planning would be for a drawing rights scheme: now she found herself, later in the year, presented with an Outline for a scheme whose label, 'Special Drawing Rights', suggested that it related to new drawing rights, but whose provisions were quite unlike the existing IMF drawing rights and instead provided for what was essentially a Bancor-type reserve asset. It was France's misgivings after the Rio meeting (September 1967) which made necessary the calling of the Stockholm meeting of the Ten in March 1968 (above, page 130), and this failed in its main purpose in that the French minister, M. Debré, persisted in his misgivings and reserved his position. It was not until September 1969 (when M. Pompidou had succeeded General de Gaulle) that France expressed willingness to participate in the SDR scheme, as provided for in the new Articles which had been adopted in the previous July.

Neither of the broad types of schemes considered in the Ossola and Emminger Reports (i.e., the drawing-rights and CRU-type schemes) nor the Bancor-type scheme eventually adopted in the Rio draft, were intended to have the flexibility of the Triffin Plan, under which the required annual increase in the new reserve medium would be brought into existence in much the same way as new bank deposits are created within a national banking system; that is to say, by the IMF buying gold, making open market purchases or by granting advances.[1] Thus under the Triffin Plan the IMF would be able to exercise in some measure the freedom of action permitted as a matter of course to the banking systems operating within each country's national boundaries, that is to say, the freedom to make new money available to those who need it, rather than to hand it out to everybody on the basis of some preconceived formula. The Emminger Report, however, flatly rejected the possibility, in the foreseeable future, of entrusting an international agency with any such freedom of action. 'We are agreed', it states, 'that deliberate reserve creation should be neither geared nor directed to the financing of balance-of-payments deficits of individual

[1] Below, p. 249.

countries'. Instead there would be a 'distribution of additional reserve assets to all participating countries in accordance with an agreed general formula', for example in proportion to IMF quotas.[1]

The adoption of the SDR scheme

In the course of the second half of 1969, the negotiations which had been under way since 1963 suddenly came to fruition. The Bretton Woods Charter was amended, *inter alia* by the inclusion of new Articles making possible the creation of a Special Drawing Account. The Amendment entered into force on 28 July 1969 following acceptance by the required three-fifths of members representing four-fifths of total voting power. The 'club' for operating the SDR scheme came into existence on 6 August: by that day the Fund had received instruments of participation in the Special Drawing Account from members together having more than the required 75 per cent of total quotas. At the Fund Annual Meeting in September, agreement was reached as to the date of the initial creation of SDRs: this was to be at the beginning of 1970.[2] Agreement was similarly reached on the amount of the SDRs to be created in the first three years: $3.5 billions in January 1970 and $3.0 billions in 1971 and again in 1972. Agreement on activation in 1970 was possible only because the EEC countries were sufficiently impressed by the evidence of a growing shortage of international liquidity (which would be intensified by the expected improvement in the US and UK balance of payments) not to insist on their earlier contention that activation had to be conditional *first* on a substantial improvement in the US balance of payments and *second* on the observance of stricter 'rules of the game' (more particularly by deficit countries) to expedite the adjustment process.

The SDR facility in outline[3]

SDRs will be more readily available than the credit that the IMF provides through drawings in the credit tranches of the General

[1] See Emminger Report, paras. 37 and 98(4).
[2] By the end of 1969, it was known that 104 countries would participate in the initial distribution. The 11 non-participants were China, Ethiopia, Iraq, Kuwait, Lebanon, Libya, Nepal, Portugal, Saudi Arabia, Singapore and Thailand.
[3] Much of this section is quoted verbatim from an article by Martin Barrett and Margaret L. Greene on 'Special Drawing Rights: a Major Step in the Evolution of the World's Monetary System', in the January 1968 issue of the *Bulletin* of the Federal Reserve Bank of New York. The text of the new Articles, with a detailed commentary, was published as a white paper in June 1968 (Cmnd. 3662).

Account. Any participating country will be able to use SDRs whenever it has a balance-of-payments or reserve need to do so. Its exercise of this right will not be subject to consultation or prior challenge nor contingent on the adoption of prescribed policies designed to restore balance-of-payments equilibrium. Moreover, SDRs are intended to provide a permanent addition to international reserves, whereas most General Account transactions give rise to only a temporary increase. Finally, the use of SDRs does not entail repayment according to a fixed schedule, as does the use of the resources of the General Account, although SDR balances must be partially reconstituted following large and prolonged use. In short, the SDRs are intended to provide systematic and regular additions to international liquidity, and to be readily available to any member of the Fund which elects to participate.

The scheme provides for the creation of specified annual amounts of a new Bancor-type reserve asset called 'special drawing rights', the value of which to any one participant rests basically on the obligation of other participants to accept them from him, up to a prescribed ceiling, in exchange for convertible currency. The SDRs thus created are distributed among the participatory countries in proportion to their IMF quotas. The amounts to be issued are for a 'basic' period of several years. The initial basic period will be three years, but the IMF may decide that any future basic period will be of a different duration.

If unexpected developments make it desirable to change the rate at which SDRs should be issued, it will be possible, under the same consultation procedure, to increase or decrease this rate for the rest of a basic period or to adopt a new basic period with a different rate of creation. Such changes will ordinarily require an 85 per cent majority vote. However, a decision to reduce the rate of issue for the remainder of a current basic period can be taken by a simple majority of the voting power of the participating countries.

The amount of all the newly-created SDRs allocated to any participating country at the time of activation and at intervals thereafter is known as its 'net cumulative allocation', and the ceiling to any participant's commitment to accept SDRs from other members, in exchange for convertible currency, is set by the provision that no participating country can be required to hold more SDRs than three times its net cumulative allocation.

Any participatory country which can demonstrate its need to

finance a balance-of-payments deficit[1] is entitled to use its SDRs to obtain convertible currencies from other participants, subject to the limitation that over a five-year period a country's average holdings will not be less than 30 per cent of the average of its net cumulative allocation over the same period. If at any given time holdings of SDRs fall below this 30 per cent average level, it will be necessary to reconstitute and hold them for a sufficient time to establish the minimum average ratio.

This feature of the 'reconstitution provisions' in the scheme is designed to prevent any tendency toward financing large and persistent payments deficits by exclusive reliance on SDRs. The reconstitution provisions also include the principle that 'participants will pay due regard to the desirability of pursuing over time a balanced relationship between their holdings of special drawing rights and other reserves'. However, the reconstitution provisions do not prevent a country from using all its SDRs when its balance-of-payments difficulties are temporary in nature. If the balance-of-payments difficulties that give rise to the use of SDRs are in fact short-lived, then a country which had utilised all its allocation of SDRs in the early part of a five-year period could reconstitute its average holding simply by minimising the use of its allocation or accumulating SDRs in the latter part of the period.

A participant entitled to make use of his SDRs may do so in either of two ways:

(1) *bilaterally*, to buy back its own currency from another participating country or to effect certain other transactions specified by the Fund,

(2) *through the Fund*, in which case the Fund designates other participants to whom the SDRs may be transferred in exchange for convertible currency, and who must thereupon accept them up to the limit of their respective ceilings.

In the latter case the Fund selects countries for designation on much the same basis as it selects currencies for drawings from the General Account (see Chapter 9) subject to the overriding proviso that the IMF will always designate any country whose average SDR holdings would otherwise fall below 30 per cent of its average cumulative allocation in the then current five-year period.

---

[1] SDRs may not be used for the sole purpose of changing the composition of a country's reserves. In other words, a country cannot use SDRs simply to build up its foreign currency balances or gold holdings. Although the use of SDRs will not be subject to prior challenge, the IMF may make representations to any country that has failed to observe this principle.

(This proviso gives the IMF a means for enforcing the reconstitution provisions, referred to above.)

Will countries respond when bilaterally invited by another participant to accept SDRs in exchange for convertible currency? Will they resent being required by the Fund to accept them? Clearly this will depend primarily on how credible it seems to the accepting country (currently, it may be presumed, in balance-of-payments surplus) that should it later go into deficit there will then be other countries to which the SDRs currently accepted can be passed on. The credibility of this option clearly depends on the adequacy of the acceptance requirement in relation to the amounts of SDRs which surplus countries would be called upon to accept. The relationship prescribed in the new Articles (see above, page 136) would almost certainly be fully adequate if *all* IMF members opted for participation and none thereafter opted out, but obviously difficulties could arise if participation were partial and unbalanced (since if the participants were predominantly deficit countries, with very few surplus countries, many members would be entitled to use their SDRs but few could be required to accept them). Fortunately this possible difficulty was foreseen in drafting the Articles, which require very widespread initial participation as a necessary condition for activation, and this condition was in fact achieved at the end of 1969, otherwise the initial distribution of SDRs in January 1970 could not have occurred. On the other hand an amendment made (at the Stockholm meeting) to the Rio draft enables countries to opt out of further participation at the end of the first year or any subsequent year, so that the mutual confidence on which the scheme is based could conceivably be eroded if surplus countries made a habit of opting out. However, apart from this possible difficulty, SDRs would appear to be an attractive reserve asset, since they are denominated in terms of gold (and hence are unaffected by devaluations) and in addition earn a return in the form of a modest rate of interest.[1]

[1]Transactions in SDRs in the first three months of the scheme (i.e. the first quarter of 1970) totalled $300 millions and in April 1970 a further $88 millions.

EUROPEAN MONETARY COOPERATION

After the liberation of Europe, the revival of intra-European trade was almost solely on the basis of bilateral payments agreements under which one of the partners, or each of them, undertook to grant limited accumulation facilities to the other. The simplest way of describing these agreements is to say that in effect one country, say Belgium, allowed her partner, say Britain, limited rights to settle in her own currency, sterling; but the actual wording of the agreements described the arrangement as being one in which the Belgian monetary authorites undertook to 'sell Belgian francs to the Bank of England . . . against sterling'[1] so that British deficits with Belgium could (to the extent permitted by the agreed 'swing') be settled in Belgium's currency.

A survey of these bilateral payments agreements is given in the eighteenth *Annual Report* of the Bank for International Settlements (published in 1948), which tells us that they

were usually concluded between governments, according to a fairly uniform pattern: the central banks, as technical agents, supplied their own currency at a fixed rate of exchange against that of their partner up to a certain limit, which was often referred to as the 'swing', since it was intended to afford room for minor fluctuations in commercial deliveries between the two countries; beyond the limit thus fixed settlements had generally to be made in gold or convertible currency.[2]

---

[1] From the Anglo-Belgian *Monetary Agreement* of November 1947, published by HMSO, Cmnd. 7264.

[2] 'Convertible currency' here meant in practice, at that time, US dollars.

By October 1947, however, it was reported[1] that

the margin of credit possible under the payments agreements concluded by some countries are almost exhausted, and this is a quasi-permanent situation. For the expansion of trade to the extent which is possible, increasingly numerous gold payments would be necessary. This situation risks hampering not only the development of trade, but actually its maintenance at the present level. . . . In these circumstances, the Committee considers that greater flexibility in the present payments system is more than ever necessary.

This need for greater flexibility was the motive behind the Agreement on Multilateral Monetary Compensation of November 1947, which came into being largely as the result of the work of the Committee of European Economic Cooperation, the committee which was set up to implement the Marshall Plan and which also brought the OEEC into being in April 1948. Fourteen of the OEEC members were parties to the Agreement, but only six (Belgium, Luxembourg, France, Italy, Netherlands and the Bizone of Germany) were 'permanent' members; the other eight were 'occasional' members, with the right to contract out of any operation arising under the Agreement.[2] The operations provided for in the Agreement were 'first-category compensations' and 'second-category compensations'. From the description of these processes which is given us by the official Agent of the Agreement, the Bank for International Settlements,[3] we see that (in the jargon we used in Chapter 3) the former comprise circular off-setting, while the latter comprise non-circular settlements between two countries achieved by transferring a third country's currency:

First-category compensations involve only a reduction of existing balances ('balances' in this context covering both debit and credit accounts). Such operations imply a 'closed circuit' of countries each of which is debtor to its immediately preceding partner, while it is itself a creditor of its succeeding partner, the last country in the chain being the creditor of the first country, thus closing the circuit. These operations are partially automatic (in so far as the 'permanent' countries are concerned) and partially optional (in so far as they apply to 'occasional' members). . . . The simple offsetting . . . of the first category can lead only to reductions of outstanding debts (and credits) and presents no

[1] By the Committee on Payments Agreements, which was set up by the recipients of Marshall Aid. Quoted in the 18th *Annual Report* of the BIS, p. 146.
[2] The occasional members were: Austria, Denmark, Greece, Norway, Portugal, Sweden, the United Kingdom and the French Zone of Germany.
[3] See the 18th *Annual Report* of the BIS, pp. 148–9.

particular difficulties—except that, in some cases, countries may for one reason or another desire to maintain certain balances in one or more particular markets and thus are unwilling to reduce them. . . .

A 'second-category operation' may be defined as a payment made by one country to another by utilising the currency of a third country. A simple example would be the payment of a Norwegian debt to the Netherlands in sterling. It is evident that such a transaction involves a limited transferability of sterling.

Unfortunately, the category of operations which was easier to effect was possible in only a comparatively small number of cases.

The working accounts of the European payments agreements show debts (and credits) entering into the compensations to the equivalent of over 700 million dollars. About 400 million of this total is net debt (or credit) which cannot be offset.[1] Of the 300 million which can be subject to compensation in theory, experience has shown that, at the present time, the maximum possibilities of the first category alone amounts to about 30–50 million. From this it follows that the possibilities for the reduction of debts (and credits) by operations of the second category are some ten times as great as those of the first category.

As a result only a very limited amount of first category compensation was possible. Second category compensation was in practice also very restricted, for it was optional even in the case of 'permanent' members and almost all the proposals were objected to by the country whose currency was to be transferred, for reasons which were explained in Chapter 3. In the event only $5 millions of first category compensations and $46 millions of second category compensations had been effected when the scheme was superseded in October 1948 by the first Intra-European Payments Agreement[2] (IEPA).

The Intra-European Payments Agreements

The first IEPA, which operated for the nine months October 1948–June 1949, differed from the preceding arrangement in that it involved all the OEEC countries and also incorporated provisions for Indirect Aid. The provisions for first and second category compensations were retained, the former being compulsory,[3] the latter remaining optional, but during the nine months that the

[1] 'Net debt (or credit)' corresponds, in the language of Chapter 3, to 'overall deficit (or surplus)'.
[2] *Agreement for Intra-European Payments and Compensations*, 1948, published by HMSO, Cmnd. 7546.
[3] Except for Switzerland and Portugal.

scheme was in operation very few compensations were in fact effected.

Indirect Aid was so called because the ECA[1] made a portion of the Marshall Aid extended to certain OEEC countries conditional on their undertaking to extend similar aid to other OEEC countries.[2] The motive of the ECA in recommending, and indeed in insisting on, the Indirect Aid provisions of the IEPA was to increase the effectiveness of aid going to needy European countries, for each $1 of aid granted was supposed to benefit the immediate recipient as well as the indirect recipient, and in both cases the help was provided in a form which made a direct contribution to the recipient's external liquidity. The countries through whom Indirect Aid was granted were those which were expected to run surpluses with other OEEC countries during the period of the scheme. The aid they received took the form of a grant of dollars from the United States: the aid they granted took the form of bilateral drawing rights in favour of each of the countries with whom a bilateral surplus was expected.[3]

Each deficit country should, in theory, have received sufficient means of settlement for covering each of its nine-monthly bilateral deficits with the other OEEC countries. In practice, as we shall see, this objective was far from being fully achieved, for the forecasts of bilateral relationships were necessarily rather wild guesses and the rigid bilateralism of the drawing rights prevented them from being utilised where they were actually needed, as distinct from where they were expected to be needed. Even where the estimates did prove reasonably accurate, this may merely have meant that countries simply adjusted their import regulations from time to time so as to make their bilateral deficits run according to plan.[4] Countries certainly had an incentive to act in this way, for the IEPA offered them no inducement to eliminate their deficits.

The total of the drawing rights provided for was initially the equivalent of 810 million US dollars (later revised to $805 millions),

[1] The Economic Cooperation Administration, the American agency administering the Marshall Plan.

[2] Indirect Aid was the second device used by the ECA to facilitate intra-European aid, for during part of 1948 the ECA made 'off-shore' purchases for dollars in various European countries and delivered them as Aid to other countries. This technique was however soon abandoned.

[3] Neither Switzerland nor Portugal participated in Indirect Aid under the first IEPA, but only Switzerland did not participate under the second IEPA.

[4] See G. D. A. MacDougall's article in the London and Cambridge Economic Service *Bulletin* of August 1950.

but in the event only $677 millions were used before the termination of the scheme, and of this amount $67 millions were used for purposes other than meeting deficits. In addition to granting a portion of these drawing rights, Britain made a further contribution by agreeing that certain other OEEC countries should draw on their sterling balances to a predetermined extent.[1]

The Indirect Aid drawing rights were in effect vicarious gifts from the United States, for the countries receiving the rights gave no quid pro quo, while the countries affording the rights were reimbursed by Conditional Aid from the ECA. It is interesting to note that in practice Conditional Aid turned out to be unconditional, in that the countries affording drawing rights which were not wholly utilised suffered no reduction in their Conditional Aid and the unused drawing rights were either cancelled or carried forward to the 1949–50 scheme.

The second Intra-European Payments Agreement, for the year July 1949 to June 1950, followed its predecessor closely except that the total of drawing rights was somewhat increased and rather over one quarter of them was multilateral, i.e. capable of being used to settle bilateral deficits with any of the participating countries. (In most of the drawing rights granted, 25 per cent, or thereabouts, was multilateral, but the rights granted by Belgium were more than half multilateral.) The multilateral portions of the drawing rights were however to be used only after the BIS had performed all possible first category compensations and had then made the fullest use of bilateral drawing rights.

Statistical post mortem

The tables which follow, Tables 6 and 7, summarise some of the most important information collected by the BIS in the course of operating the two Payments Agreements over the whole 21 months from October 1948 to June 1950. Columns 1 and 2 of the former table set out the BIS's figures of the total of the *bilateral* deficits and surpluses of each participating country[2] with each of the other participants *in each separate month*. The bilateral deficit or surplus of any one participant with any other participant in each month was calculated by the BIS by simply noting the

[1] Similar contributions were offered by several other countries, but much smaller in amount that Britain's.
[2] Switzerland is however excluded, since she did not take part in Indirect Aid.
  Eire and Iceland, being members of the Sterling Area, are not shown separately from the UK. Likewise Luxembourg is included with Belgium and Trieste with Italy.

TABLE 6

INTRA-EUROPEAN PAYMENTS AGREEMENTS

DEFICITS AND SURPLUSES AS BETWEEN THE PARTICIPATING COUNTRIES, OCTOBER 1948 TO JUNE 1950

(All figures are expressed to the nearest million[1] of US dollars)

Country	Total of *Monthly* Bilateral Deficits and Surpluses with each of the other Participants		'Reciprocal' Deficits and Surpluses	Total of Bilateral Deficits and Surpluses, *taking the Period as a whole*		Overall Deficit or Surplus with all other Participants, *taking the Period as a whole*	
	Deficits	Surpluses		Deficits	Surpluses	Deficit	Surplus
	1	2	3	4	5	6	7
Austria	170	12	7	163	5	158	—
Belgium	151	722	151		570		570
Denmark	201	174	122	79	51	28	
France	453	454	296	157	158		1
Greece	241	7	7	233		233	
Italy	107	412	96	11	316		305
Netherlands	552	298	186	366	112	254	
Norway	260	41	32	228	10	218	
Portugal	139	47	30	109	16	93	
Sweden	143	300	103	40	197		157
Turkey	161	83	63	98	20	78	
United Kingdom	946	1,025	544	402	481		79
Western Germany	502	452	260	242	192	50	
TOTAL	4,025	4,025	1,897	2,128	2,128	1,112	1,112

[1] In this and later tables the process of rounding leads to small discrepancies in the additions.

TABLE 7

INTRA-EUROPEAN PAYMENTS AGREEMENTS
DRAWING RIGHTS UTILISED TO MEET DEFICITS,
OCTOBER 1948 TO JUNE 1950

(All figures expressed to the nearest million of US dollars)

Country	On a Bilateral Basis		On an Overall Basis	
	Amount Received	*Amount Granted*	*Amount Received*	*Amount Granted*
	1	*2*	*3*	*4*
Austria	152	4	148	
Belgium	9	434[1]		425
Denmark	35	7	28	
France	321	56	265	
Greece	199	0	199	
Italy	0	80		80
Netherlands	206	32	175	
Norway	131	11	120	
Portugal	16	3	13	
Sweden	8	85		77
Turkey	75	34	41	
United Kingdom	62	362		300
Western Germany	106	213		107
TOTAL	1,319	1,319	989	989

monthly movements of each country's official holding of the other's currency, before the BIS had arranged any end-of-the-month adjustments in the form of Indirect Aid, of first and second category compensations, and of gold or dollar settlements. Thus the United Kingdom's bilateral deficit with Belgium in (say) January 1949 would comprise the month's change in Belgium's official holding of sterling, minus the month's change in the United Kingdom's official holding of Belgian francs. The bilateral deficits and surpluses on which Table 6 is based are therefore affected by movements in one participant's holding of another's currency due to receipts from, or payments to, a third country. Such cases would occur in practice mainly as a result of the widespread use of sterling for making settlements outside the United Kingdom. If, for example, Belgium settled with Brazil in sterling this would reduce the UK–Belgian deficit, as calculated by

[1] Including drawings on the loans which Belgium made available in addition to Drawing Rights proper, under the second IEPA.

this BIS.[1] (The fact that the BIS calculated bilateral deficits and surpluses in this way had important consequences in the working of the European Payments Union, as we shall see in the next chapter.)

The figures in columns 4 and 5 of Table 6, relating to the bilateral deficits and surpluses of each participant with each of the other participants *taking the 21-month period as a whole*, are less than the totals of *monthly* bilateral deficits and surpluses (columns 1 and 2) since the process of cumulation gives rise to a considerable amount of cancellation. For example, in some of the 21 separate months the United Kingdom had bilateral deficits with Belgium (total $148 millions) while in the other months of the period Belgium had bilateral deficits with the United Kingdom (total $44 millions): in column 1 *all* these deficits would appear— $148 millions as part of the United Kingdom total and $44 millions as part of the Belgian total—but in Column 4 only the United Kingdom deficit for the period as a whole ($104 millions) would be recorded. In general terms, the difference between the two columns arises from what may be termed 'reciprocal deficits' —i.e. from bilateral deficits of A with B in some months balanced by bilateral deficits of B with A in other months. The total of 'reciprocal deficits' is shown in column 3, and since a reciprocal deficit is (by definition) one which is balanced by a surplus in the same bilateral relationship, the same column also serves to show the total of reciprocal surpluses (accounting for the difference between columns 2 and 5).

Columns 6 and 7 of Table 6 have been calculated as the differences between columns 4 and 5, and thus give the *overall* deficit or surplus of each participant with all the other participants in the 21-month period as a whole. If we refer to the last line of column 6, we see that the total overall deficits among the participants in the 21-month period as a whole was $1,112 millions, whereas the total of bilateral deficits was on the same basis $2,128 millions, so that the total of 'compensable' deficits was some $1,000 millions. However, only very little of this last amount—less than

---

[1] If Belgium's settlement in sterling had been not with Brazil but with another participant, say France, but the settlement was not made through the machinery of the IEPA (so that the BIS did not record the transaction as a second category compensation) the BIS's figures of each of the bilateral deficits between the three countries concerned (Belgium, France and Britain) would thereby be 'distorted'.

According to the Bank of England's *Report* for the year ended 28 February 1950, p. 10, £48 millions of sterling were in 1949 transferred by OEEC countries to other countries outside the Sterling Area, £100 millions were received by OEEC countries from outside the Sterling Area, and £48 millions were transferred between Britain's fellow members of the OEEC.

$100 millions in fact—was covered by first and second category compensations arranged under the IEPA; this must be attributed partly to the fact that deficits only rarely occurred in closed circuits, partly to the reluctance of countries to allow their currencies to be transferred.[1]

The second of the two tables, Table 7, summarises the Indirect Aid operations under the two Agreements. The point which calls for comment is the apparent inadequacy of the amount of drawing rights actually utilised to cover deficits, namely $1,319 millions on a bilateral basis, or $989 millions on an overall basis. Admittedly the latter amount was not far short of the total of overall deficits ($1,112 millions), but since so little was achieved under the IEPA provisions for first and second category compensations a large additional amount of bilateral drawing rights could usefully have been provided to complete the clearing of the compensable deficits. This indeed seems to have been the intention of the two Agreements, but it was only very imperfectly realised, as will be seen by comparing the total of $1,319 millions of bilateral rights utilised with the total of $2,128 millions of bilateral deficits shown in column 4 of Table 6.

In view of the apparent inadequacy of the drawing rights available under the two Agreements, it was unfortunate that some of the rights originally provided for had to be cancelled or left unused. The first scheme was particularly liable to be 'wasteful' of drawing rights,[2] since these were established on a rigid bilateral basis, which meant that rights which in the event proved to be over-generous could not be used elsewhere. Rather surprisingly, a somewhat larger amount was 'wasted' under the second scheme, even though a portion of the drawing rights was multilateral; an explanation is perhaps to be found in the changes in exchange rates which occurred in September 1949,[3] which considerably altered the previous pattern of intra-European deficits.

---

[1] It will be recalled from footnote 1 on p. 146 that in addition to the second category compensations arranged under the IEPA there were other transfers of sterling of a second category type—i.e. as between two of Britain's fellow members of the IEPA. Such transfers effected outside the IEPA machinery were not included in the BIS's statistics of first and second category compensations.

[2] Above, p. 142.

[3] See below, Chapter 18.

I 2

THE EPU, EMA and EEC

The next scheme for intra-European payments, the European Payments Union (EPU),[1] though carrying on some features of its predecessors, was much more nearly comparable, in its aims and its machinery, with the IMF (and even more with Keynes' Clearing Union[2]) than with the previous European schemes. First, the 'aid' provisions of the 1948–9 and 1949–50 schemes reappeared under the alias of 'Initial Credit (and Debit) Positions'[3] but their total amount was relatively small. Second, the little used provisions in the IEPA for first and second category compensations were superseded by machinery which *automatically* cleared all compensable deficits, irrespective of their size. Third, the same machinery also ensured that 'reciprocal deficits' were settled *automatically*, instead of inadequately (and indeed unintentionally) under the IEPA. Fourth, the EPU agreement, again unlike the IEPA, included provisions designed to correct, as well as to accommodate, intra-European disequilibria.

The machinery of settlement

The *modus operandi* of the EPU was basically as follows:

(1) Each month the Union took over all bilateral surpluses and deficits of each of the members. If for example during July

---

[1] The Agreement has been published by HMSO. See *Documents Relating to the EPU* and *Agreement for the Establishment of an EPU*, Cmnd. 8064.
[2] Above, pp. 84 and 111–12.
[3] Further aid provisions were introduced after the first year's operations, in the form of 'Special Resources'.

1950 Belgium ran a bilateral surplus with Britain, this would be treated as a surplus with the Union in the case of Belgium and as a deficit with the Union in the case of Britain, and Britain would not be called upon to make any settlement direct with Belgium. The sum of all Belgium's bilateral surpluses with other members in July 1950, minus all her bilateral deficits, would be recorded by the BIS[1] as Belgium's 'net position' for the month, and similarly for the other members.

(2) The monthly net positions of each member since mid-1950 were recorded by the BIS, with the appropriate sign, and cumulated, so that at the end of each month each member had a 'cumulative net position' with the Union. Since in the calculation of each member's cumulative net position, all his monthly bilateral deficits to date were set off against all his monthly bilateral surpluses, it follows that all compensable and all reciprocal deficits (and surpluses) between members were simply cancelled out.

(3) At the end of each month the change in a member's cumulative net position, as compared with a month ago, had to be settled as between the member and the Union. Either the member had to settle with the Union (if he had a cumulative net deficit which had increased or a cumulative net surplus which had diminished) or the Union had to settle with the member (if he had a cumulative net surplus which had increased or a cumulative net deficit which had diminished).

(4) The means prescribed for settling any change in a member's cumulative net position did not depend on why that change occurred. It did not, for instance, make the least difference to the British monetary authorities whether British tourists chose to visit Switzerland rather than Norway, whether British importers bought in Germany or in Greece, or whether British exports went to Turkey or to Belgium—though prior to the EPU there was a strong incentive for preferring the latter alternative in each of the three examples (as being much less likely to cause an outflow of gold). The EPU thus provided machinery for fully multilateral settlement between its members.

(5) The principal means of settlement (whether from a member to the Union or from the Union to a member) were gold (or US dollars) and so-called 'credits'. The latter were in effect IOU's denominated in the borrower's currency which the lender undertook to accumulate up to a certain ceiling. Thus according to the

---

[1] In its capacity as the Union's agent. The BIS calculated the surpluses and deficits for the Union in exactly the same way as it did for the IEPA. See p. 143.

nomenclature we adopted in Chapter 3, EPU credits can best be classed as 'accumulation facilities'. When the Union granted credit to a member, it accumulated IOU's expressed in terms of his currency, and when a member granted credit to the Union, he accumulated IOU's expressed in terms of the Union's 'unit of account'.[1] This unit of account was thus in a sense a new international currency, like the bancor of Keynes' Clearing Union, but it was not such a 'full-blooded' currency as Keynes' would have been in that it could not be transferred from one holder to another: the value of the Union's IOUs to a member holding them was solely as a means of settling with the Union in future months and as a claim on the Union's assets when the Union was disbanded.[2]

A major difference in the *modus operandi* of the EPU and the IMF General Account is thus that in the former the members did not make any initial contribution of their currencies to a common pool, but merely paid in their currencies (or promises thereof) as required, when they got into deficit with the Union. Moreover, since there was not a common pool, the Union could not settle with a surplus member in his own currency: hence the need for providing the Union with a new means of settlement—its 'unit of account'.

(6) The Union's 'unit of account' also served as the accounting unit in which members' cumulative net positions were recorded. The translation of amounts expressed in units of a member's own currency (sterling in Britain's case) into so many of the Union's units of account was achieved by the provision that for this purpose the Union's unit of account should have the same gold value as the US dollar.

(7) The formula for settling the proportion between gold (or dollars) and credit in any particular monthly settlement depended prior to July 1954 on the '*quota*' allocated to each member (see Table 8) and a formula which related the gold/credit proportion to the member's cumulative deficit or surplus expressed as a percentage of his quota. The relevant formula, as originally prescribed, is shown in Table 9, together with the minor amendments which were made as from mid-1953. (From mid-1954 to August 1955 the gold/credit ratio became invariably 50 : 50 and thereafter 75 : 25 until the demise of the Union at the end of 1958.)

---

[1] These IOU's bore interest at a rate which depended on various considerations, but which was never in excess of 3 per cent per annum.
[2] See below, pp. 158–60

TABLE 8

(Expressed in millions of US dollars)

Country	Quotas	Country	Quotas
Austria	70	Norway	200
Belgium	360	Portugal	70
Denmark	195	Sweden	260
France	520	Switzerland	250
Germany	500	Turkey	50
Greece	45	UK	1,060
Iceland	15		
Italy	205	Total	4,155
Netherlands	355		

TABLE 9

SCALE FOR DETERMINING, FOR ANY TRANSACTION OF THE EPU,
THE PROPORTION WHICH REQUIRED SETTLEMENT IN GOLD OR
DOLLARS, MID-1950 TO MID-1954

DEFICIT MEMBERS

Cumulative Accounting Position[1] of the Member Concerned, dating from mid-1950	*Percentage of gold or US dollars in monthly settlement received or made by the Union*	
	Originally	*Later*
Deficit in excess of member's quota	100	100
Deficit between 80 and 100% of member's quota	80	70
Deficit between 60 and 80% of member's quota	60	50
Deficit between 40 and 60% of member's quota	40	40
Deficit between 20 and 40% of member's quota	20	30
Deficit between 10 and 20% of member's quota	0	20
Deficit between 0 and 10% of member's quota	0	0

SURPLUS MEMBERS

Cumulative Accounting Position[1] of the Member Concerned, dating from mid-1950	*Percentage of gold or US dollars in monthly settlement received or made by the Union*
Surplus between 0 and 20% of member's quota	0
Surplus between 20 and 100% of member's quota	50
Surplus in excess of member's quota	not specified

[1]Defined on p. 153.

To provide for the contingency that the Union's receipts of gold and dollars might fall short of its payments, the ECA contributed an initial 'kitty' of 350 million US dollars.

The significance of the principle on which the EPU formula for gold payments is based will be seen if we contrast it with the principle on which gold payments had previously been required under the bilateral agreements, with two-way swings, which linked many of the members of the IEPA. Under her bilateral agreement with (say) Belgium, Britain would lose gold if her cumulative bilateral deficit with Belgium took her to the limit of the agreed swing, and this gold would never come back to Britain unless she thereafter ran a surplus large enough and persistent enough not only to wipe out her cumulative deficit but also to build up a cumulative surplus in excess of the swing. Thus gold lost under a bilateral agreement did not normally begin to return for a long time, if at all. On the other hand, gold losses to the EPU would begin to return immediately a member had a current surplus in any single month, i.e. he began to get gold back without having to eliminate his cumulative deficit, let alone build up a cumulative surplus.

It is now appropriate to mention two subsidiary provisions, relating to settlements, in the EPU agreement.

First, the equivalent of Indirect Aid under the EPU was arranged by giving the vicarious providers of the Aid 'Initial Debit Positions' in the Union and the recipients of the Aid 'Initial Credit Positions'; thus such Aid became part of the ordinary settlement machinery. (Subsequently these 'Aid' provisions in the original agreement were continued by the so-called 'Special Resources' procedure, under which the United States contributed dollars to the Union in order to discharge the liabilities to the Union of certain deficit countries.)

Second, if a member had an amount of his currency or of his liquid debts held by other members as at 30 June 1950, due e.g. to the operation of earlier monetary agreements, he had either to make an agreement to amortise the balances or to allow them to be used by the holders as 'existing resources' for settling any net deficit with the Union. Any balance given the status of 'existing resources' therefore corresponded broadly to an initial net credit position for the holder and to an initial net debit position for the other party. The main balances to be settled under these provisions were the sterling balances of various members, particularly Italy, Sweden and Portugal, the total amount of which on the date in question was about £200 millions. Britain indicated that she was prepared that all this sterling could be used for settling deficits with the EPU. If (as indeed actually happened) the use of sterling 'existing resources' involved Britain in gold payments to the Union, she was (by a special agreement) to be reimbursed by the ECA.

The settlement of a member's cumulative net position with the Union by the use of Existing Resources, Initial Positions, or Special Resources, was known as 'ante-quota' settlement, and what remained of a member's cumulative net position after ante-quota settlements had been effected was known as his 'cumulative *accounting* position'.[1] It was a member's cumulative accounting position, not his cumulative net position, which was relevant to the formula given in Table 9 for deciding in any month the proportion in which gold (or dollars) and credit had to be mixed in making settlements.

A statistical illustration

A practical example of how settlements were effected under the EPU is given in Table 10, which summarises the first three months' operations. Column 3 of the table shows each member's cumulative net position, i.e. the cumulative overall surplus (marked +) or deficit (marked −) of each member country with all the other members, taken together. As in Table 6, the total of the overall surpluses is necessarily equal to the total of the overall deficits. Column 4 shows the amount of existing resources which deficit countries holding such resources chose to use in settling with the EPU (marked −) and the amount and 'nationality' of the currencies which the EPU thereby acquired (marked +). The excess of column 3 over column 4 was used, as shown in column 5, to cancel an equivalent amount of a deficit country's initial credit position (marked −) or of a surplus country's initial debit position (marked +), to the extent that such initial positions had been created. In so far, however, as initial positions (*a*) had not been created, or (*b*) had been created in the wrong sense—i.e. if a deficit country had been provided with an initial debit position, or vice versa, or (*c*) were inadequate to meet the excess of column 3 over column 4, a balance remained (column 6) corresponding to the member's cumulative accounting surplus (marked +) or deficit (marked −), which had to be settled in credit (column 7) or in gold or dollars (column 8).

It should be noted that Table 10 merely shows how the *overall* deficits and surpluses were settled over the three-month period as

[1] The change in a member's cumulative accounting position, as between the beginning and end of a month, thus corresponds to the amount requiring settlement, after the end of the month, in gold (or dollars) and credit.

TABLE 10

EPU OPERATIONS, THIRD QUARTER 1950

(All figures are expressed to the nearest million US dollars)

One fifth of Original Quotas	Country[1]	Overall Surplus (+) or Deficit (−)	Use of Existing Resources	Use of Initial Positions	Cumulative Accounting Position	How settled	
						Credit	Gold
1	2	3	4	5	6	7	8
14	Austria	−8		−8	0		
72	Belgium	−3	−3		0		
39	Denmark	−18	−2		−16	−16	
104	France	+187	+1		+186	+145	+41[2]
64	Germany	−185	−12		−173	−142	−31[3]
9	Greece	−43	−1	−42	0		
3	Iceland	−2		−2	0		
41	Italy	+2			+2	+2	
66	Netherlands	−41		−30	−11	−11	
40	Norway	−11		−11	0		
14	Portugal	+18			+18	+16	+2[2]
52	Sweden	+6		+6	0		
10	Turkey	+1			+1	+1	
212	UK	+96	+16	+80	0		
740	Total	±310	±18	−92 +85	−200 +207	−169 +164	−31 +43

a whole. In addition to the total of $310 millions of overall deficits (or surpluses) shown in Table 10, there was in the three months a further total of nearly $300 millions of 'reciprocal' deficits and 'compensable' deficits. These were of course settled automatically by mutual cancellation.

Amendments to the EPU

The EPU was in operation for the eight and a half years from the middle of 1950 to December 1958 and in the course of this period various changes were made (particularly on the renewal of the

[1] Switzerland excluded.
[2] Being half the excess of the country's cumulative accounting surplus over one fifth of its quota.
[3] Being 0 per cent of 64 (see col. 1) plus 20 per cent of 64 plus 40 per cent of 45. (The cumulative accounting deficit of 173 must be regarded as being made up of 64 + 64 + 45.)

Union at mid-1954 and at mid-1955) with a view to reducing the amount of outstanding credit, to simplify the arrangements for the monthly settlements and to make these settlements 'harder' in terms of gold or dollars. In particular:

(1) As from mid-1954 the functioning of the EPU was simplified by providing, as a general rule, for the settlement of future monthly surpluses and deficits on a uniform basis of half gold and half credit and not, as had obtained hitherto, on the basis of the scales given above in Table 9 (which depended on the member's cumulative accounting position with the Union).

(2) In August 1955 the 50 : 50 basis of settlement was changed to one of 75 gold to 25 credit.

(3) Various bilateral arrangements were concluded between extreme creditor and debtor countries, under which the debtor countries agreed to repay to the creditors, in gold, part of the debts owing by the debtors and to the creditors in the Union. In each case repayments consisted of an initial instalment and a balance to be paid over a certain number of years. Each of these bilateral payments cancelled an equal amount of the debt due to and owed by the Union.

(4) In addition to the repayments received from the debtor countries under the bilateral agreements, the creditor countries also had some of their claims on the Union discharged by gold payments made out of the Union's own 'kitty' of gold and dollars.

None of the above changes nor any others made in the course of the Union's lifetime was permitted to make more than minor changes in the cumulative credit 'swings' (between the Union and its members) which were originally agreed in 1950 (i.e. 40[1] per cent of the original quotas). Such changes as did occur were mainly either temporary increases (for members reaching either of the limits of their 'swing') or adjustments made to take account of the increasing importance of several member countries in intra-European trade.

The wider area of multilateral settlement

Owing to the way in which the BIS calculated surpluses and deficits,[2] the effective area of multilateral settlement under the EPU was very much greater than that comprised by its European

[1] It will be seen that the average of the percentages shown in each section of Table 9 is 40 per cent.
[2] See above, pp. 143 and 149.

members, owing to the fact that several members' currencies were the usual, or even the sole, media for making international settlements in other large areas of the world. Of the Western European currencies thus used for making international settlements, sterling was much the most important, as we shall see in Chapter 13, but the Belgian, Dutch, French and Portuguese currencies were also used extensively, or even exclusively, within their respective empires.

As an example of the wider area of multilateral settlement facilitated by the EPU, we may note that France (or any other Continental member of the Union) had no monetary incentive to prefer making payments to (or getting receipts from) Australia rather than Britain, since her sterling holdings (and therefore her cumulative net position in the EPU) was affected in precisely the same way in the two cases.

However, the wider area of settlement was not always perfectly multilateral: thus Britain obviously had some incentive to prefer a bilateral deficit with Australia to one with France, unless she expected Australia to spend her sterling earnings in the OEEC area or in some other country which was unwilling to accumulate sterling.[1]

Correction of disequilibria

The EPU was however not simply a scheme for providing additional liquidity to accommodate intra-European disequilibria; it was also, unlike the IEPA, an agreement to correct such disequilibria. The relevant provisions[2] can be summarised thus:

First, as we have seen, the provisions requiring debtors to settle partly in gold or dollars provided them with an incentive, lacking entirely under the IEPA, to correct their external deficits.

Second, restrictions on trade were to be reduced. A separate OEEC scheme, involving all the EPU members, required each country to 'liberalise' (i.e. to free from all quantitative restrictions) a proportion of its imports on private account from other member countries. The main features of the scheme are set out in the next section of this chapter. This liberalisation was advantageous, not only because it facilitated international specialisation on the basis of comparative costs, but also because it enabled international disequilibria to be more readily dealt with by comparatively minor movements in relative prices. (See pp. 60 and 64.)

[1] This assumes that Australia would not become so surfeited with sterling as to be liable to leave the Sterling Area altogether.
[2] See Sections IV and V of *Documents relating to the EPU*.

Third, the EPU, by putting liquidity on a fully multilateral basis, made it unnecessary for members to discriminate in respect of their imports as between one member and another. Hence members undertook to avoid such discrimination.

Fourth, an exception to the rule of non-discrimination was provided in the form of the equivalent of the IMF's Scarce Currency Clause, allowing for discrimination against a member who had achieved an excessive creditor position. This provision was, however, impossible, to invoke in practice, since it required the unanimous consent of the member countries, including the member against whom the discrimination would be applied.

Fifth, there was in the EPU Agreement a contrary provision to deal with a country which developed an excessive debtor position. A country in this situation might 'suspend on a temporary basis measures taken by it for the liberalisation of trade'.

Trade liberalisation

The decision to liberalise trade between the OEEC countries (in the sense of freeing it from quantitative restrictions) dates back to a proposal made by Sir Stafford Cripps at an OEEC meeting in June 1949.[1] This proposal crystallised into an OEEC decision that countries should 'liberalise' 50 per cent of their trade by 15 December 1949 or show good reasons why this was impossible.

The 50 per cent targets applied separately to 'food and feeding stuffs, raw materials, and manufactured goods', and in the OEEC's *Second Report* of February 1950 (p. 224) it was claimed that 'most member countries have reached, or even exceeded, the targets thus laid down'. A further resolution was adopted by the OEEC in January 1950, to the effect that 'member countries must make it their aim to remove, as soon as . . . a Payments Scheme comes into force, quantitative restrictions on at least 60 per cent of their imports on private account from other member countries taken as a group'.[2]

Subsequently the target was raised to 75 per cent to be achieved if possible by February 1951. Subsidiary targets of 60 per cent applied separately to food and feeding stuffs, raw materials, and manufactured goods, and in addition member countries undertook to liberalise fully (by August 1951) their imports of certain specific categories of goods, collectively known as the 'common list'.[3]

The achievement of the 75 per cent target by almost all OEEC members was followed by a further raising of the target. By the

[1] *Economist*, 2 July 1949, p. 32.
[2] *Second Report*, p. 226.
[3] Articles 2 and 4 of the *Code of Liberalisation*, published by the OEEC in July 1951.

end of the 1950s the target had been raised to 90 per cent, with subsidiary targets of 75 per cent for each of the three categories of commodities mentioned above. Soon afterwards virtually complete liberalisation was achieved by all the economically advanced countries within the OEEC.

The percentage figures used to express these various targets were in all cases the proportion of imports on private account (falling within the specified categories) not subject to quota restrictions, the calculation being made on the basis of the value of goods in each category imported in the 'base year', 1948.[1] The targets did not represent the upper limit of what members undertook to do, in that they agreed to 'take the necessary measures for the progressive elimination between one another . . . of quantitative restrictions on the import of commodities, as fully as their economic and financial position will permit'.[2]

There can be little doubt that the success of trade liberalisation within the OEEC area was very greatly facilitated by the existence of the EPU, with its multilateral arrangements for relatively 'soft' settlements.

Liquidation of the EPU

It will be apparent from the constitution of the EPU, as briefly outlined above,[3] that the acceptability to a surplus country of its claims on the Union derived entirely from their value as a means (*a*) for settling future deficits or (*b*) for obtaining a share of the Union's assets should the country withdraw from the Union or the Union be disbanded. Thus the break-up provisions of the original EPU agreement[4] were of particular importance, since they had to be generous enough to the Union's creditors to secure the adherence of countries (such as Belgium) which expected to have overall credit positions, while at the same time not imposing on the Union's debtors burdens so onerous that prospective debtors would be deterred from joining.

To this end, the break-up provisions were aimed at (*a*) giving the creditor members of the Union, on liquidation, first a claim to the Union's gold and dollars, and second a right to have the greater part of the balance of their credit paid to them by the larger and more stable member countries; and (*b*) giving the debtor members, on liquidation, the right to discharge their

[1] 1949 in the case of Germany and 1952 in the case of Austria.
[2] Article 1a of the *Code of Liberalisation.*
[3] Above, p. 150.
[4] Annex B of Cmnd. 8064 and Annex III of *Documents Relating to the EPU.*

debts to the Union in the currencies of the other Union members, not in dollars, and to spread a considerable part of the repayments over a long period of years. (It will be obvious that the task of reconciling the interests of prospective creditors and prospective debtors was greatly facilitated by the gift of $350 millions from the ECA.)

The break-up provisions were reconsidered in detail in 1955, simultaneously with the drafting of the European Monetary Agreement (below, page 160), but no major change of principle was introduced, so that when, in December 1958 (at the time of the move by twelve of its members towards the greater convertibility of their currencies), the EPU was eventually superseded by the EMA,[1] the liquidation procedure actually adopted conformed very closely to the terms of the break-up provisions in the original agreements.

The final assets and liabilities of the Union, which had been brought into equality (as shown in Table 11) by the transfer of surplus assets to a fund set up under the EMA, were liquidated as follows:

(1) The gold and dollar holding of the Union, amounting to $167 millions, was distributed to the creditor-members in proportion to their share in their total final position of $1,315 millions. Thus (in $millions) Germany got 130, Belgium 20, and the Netherlands 15, while Italy, Austria and Sweden together received 2.

(2) A special credit of $150 millions granted to France earlier in 1958 was due to be repaid (by instalments) as to $118 millions to Germany and the four other members who had made this sum available. The balance of $32 millions became repayable by France to the six creditor members, the amount being allocated in the same proportions as the 'kitty' of $167 millions referred to in (1) above. By this rule, 25 of the 32 millions became due to Germany.

(3) The final position of each of the creditor members was converted into bilateral claims on the other members, the amount of the position being divided between these members in proportion to their respective quotas.

(4) Likewise, the final position of each of the debtor members was

[1] Making use of a procedure agreed in 1955, six members of the EPU, namely Belgium (with Luxembourg), France, Germany, Italy, the Netherlands and the UK (with Ireland), brought the EPU to an end and the EMA into force by declaring their intention of applying the EMA in connection with the restoration of non-resident convertibility for their currencies. Immediately afterwards six other EPU members (Austria, Denmark, Norway, Portugal, Sweden and Switzerland) also made their currencies convertible for non-residents. Finland (not a member) followed suit.

converted into bilateral debts to each of the other members, the amount of the position being divided between these members in proportion to their respective quotas.

TABLE 11

FINAL BALANCE SHEET OF THE EPU

(All figures in millions of US dollars, rounded to nearest million)

LIABILITIES *Final Positions of Creditor-* *Members*		ASSETS *Final Positions of Debtor-* *Members*	
Germany	1,027	Iceland	7
Belgium	154	Switzerland	12
Netherlands	121	Greece	12
Italy	7	Turkey	34
Austria	5	Portugal	36
Sweden	1	Denmark	66
		Norway	87
		UK	379
		France	485
	1,315		1,117
Special Credits[1]		*Special Credit*	
from Germany	100	*to France*[1]	150
from other members	18		
		Gold and US Dollars[2]	167
	1,434		1,434

It will be noted that, since the final assets and liabilities of the Union had been brought to equality, each creditor member was, in effect, repaid in full. Thus in the case of Germany, her final position of $1,027 millions was repaid as to $130 millions under (1) above, as to $25 millions under (2) above, while the net balance of bilateral debts created under (3) and (4) above was $872 millions in her favour.

The European Monetary Agreement[3]

The European Monetary Agreement came into force immediately upon the termination of the European Payments Union at the

[1] In February 1958 the Union arranged a credit of $150 millions to France, of which $118 millions was provided by Germany, Austria, Belgium, Italy and Switzerland, the balance being taken from the Union's own 'kitty' of dollars.
[2] After transferring the EPU's capital of $272 millions to the European Fund, set up under the EMA—this amount comprising $237 millions of gold and convertible currencies and $35 millions of long-term loans to Norway and Turkey.
[3] Much of this section is quoted verbatim from the 29th *Annual Report* of the BIS, pp. 220–24. The text of the EMA was published by the OEEC on 5 August 1955, and a Supplementary Protocol slightly amending the Agreement on 27 June 1959.

close of business on 27 December 1958. This Agreement, prepared in the spring and summer of 1955[1] and signed on 5 August of that year, was designed to ensure the maintenance of monetary co-operation between the OEEC members in the event of the restoration of convertibility for the major European currencies. This, in fact, took place simultaneously with the coming into force of the Agreement, the text of which remained virtually unchanged.

The Agreement has two principal features: the European Fund and the Multilateral System of Settlements. The former has a capital of $600 millions (237 millions of gold and dollars transferred from the EPU, *plus* $35 millions of long-term claims from Norway and Turkey, also transferred from the EPU, *plus* $328 millions in gold to be called up from member countries as and when required) and exists to provide short-term credit (up to two years) to any member country to enable it to withstand temporary overall balance-of-payments difficulties, in cases where these difficulties endanger the maintenance of the level of its intra-European trade liberalisation measures. Such assistance is however not automatic: a member in difficulties can apply for help, but the decision as to whether he gets it rests in the first place with the EMA Board of Management, which has in fact given its agreement to only very small amounts of assistance.

The Multilateral System of Settlements provides a framework within which transactions between member countries can in normal circumstances be settled through their foreign exchange markets,[2] although a multilateral clearing is provided for if needed. There are however a number of important changes introduced by the supersession of the EPU by the EMA's Multilateral System of Settlements. *First*, there is no longer any automatic credit element, and all settlements have to be 100 per cent in US dollars. *Second*, settlement of currency balances which are reported is made no longer at parity with the US dollar but at official buying and selling rates, the spread between which is such as to make it slightly advantageous (in normal circumstances) to effect settlements outside the EMA by transactions on the foreign exchange markets. *Third*, though the EMA initially carried over from the EPU the provision that each member's official holdings of other members' currencies should be convertible at pre-determined rates of exchange (and thus be guaranteed against

---

[1] See below, p. 244.
[2] For the re-establishment of the foreign exchange markets since the second world war, see below, p. 184.

I.M.C.—F

devaluation) a revision of the EMA constitution at the beginning of 1963 limited the guarantee to minimal working balances.[1] Taken together, the effect of the three changes just described has been to make the EMA's Multilateral System of Settlements little more than a dead letter.[1]

The OECD

In September 1961 the OEEC was re-constituted as the OECD (Organisation for Economic Cooperation and Development). The membership remained unchanged, except that the United States and Canada now became full members.[2] This change made no difference to the European Monetary Agreement, but in view of the successful completion of the OEEC's activities in the field of Trade Liberalisation, no provision was made for their continuance by the OECD. However, the OECD has come to be the forum for the coordination of the members' policies for economic aid to the under-developed countries, and also (as we have seen in Chapters 10) for the surveillance of their balance-of-payment problems.

The European Economic Community

The Treaty of Rome, which came into effect in January 1958 and thereby established the European Economic Community, incorporates a small chapter (Chapter 2, entitled *Balance of Payments*) devoted essentially to questions of international monetary cooperation. This Chapter provides for the setting up of consultative machinery (including a Monetary Committee) for enabling the EEC Commission and the six members of the Community to discuss and (if possible) coordinate their policies and activities in respect of international monetary questions. These consultative arrangements are in operation and there is no doubt that in consequence the Six are prepared to discuss their affairs at Brussels in a more intimate and detailed fashion than is usual among sovereign states. It would however be premature to claim that the Six have yet reached the stage of being able to resolve differences arising between themselves in the field of monetary cooperation and thus to present a common front to the rest of the world. At the most one can say that in the prolonged negotiations which led up to the amendment to the IMF charter

[1] Prior to the devaluation of sterling in November 1967 settlements were made under the Scheme only on three occasions and for small amounts. However further settlements were made (totalling $20 million) on the devaluation of sterling in November 1967, and again (totalling $25 million) on the devaluation of the French franc in August 1969.

[2] Japan joined in 1964.

in 1969, providing *inter alia* for the establishment of Special Drawing Rights, the Six constantly attempted, as from 1966, to reach prior agreement among themselves and occasionally succeeded in doing so, though effectively the negotiating forum was the Group of Ten.

In one respect, however, the Rome Treaty envisages something more than mere consultation on monetary matters as between its six signatories, in that one of the Articles in Chapter 2 (Article 108) provides for the possibility of a member of the Community being afforded 'mutual assistance' by 'the granting of limited credits by other Member States, subject to the agreement of the latter'. So far, however, no financial assistance of this nature has been afforded under Article 108.

Nevertheless, this should not be taken to imply that rapid progress may not be made in the future in the field of monetary cooperation between the members of the Community. Certainly the EEC Commission has for many years wanted to see rapid progress in this field, as was evident from the chapter on *Monetary Policy* in the Commission's *Action Programme for the Second Stage*, published in Brussels in October 1962. More recently, in February 1968, the Commission prepared a memorandum on the desirable action of the Community in the monetary field. In this memorandum, it was suggested that the Monetary Committee and the committee of the governors of the Community's central banks should carry out studies on the following problems:

(1) the possibility of member states committing themselves not to go forward with a change of parity except by joint agreement;

(2) the elimination between the currencies of member states of daily fluctuations in exchange rates around the parity-levels and the adoption of margins of fluctuation identical with each other vis-à-vis non-member countries;

(3) the setting-up within the framework of the Community of a mutual assistance arrangement in application of Article 108 of the Treaty, for example in the form of a multilateral network of reciprocal credits, which the institutions concerned might call upon in case of need;

(4) the definition of a European monetary unit which would be used in all the fields of Community action requiring a common denominator.

At a conference of Ministers of Finance which took place later in 1968, terms of reference were given to the Monetary Committee to carry on its work on the future of monetary relations within the EEC. The practical outcome of this work has thus far been an *agreement on short-term monetary assistance* which came into operation in February 1970. According to a press report[1] in January 1970,

A Council meeting of Ministers of Finance and Economic Affairs reached agreement on new methods of short- and medium-term consultation on economic policy, and gave their Central Bankers the green light to set up a new $2,000m. system of short-term mutual drawing rights for use by member States in monetary difficulties.

The Ministers also held a preliminary discussion on . . . proposals drawn up by the Monetary Committee for the transformation of the short-term monetary support scheme into medium-term financial aid. But work was not far enough advanced for decisions to be taken, and the Monetary Committee was asked to continue its labour and will report back.

Under the short-term support system drawn up by the central bankers:

(1) $1,000 millions will be automatically available as three-month credits renewable for a further three months. Each member state will be able to call on its partners up to the limit of its own quota, the quotas of the members being as follows:

	$ millions
France	300
Germany	300
Netherlands	100
Belgium	100
Italy	200
	1,000

(2) A second $1,000 millions will be mobilisable at the request of one or other of the member states, but this further instalment will be conditional, that is to say, subject to consultations and recommendations on the policies of adjustment to be adopted by the member requesting the drawing.

As regards consultation on economic policy, the six governments accepted proposals from the Commission and the Monetary Committee for more intensive consultation as to their policies for controlling the pressure of demand in their respective economies, and for the coordination of their medium-term economic policies.[2]

A programme of further recommended reforms was put forward by the Commission in March 1970:

[1] *Financial Times*, 27 January 1970.
[2] See the report in *Le Monde*, 28 January 1970, p. 29.

The Commission's new proposals call for concerted action by the member states in three distinct stages.

A first preliminary stage would run from now until the end of 1971. During this time the Six would set up the medium-term scheme for financial aid to countries in monetary difficulties, increase coordination between monetary authorities, introduce value added tax throughout the community, harmonise taxation of capital and take steps to free capital movements.

Transition to the second stage, to the end of 1975, would be automatic. In this stage, the Six would reduce the margins of fluctuation between their currencies, and their central banks would adopt common intervention policies on exchange markets. The member States would agree to common guidelines on credit policies, and, in 1973, adopt a policy of 'joint management' of their Special Drawing Right allocations.

During the same period, the Six would increase the coordination of economic policy to ensure the 'convergence' of national economies, and harmonise the rates of . . . taxation. Steps would be taken to 'reinforce' capital markets to prepare for the free movement of capital . . . .

In the third and final stage, margins of fluctuation between community currencies would be abolished, the Six's exchange rates would be 'irrevocably' fixed in relation to each other, a European reserve fund would be set up, and a council of central bank governors established. All tax frontiers inside the community would be abolished and complete freedom of capital movements would be achieved.[1]

Despite all this activity at Brussels, the fact remains that to date (July 1970) no finance has yet been furnished under Article 108. The rescue operation for the benefit of the Italian lira in March 1964 (see below, page 260) was *not* organised under the auspices of the EEC, nor were those for the French franc in 1968–9 (below, page 269). Even in March 1970, the Italians sought facilities

in New York to support the lira instead of trying to activate the Community's new short-term mutual assistance programme . . . the feeling was that the Italians passed over a good chance to force the member Governments to put some flesh on article 108 of the Rome Treaty, which provides for community assistance to member countries in payment difficulties. . . .[2]

[1] *Financial Times*, 6 March 1970.
[2] *Financial Times*, 18 March 1970.

I3

STERLING BEFORE 1959[1]

Sterling deserves an important place in a study of international monetary cooperation, first because before the second world war it had a much stronger claim than any other country's currency to be called an *international* currency, second because even in the post-war period it has shared with the US dollar the honour of being the only national currencies in widespread use internationally, third because the British monetary authorities have consciously used it as a means of international monetary cooperation, and fourth because the history of the Sterling Area exchange controls provides an illuminating case study of what can (and what cannot) be done by restrictions of this kind.

Sterling under the gold standard

The gold standard was neither invented nor consciously planned. It grew up gradually as a gold currency standard in the eighteenth and nineteenth centuries, gaining more and more adherents with the passage of time and enjoying its heyday from the end of the Franco-Prussian War (when the German Empire adopted gold as its standard) until the outbreak of the first world war. The standard suffered a partial eclipse as the result of that war, but was revived in the nineteen-twenties as a gold bullion standard, only to collapse, more or less completely, in the early nineteen-thirties.

[1] I am indebted to the editor for permission to reproduce in this chapter extracts from my article on 'Sterling as an International Currency', which appeared in the June 1948 issue of the *Economic Record*.

Both versions of the gold standard have already been described in Chapter 2, but only in their bare essentials, so that certain important practical features were passed over without comment. In particular, any realistic description of either version of the gold standard must recognise that in practice gold accepted sterling as in some respects an equal partner. Certainly sterling was much the more *active* partner, for unlike gold it could be transferred from one country to another almost without expense. But sterling was also prized along with gold as an asset suitable for holding as a store of value, and in the case of many countries, not only the working balances of the commercial banks, but also part or even the whole of the official reserve of the central bank, were kept in the form of sterling: to a considerable extent the gold standard was a gold *exchange* standard.[1]

Why, under the gold standard, was sterling so widely used as an international currency? *First*, Britain had a voracious appetite for imports and (partly in consequence of this) British investors were willing to make considerable overseas loans, with the object of developing the export potential of Britain's suppliers. As a result, the whole world was constantly supplied with sterling. *Second*, since Britain's overseas loans were sterling loans, the borrowing countries committed themselves to meet a debt service in sterling, and this naturally provided a strong inducement to hold a reserve of sterling. *Third*, since many countries had an extensive import trade with Britain, it was quite convenient for them to conduct at least a considerable proportion of their overseas transactions in sterling, and to hold working balances in London. *Fourth*, the sterling prices of British goods were reasonably stable, so that there was no great danger that working balances or official reserves of sterling would suffer a severe depreciation in purchasing power. *Fifth*, sterling was almost continuously convertible into gold by virtue of the Bank of England's willingness to buy and sell gold freely at a fixed price. *Sixth*, sterling could be lent in London with complete safety and thus earn interest. *Seventh*, sterling enjoyed unrestricted transferability, and this, in conjunction with London's unrivalled credit facilities, the acceptance houses and bill market, made the bill on London, a sterling bill, the world-wide instrument for financing international trade. *Eighth*, the currencies of such countries as would *not* accept sterling without limit could always be bought as required in London. Thus there was no need for (say) Australia to hold stocks

[1] See footnote 4 on p. 168.

of marks or francs, or even to hold stocks of gold with which to buy these currencies; she could always get them whenever she needed by buying them for sterling.

The pre-war Sterling Area

Early in the nineteen-thirties the gold standard virtually collapsed; most countries apart from the Gold Bloc (France, Italy, Switzerland, Holland and Belgium) gave up the attempt to maintain a stable exchange rate with gold. The seceding countries were, however, for the most part keenly aware of the disadvantages of freely fluctuating exchange rates, and many of them chose to stabilise the value of their currencies in relation either to sterling or to the US dollar, both of which were then completely unrestricted in their transferability. (Indeed before the war, exchange control in any form was very rare outside Germany, Italy, the USSR and the eastern European countries.[1]) The countries which decided in favour of a stable exchange rate with sterling came to be known as the Sterling Area, which by 1933 comprised the whole of the British Empire except Canada and Newfoundland, most of the Scandinavian and Baltic countries and a few others.[2]

To the countries which joined the Sterling Area the transition from the gold standard to the new regime involved little change in their monetary policy. They still declared an official exchange rate, though now not with gold but with sterling. Their official reserves now consisted almost entirely of sterling, not gold,[3] but for most members of the area this did not involve any considerable departure from their practice under the gold standard. Their official agencies also bought and sold sterling freely at the official rate, just as previously they had bought and sold gold.[4] Moreover, though they reserved the right to prevent an undue depletion or accumulation of their sterling reserves by varying their official exchange rates with sterling, in practice this right was rarely (if

[1] Certain other countries temporarily imposed controls on capital payments in the early 1930s.
[2] The Sterling Area eventually included the Colonial Empire and Mandates, the Southern Dominions, Eire, Egypt, India, Iraq, Portugal, Siam, Iran, Estonia, Sweden, Norway, Finland, Denmark and Latvia.
[3] South Africa, though regarded as a member of the Sterling Area, continued to keep her official reserves mainly in the form of gold. She held sterling only as a working balance.
[4] Even under the gold standard, most of the countries which later joined the Sterling Area had made effective their official exchange rates with gold by buying and selling sterling (which could be exchanged for gold in London) freely at the appropriate price. Such countries were said to be on the gold *exchange* standard.

ever) exercised. The *modus operandi* of the Sterling Area was indeed so similar to that of the gold standard that we may reasonably describe the members of the area as adhering to the sterling *standard*.[1]

We see then that after the collapse of the gold standard a considerable part of the world retained sterling in use as an international currency. What of the rest of the world? The banks of countries outside the Sterling Area continued their practice, which had grown up under the gold standard, of keeping most, or even all, of their working balances in the form of sterling. Moreover, sterling was in use throughout the world as much the most popular means of making international payments, as it had been under the gold standard. For indeed the attractiveness of sterling as an asset and as a means of payment had been little diminished by Britain's departure from the gold standard. Though in the years 1931–4 sterling had depreciated by some 40 per cent in relation to the gold bloc currencies which had not been devalued (e.g. the French and Belgian francs), it had maintained its value in relation to other currencies, and the subsequent devaluations of the gold bloc currencies reduced the relative depreciation of sterling to only about 20 per cent.[2] Moreover, sterling was not in this period subject to short period fluctuations in value, thanks to the operations of the Exchange Equalisation Account, whose *modus operandi* was briefly described in Chapter 2.[3] Finally sterling remained throughout a fully acceptable means of settlement with the extensive Sterling Area. It is not therefore suprising that right up to the time that war became imminent sterling

---

[1] See above, p. 41.
[2] According to the footnote on p. 129 of *International Currency Experience*, published by the League of Nations in 1944, the value in sterling of other currencies changed as follows after Britain left the gold standard in 1931. All figures are percentages of the exchange rates prevailing in December 1930.

Country's currency	1932	1934	1936
Argentine	113	97	97
Brazil	120	84	90
Australia	73	86	86
Sweden	100	93	93
India	100	100	100
Canada	130	99	99
USA	149	98	99
Czechoslovakia	149	139	118
Italy	149	159	99
Belgium	149	165	120
France	149	165	118

[3] Page 30.

should remain in world-wide use as a means of international settlement.

War time

In the early stages of the war the Sterling Area lost all its European members and soon came to consist only of the British Empire (excluding Canada and Newfoundland), Egypt and the Sudan, Iraq, Iceland and the Faroes. When the exigencies of war demanded the official rationing of international payments the Sterling Area countries concentrated mainly on controlling payments into and out of the Sterling Area *as a whole*, leaving payments between one Sterling Area country and another almost entirely free.[1] There was however no single authority responsible for exchange control in the Sterling Area, for the Dominions within the Area retained full autonomy and only the UK and the Colonial controls were responsible to Whitehall. The autonomy of the Dominion members of the Area was such that they retained three rights: they could freely authorise the transfer of sterling to any part of the Sterling Area, they could also authorise the transfer of sterling to non-sterling countries, and they enjoyed unrestricted access to the Exchange Equalisation Account in London for converting their sterling into gold or into US dollars. Naturally the second and third of these rights were used with due restraint. The Exchange Equalisation Account itself underwent a certain change of function: instead of continuing as the official agency for buying and selling sterling in the gold and foreign currency markets it became, once these markets were made illegal, simply the Sterling Area's common pool of gold and foreign currencies (more particularly US dollars). Into this pool flowed the foreign currency earnings of residents not only in the UK but also in the outer sterling area countries, each of which enforced regulations designed to ensure the surrender of foreign currency earnings to its own exchange control authority, which in turn sold them to the Exchange Equalisation Account for sterling.

The UK exchange control operated by canalising all exchange transactions through 'authorised dealers', namely the Bank of England, the Joint Stock banks, and a number of merchant bank and acceptance houses, all of which were permitted to deal with all countries, and the London offices of various Dominion, Colonial and foreign banks, each of which was permitted to deal with one

[1] The UK control did not restrict payments within the Sterling Area at all. Some Dominions had such restrictions, but they were very mild in practice.

overseas country or a limited number of countries. Apart from the Exchange Equalisation Account, these dealers became virtually the only lawful British holders of foreign currencies, for the only currencies (apart from sterling) against which British exporters were allowed to sell their goods (the so-called 'specified' currencies, of which the most important was the dollar) had always to be sold for sterling (at the appropriate official price) to an authorised dealer.

The authorised dealers, and they alone, could (1) buy and sell foreign currencies for sterling, (2) get gold and foreign currencies (in particular dollars) from the Exchange Equalisation Account,[1] (3) transfer sterling as between the account of a UK resident and that of a resident in a foreign country, and (4) transfer sterling as between the account of a resident in one foreign country and that of a resident in another foreign country. The word 'foreign', in this connection, means 'outside the Sterling Area', for the transfer of sterling within the Area was not subject to the British control. In addition the authorised dealers became legally the sole inter-mediaries in the export and import of bank-notes and of nego-tiable securities. By virtue of these measures, the authorised dealers, and they alone, were in a position to exchange sterling against gold and foreign currencies;[2] they also controlled all inward and outward sterling payments between residents of the United Kingdom (but not of the outer Sterling Area) and foreigners, and the transferability of sterling as between different foreign countries. This machinery for exchange control, set up early in the war, remained basically unchanged up to the time of the resumption of non-resident convertibility in December 1958 (see below, page 187) and even today some of the original structure remains.

How was the machinery used? First, in dealing with the other Sterling Area exchange controls, the British dealers simply trans-ferred sterling on request. Second, all transactions between United

---

[1] Originally the Bank of England (as manager of the Account) quoted nearly equal buying and selling prices for each 'specified' currency when doing business with the authorised dealers. In October 1950, however, when Canada cancelled the official par value of the Canadian dollar (below, p. 239), the Bank ceased to quote an official rate for this currency. Then in December 1951 the Bank widened the margin between its buying and selling rates for the other specified currencies, and by this and subsequent changes contrived to give the authorised dealers an increas-ing freedom to deal among themselves in the other specified currencies. These changes, which are described below, p. 184, did not however imply any substantial relaxation of the British control regulations, as they affected the British public.
[2] Except for the 'free' markets in certain foreign countries. See Chapter 14.

Kingdom residents and foreigners were subject to the closest scrutiny and vetoed if the war effort so demanded. Third, transfers of sterling as between residents of different countries were in many cases restricted. Fourth, foreigners were made to accept payments from the Sterling Area exclusively in sterling and only in certain cases did they enjoy a right of conversion—i.e. of getting gold or dollars for their sterling, at the official selling price, from the Exchange Equalisation Account.[1]

In practice the British control, like the other Sterling Area controls, came to distinguish between foreign countries which would accept inconvertible sterling and those which would not. This was the historical origin of the distinction between 'soft' and 'hard' currency countries. In dealing with a hard currency country (like the United States or Canada) the Sterling Area controls would be less likely to authorise a transaction involving a payment by the Area, and more likely to authorise one involving a receipt by the Area, than in dealing with a soft currency country. Moreover, though the sterling held by hard currency countries was transferable almost without restriction and freely convertible into US dollars, the sterling accounts of other countries were mostly subject to a system of currency control known as the *Special Accounts* system. The sterling earnings of the countries in question were paid into Special Accounts, and sterling in Special Accounts was not convertible into gold or dollars and could not normally be used for making international payments except to the Sterling Area. There were some exceptions to the latter restriction: for instance country X might be allowed to draw freely on its Special Account to make payments not only to the Sterling Area but also to certain specified countries Y and Z[2] and even to make payments to other countries if the transaction requiring the payment had been specifically approved by the British exchange control. But apart from these relatively minor relaxations, the Special Accounts system virtually put an end to the use of sterling for making payments between two soft currency countries outside the Sterling Area, and thus considerably detracted from the usefulness of holding sterling.

[1] Only banks classified as authorised dealers had direct access to the Exchange Equalisation Account, but other holders of convertible sterling could have access through an authorised dealer.

[2] Thus the Special Accounts arranged for the Central American countries, the so-called Central American Accounts, permitted each Central American country to spend its sterling earnings either in the Sterling Area or in any other Central American country. The Central American Accounts were however unusual in the number of choices open to the holders.

Why during the war period were many allied and neutral countries willing to accept sterling with all the limitations imposed by the Special Account system? They did so to a certain extent because they wanted to use it to buy imports, but in many cases this was not the whole explanation, for certain countries (e.g. Argentina) had such a large export surplus with the Sterling Area that their willingness to accept sterling in practice implied a willingness to accumulate sterling. Some of these countries in fact accumulated very large sterling balances in the course of the war. Their willingness to do this partly reflected their faith in the value of sterling after the war, but it must also be remembered that at this time Britain was the only large market for these countries' exports.

The first advance to convertibility

After the liberation of Europe the British government took a very active part in the negotiation of the bilateral agreements, to which reference was made at the beginning of Chapter 11. In particular, agreements were concluded with Belgium, Czechoslovakia, Denmark, France, Holland, Norway, Portugal, Sweden and Switzerland. These agreements, though by no means identical in their terms, followed a fairly uniform pattern; they all provided for a fixed rate of exchange, and in each case Britain's partner undertook to accept sterling from the Sterling Area and in return was permitted to use its sterling freely to make payments to the Sterling Area. The post-liberation agreements thus to some extent followed the model of the war-time Special Accounts, but not however in all respects. In the first place most of the new agreements incorporated a so-called 'gold clause', which prescribed maximum 'swings' beyond which each party's requirement of the other's currency had to be settled in gold. The 'swings' permitted by the agreements were frequently different in the two directions, Britain undertaking to accumulate her partner's currency up to the equivalent of X dollars, and her partner to accumulate sterling to the equivalent of Y dollars. The other important difference between the post-war agreements and the war-time Special Accounts was that the former were less strictly bilateral than the latter, since provision was frequently made for fostering transferability on an administrative basis, as opportunity offered.

The next steps which were taken to reinstate sterling as an international currency were the result of the Anglo-American Loan Agreement, which was negotiated in 1945 and came into force on

15 July 1946. Under Sections 7, 8(i) and 8(ii) of this Agreement,[1] Britain committed herself to abolish her exchange restrictions on current transactions much sooner than the end of the Transitional Arrangements under the IMF Agreement.[2] Section 8(i), which became operative immediately, precluded the United Kingdom from imposing restrictions on payments and transfers, for current transactions, from the United Kingdom to the United States, or on the use of virtually all sterling owned by US residents. (Section 8(i) did not however preclude Britain from imposing quantitative trade restrictions, as distinct from exchange restrictions, on imports from the USA,[3] though Section 9 required that after the end of 1946 such restrictions should be applied, with certain exceptions, in a non-discriminatory manner.) Section 8(ii), which was to become operative one year after the Agreement came into force, precluded the United Kingdom from imposing 'restrictions on payments and transfers for current transactions' from the United Kingdom to any other country, with the following exceptions:

First, restrictions were permitted if imposed in conformity with the IMF Agreement under the Scarce Currency Clause, or by special authorisation of the Fund under Article VIII.

Second, the United States government could waive the United Kingdom's undertaking in exceptional cases.

Third, restrictions were permitted if needed 'to uncover and dispose of assets of Germany and Japan'.

Fourth, restrictions were permitted on the use of sterling already held by third countries and their nationals.

The fate of the sterling balances already in existence was dealt with in Section 10 of the Agreement, which provided that such balances should either be 'adjusted as a contribution to the settlement of war and post-war indebtedness and in recognition of the benefits which the countries concerned might be expected to gain from such a settlement', or 'be released at once and convertible into any currency for current transactions' or blocked initially but released in a similar manner over a period of years.

The last section we have to consider, Section 7, which was also to become operative one year after the Agreement came into force, was addressed to Britain as custodian of the whole Sterling

[1] Published by HMSO as a White Paper in 1945.
[2] See above, Chapter 8.
[3] See article by Knapp and Tamagna, 'Sterling in Multilateral Trade', in the *Federal Reserve Bulletin*, September 1947.

Area's gold and foreign currency reserve, and required that (with one minor exception) 'the sterling receipts from current trans-actions of all sterling area countries . . . will be freely available for current transactions in any currency area without discrimination'.

Britain worked to implement the provisions of the Loan Agreement mainly by means of two devices, *American Accounts* and *Transferable Accounts*. The former accounts were arranged, mostly in 1945, with the United States, the Philippines, Colombia, Costa Rica, Cuba, Bolivia, the Dominican Republic, Ecuador, El Salvador, Guatemala, Haiti, Honduras, Mexico, Nicaragua, Panama, Venezuela, Chile and Peru. (The last two named countries subsequently left the American Account area.) The Transferable Accounts were negotiated, mainly in the first half of 1947, with the following countries: Argentina, Brazil, Uruguay, Belgium, Holland, Portugal, Spain, Norway, Finland, Italy, Czechoslovakia, Egypt and the Sudan, Iran, Ethiopia, Sweden, Canada and Newfoundland. Thus the countries of the world could in July 1947 be grouped roughly under four headings: the Sterling Area, the American Account Area, the Transferable Account Area, and 'all others'.

So far as the Sterling Area was concerned the implementation of the Loan Agreement required that the United Kingdom and Colonial exchange controls should lift any restrictions which had hitherto been imposed on current payments to countries outside the Area, and that the United Kingdom should eliminate all discrimination against the United States in her quantitative trade restrictions. At the same time the Dominion members of the Area were of course free to follow suit if they chose to do so.

With regard to the American Account Area, the Loan Agreement was implemented by permitting current payments to be made into American Accounts both from accounts of residents of the Sterling Area and from Transferable Accounts, and by providing that the British authorities should on demand freely convert into US dollars all sterling paid into American Accounts.

Transferable Account arrangements worked in a more complicated fashion than those for American Accounts, for unlike American Accounts they incorporated provisions aimed at fostering the use of sterling as an international currency. Let us consider the Transferable Account arrangements which would have been made with an imaginary country, Ruritania. First of all, if Ruritania was a country which had, during the war, accumulated a large balance of sterling, there would probably be an arrangement to block part of this balance, or to hypothecate it for some specified purpose. Then there would be an undertaking by Ruritania to accept sterling from all other countries in settlement of current (though not capital) transactions. In return Britain would offer Ruritania important concessions. Ruritania would be permitted to draw freely on the sterling 'at the disposal' of her monetary authorities (i.e. on the sterling accruing to the new Ruritania Transferable Accounts from future current transactions or from existing balances which had not been blocked) to make *current* payments to virtually all countries, including the American Account countries. This last concession, the right to transfer sterling for current purposes to American Accounts, was of course of great significance, since the British authorities were committed to convert into dollars all the sterling thus transferred.

Thus the Transferable Account countries, unlike the American Account countries, in effect agreed to use *and hold* sterling as an international currency. First, they agreed to accept sterling from all countries in payment for exports or for any other current purposes. Second, they agreed to retain the sterling they earned until such time as they needed to use it for buying imports or making other current payments.[1] In effect therefore they committed themselves to sterling both as a means of international payment and as an international store of value.

The miscellaneous group of countries which we have labelled 'all others' had not by July 1947 been brought within the provisions of the Loan Agreement. This group included one country (Switzerland) which preferred to continue on the basis of her bilateral agreement, certain bilateral agreement countries with whom (it was hoped) Transferable Accounts would soon be negotiated,[2] two ex-enemy countries (Germany and Japan) whose overseas payments were still controlled in detail by the Allies, and finally a small residual group of countries which were unable or unwilling to operate an effective exchange control.[3]

The provisions in Section 10 of the Loan Agreement, concerning

[1] However, a number of countries had Transferable Accounts agreements which provided for a limited 'swing', beyond which settlement had to be made in some means other than sterling (usually gold or US dollars).
[2] The United States granted a postponement until 15 September 1947, of Britain's obligations under the Loan Agreement in respect of fourteen countries: Austria, Bulgaria, China, Denmark, France, Greece, Hungary, Paraguay, Poland, Rumania, Thailand, Turkey, the USSR, Yugoslavia.
[3] The principal countries in this group were Afghanistan, Albania, Korea, Liberia, Nepal, Saudi Arabia, Cyrenaica, Eritrea, Tripolitania and Yemen.

the treatment of already existing sterling balances of overseas countries, were not closely adhered to. At the middle of 1947 about £3½ billions were outstanding[1] (mostly in the form of British Treasury Bills), of which about one half was covered by short-term blocking arrangements. None of the balances had been cancelled (and indeed none have since been cancelled, apart from £46 million gifts from Australia and New Zealand). Nor had any of the blocking arrangements been put on a long-term basis. Hence there was in July 1947 a vast amount of 'old' sterling in existence which either had the full status of 'current' sterling or had this status withheld merely by short-term agreements.

The retreat from convertibility

The measures which were taken for increasing the transferability of sterling were followed by such a drain on the Sterling Area gold and dollar reserve that on 20 August 1947, after consulting the United States government, Britain suspended the right of Transferable Account countries to use sterling from their Transferable Accounts for making current payments to American Accounts. How did this suspension of convertibility affect the three major areas: the Transferable Account Area itself, the Sterling Area and the American Account Area? To take the last Area first, the legal rights attaching to American Accounts were unaffected, for all sterling accruing to these accounts could still be freely converted into dollars. But it was no longer possible for the American Account countries to earn sterling from the Transferable Account countries. The *Sterling Area* was not directly affected by the suspension of convertibility, but the world-wide dollar shortage, of which the suspension of convertibility was a symptom, was a most serious matter to most Sterling Area countries and led to certain changes in the Area's currency arrangements. In particular, South Africa decided to modify the war-time procedure under which her exports of gold were always sold in London for sterling,[2] and Sterling Area countries generally

---

[1] The comparable pre-war figure was £½ billion.

[2] South Africa has a large output of new gold, almost all of which is retained in her official reserves or exported. During the period that she was selling her gold exports exclusively to Britain, she made payments to other countries exclusively by drawing on her sterling holdings. Under an agreement negotiated in October 1947 South Africa undertook to sell in London only such gold as was required to meet her sterling deficit and to make a loan of £80 millions; the rest of her gold exports could at her discretion be sold elsewhere, for example in the United States. (In subsequent years there were modifications in the agreement, which lapsed altogether in 1955.)

agreed to limit their dollar expenditure in accordance with principles arrived at in discussion with the British government. (In certain cases, for example Eire and India, expenditure was for a time limited by agreement to fixed annual amounts.)

A later development, affecting both the American Account Area and the Sterling Area, was the reimposition by the latter of discriminatory restrictions directed against the United States. The Dominion members of the Sterling Area were of course free agents in this matter but Britain was tied by the Loan Agreement. Britain however claimed that discrimination in favour of her colonies was not a breach of the Agreement[1] and in fact reintroduced such discrimination towards the end of 1947. Later on the United States supported the schemes (to which reference was made in Chapter 12) for liberalising trade in Western Europe, and agreed that Britain (and her colonies) should participate in them, even though they involved discrimination in favour of trade between members of the OEEC.

With regard to the *Transferable Account* countries, the suspension of convertibility was so serious a matter that the relevant payments arrangements had in effect to be renegotiated. Some of the countries went back to their earlier 'bilateral' status, modified in most cases by 'administrative transferability'. This meant that such countries would accept sterling, at any rate up to a prearranged swing, in settlement from the Sterling Area and could in turn always use their sterling to make payments to the Sterling Area, but that other transfers of sterling to them or from them were subject to the approval of both their own monetary authorities and the British exchange control. Canada came to enjoy something closely akin to American Account status. The other countries in question continued with their Transferable Account arrangements, with however the important difference that their sterling could now be transferred automatically only to the Sterling Area and to other Transferable Account countries: transfers to other countries were henceforth at best only on an administrative basis and in the case of American Account countries were prohibited altogether.

The countries which continued their Transferable Account status after the suspension of convertibility in August 1947, and those which acquired this status later on, were broadly speaking

[1] The British case was based on the doctrine that members of a group of countries which have, like Britain and her colonies, a common quota in the IMF should be entitled to discriminate in favour of one another against countries outside the group when the group as a whole is in balance-of-payments difficulties.

those whose monetary authorities could be trusted to keep to the new and more stringent rules of the Transferable Account game, and whose sterling receipts and payments could be expected to stay reasonably in balance.

The British monetary authorities were not inclined to give Transferable Account status to countries which would have tended to be persistently short of sterling (e.g. Greece[1]), since the difficulty which such countries already had in settling their accounts with the Sterling Area would have been aggravated if they had been free to settle in sterling outside this Area. Nor, on the other hand, did the British authorities want to give Transferable Account status to countries which would have tended to accumulate sterling persistently. This was clearly the case where a country required settlement in gold beyond a limited swing (as in the case of Belgium, Portugal, Switzerland or Argentina, for example[2]), but even in the absence of such a provision a Transferable Account arrangement would have caused difficulties. Take for example Argentina. Argentina tended in the period after August 1947 to accumulate sterling almost to the point of satiety, so that she had no desire to incur an obligation to accept sterling from countries outside the Sterling Area, and Britain for her part was also anxious to restrict transfers of sterling to Argentina, for the more Argentina was satiated with sterling the less ready she would be to continue her supplies of meat and other products to the British market. (Of course transfers of sterling *from* Argentina did not give rise to comparable difficulties and were in fact frequently permitted on an administrative basis.)

August 1947 to February 1954

The developments which occurred immediately after 20 August 1947 resulted in the regrouping of the countries of the world under four headings,[3] from the point of view of the transferability of sterling. The membership of each group changed from time to time but in February 1954 was as set out in Table 12. The characteristics of each group can be summarised briefly as follows, so far as unblocked sterling is concerned:

(1) *The Sterling Area.* Within this Area unconditional transferability was the rule, qualified by certain local controls mainly on

[1] Greece was, however, given Transferable Account status in 1951.
[2] A more extreme example was Canada where (as in the period before 1947) the monetary authorities would not undertake to accumulate sterling, so that the Sterling Area had to settle with Canada in gold or in Canadian or US dollars.
[3] Plus most of the 'small residual group' listed in footnote 3, p. 176.

TABLE 12

Sterling Area
(alias 'Scheduled Territories')

The United Kingdom
The Outer Sterling Area:
British Colonial Empire
Australia
New Zealand
India
Ceylon
Pakistan
Burma[2]
Eire
Iceland
Iraq[2]
Jordan
Libya
South Africa

American Account
Countries

United States
Bolivia
Canada[1]
Colombia
Costa Rica
Cuba
Dominican Republic
El Salvador
Ecuador
Guatemala
Haiti
Honduras
Mexico
Nicaragua
Panama
Philippine Republic
Venezuela

Transferable Account Countries

Austria
Chile
Czechoslovakia
Danish Monetary Area
Egypt
Ethiopia
Finland
Greece
Italian Monetary Area
Netherlands Monetary Area
Norway
Poland
Spanish Monetary Area
Sudan
Sweden
Thailand
USSR
Western Germany

'Bilateral' Countries[3]

Argentina
Belgian Monetary Area
Brazil
Bulgaria
French Monetary Area
Hungary
Israel
Japan
Lebanon
Paraguay
Peru
Portuguese Monetary Area
Rumania
Switzerland
Syria
Tangier
Turkey
Uruguay
Vatican City
Yugoslavia

[1] Canada was not officially an American Account country, but had a very similar status.
[2] Iraq left the Sterling Area in 1959, and Burma in 1966.
[3] Despite the label 'bilateral', these countries might in many cases receive sterling from, and pay sterling to, other bilateral countries or Transferable Account countries, on a basis of 'administrative transferability'.

capital transactions. Payments into the Area were unrestricted and could always be made in sterling. Payments out of the Area required authorisation by the British or the local controls, according to the domicile of the payer. In the case of the United Kingdom, the exchange control on capital transactions and on imports of services (e.g. tourists' expenditure) was strict, but permission to pay for imports of goods was automatic if an import licence had been obtained.[1] Thus the effective restrictions were largely restrictions on trade rather than on payments and the same was true of most of the other countries of the Area.

(2) *American Account countries*. Once sterling reached an American Account the Sterling Area controls placed no restriction whatever on its transfer to any countries other than those on the 'bilateral' list in Table 12. Transfers to 'bilateral' countries were subject to administrative approval but were allowed liberally. The British authorities would on demand always convert American Account sterling into US dollars.

(3) *Transferable Account countries*. Sterling on Transferable Account was not convertible into US dollars or any other currency. However, Transferable Account sterling enjoyed automatic transferability for *current* payments to other Transferable Account countries and to the then members of the 'small residual group'[2] and was accepted for all payments to the Sterling Area. The use made of sterling by the Transferable Account countries, other than for making payments to the Sterling Area, was indeed very considerable.[3]

(4) *Bilateral countries*. The position in February 1954 was that, except in the case of Argentina, Bilateral Account sterling was not convertible into gold or dollars.[4] It was accepted for all payments to the Sterling Area, but for payments outside this Area it enjoyed

[1] So far as earnings from exports are concerned, the control was intended solely to ensure (1) that exporters exacted payment either in the appropriate brand of sterling (e.g. exporters to America could not accept, say, French Account sterling) or in a specified currency; and (2) that all specified currencies earned were duly surrendered.
[2] This group in February 1954 was substantially the same as listed in footnote 3, p. 135, except for three additions—China, Formosa and Iran, and two deletions—Cyrenaica and Tripolitania. Cyrenaica and Tripolitania are now united as the United Kingdom of Libya, which joined the Sterling Area in January 1952.
[3] See the Bank of England's *Report* for the year ended 28 February 1953, p. 11.
[4] Britain's bilateral agreement with Argentina provided that Argentina should accumulate sterling only up to a limited swing, beyond which settlement would be in gold. The same arrangements applied, prior to the formation of the EPU in 1950, to Belgium, Portugal, Switzerland and certain other European 'bilateral' countries, but these conversion arrangements were terminated when the EPU came into force.

only administrative transferability. It should be noted, however, that the facilities for administrative transferability were widely used, as is shown by the figures quoted in the Bank of England's annual *Reports*.

None of the above remarks applies to blocked sterling. The estimated total of all sterling balances as at the end of June 1952 was about £3·4 billions, of which about one billion was blocked by agreement with the holders. Details are given in Table 13, and

TABLE 13[1]

ESTIMATED BALANCES OF NON-RESIDENT STERLING
AT MID-1952

(*In £ million*)

Country	Total	Blocked
Sterling Area Countries		
Australia	233	
New Zealand	72	
South Africa	73	
Eire	211	
India	670	} 697[2]
Pakistan	101	
Ceylon	65	30
Iraq	50	
Burma	59	
Colonial Empire	1,042	
Other Countries		
Egypt	190	185
Thailand	42	
Japan	127	
OEEC Countries	349	81[3]
Errors and Omissions	113	
Grand Total	3,397	993

it will be seen that much the largest holdings of blocked sterling were those of India, Egypt and Pakistan. Until 1950, all the blocking was on a short-term basis, the relevant agreements needing to be renegotiated at intervals of a year or so, but the Colombo Plan of October 1950[4] laid down a long-term pro-

[1] From the BIS's report on *The Sterling Area*, January 1953.
[2] Includes £157 millions hypothecated to cover pension obligations.
[3] Portuguese government loan to the UK.
[4] Cmnd. 8080.

gramme for the release of part of the blocked sterling held by India, Pakistan and Ceylon, and early in 1951 similar arrangements were made with Egypt. Thanks to these arrangements, and to subsequent bilateral agreements with the four countries concerned, the sterling balances which they held were progressively unblocked, the latest date for completion specified in these agreements being 1963. In the case of the Portuguese loan, the amount still outstanding at the end of March 1966 was about £33 millions, and final repayment is due by 1973.

The end of bilateralism

In March 1954 'Bilateral' status was abolished and Transferable Account status extended to virtually all countries outside the Sterling and American Account areas. Combined with this extension of the Transferable Account area there was a liberalisation of the transferable account system as such. First, Britain no longer insisted on the quid pro quo which had previously been exacted from any country wishing to qualify for Transferable Account status, namely that it should undertake to accept in sterling any current payments made to it by another Transferable Account country or from the Sterling Area. Second, the whole distinction between current and capital transactions was swept away, transferability being made automatic in both cases. The previous arrangements governing the Sterling Area, the American Account Area and blocked sterling were not affected by these changes. However, as we shall see in the next section, a new brand of sterling, 'registered sterling', was introduced simultaneously with the extension and liberalisation of Transferable Accounts, as the result of the re-opening of the London gold market.

The motive of the British authorities in abolishing 'Bilateral' status and liberalising the transferable account system seems to have been that the need for restrictions was diminishing—in that the Bilateral countries which had originally been either chronically short of sterling, or chronically satiated with it, had gradually achieved a more balanced position.[1] The relevant restrictions had indeed been increasingly inoperative for some considerable time. Their nature was such that their rigorous enforcement would have required a most detailed scrutiny of traders' and bankers' transactions, so detailed in fact that enforcement had never been com-

[1] See the article on 'Convertibility' by J. R. Sargent in *Oxford Economic Papers*, February 1954.

pletely rigorous, and with the transition to more favourable circumstances the standard of enforcement was allowed to become still less exacting. By March 1954 it was clear that the regulations then abolished had long been honoured more in the breach than in the observance.[1]

The London foreign exchange market

As the result of changes introduced in 1950 and 1951, to which reference has already been made in a footnote on page 171, the Exchange Equalisation Account's buying and selling prices for 'specified' foreign currencies[2] had in one case (the Canadian dollar) been abolished and in all others amended so as to allow a wider margin between the buying and the selling price, and at the same time the authorised dealers were left free to deal among themselves in these currencies. Let us take as an example the US dollar, whose parity rate had been $2.8 per £ since the devaluation of sterling from $4.0 in September 1949. Prior to December 1951 the Account had bought US dollars at 2.79⅞ per £1 and sold them at 2.80⅛ per £1, but thereafter the Account undertook to buy at 2.78 and sell at 2.82 (nearly the maximum spread allowed by the IMF): in consequence US dollars henceforth changed hands between authorised dealers, and between them and the public, at a price which fluctuated within the limits of 2.78–2.82 per £1.

Before May 1953 the market in foreign currencies was wholly bilateral, except for freedom of arbitrage between US and Canadian dollars. Thus authorised dealers, when dealing with Brussels, could do so only in sterling against Belgian francs. But in the course of 1953 authorised dealers were permitted to undertake spot arbitrage transactions as between any of the following countries: France, Switzerland, Belgium, Netherlands, Western Germany and the Scandinavian countries.[3]

These arrangements were later extended to include forward operations for periods up to three months ahead, but otherwise remained virtually unchanged until the introduction in December 1958 of non-resident convertibility, to which reference will be

[1] See *The Banker*, April 1954, p. 183.
[2] The list of specified currencies changed slightly from time to time, but by the end of 1956 had settled at a total of thirteen, namely the currencies of the USA, Canada, Austria, France, Switzerland, Belgium, Norway, Sweden, Denmark, Holland, W. Germany, Portugal and Italy.
[3] And subsequently Italy in 1955 and Austria in 1957.

made in the final section of this chapter. Part of this later story can however conveniently be mentioned here: in January 1960 the Account ceased to quote official buying and selling prices for any of the specified currencies except the US dollar. Moreover, since exporters could thereafter accept payment in virtually *any* convertible currency, the distinction between specified and non-specified currencies ceased to have any practical significance.

The reopening of the London foreign exchange market fundamentally changed the *modus operandi* of the Exchange Equalisation Account. Instead of being a party to every exchange transaction, as it had been since the introduction of the war-time exchange control, it was able to revert to its pre-war practice of simply intervening in the market, though now (on account of the IMF Agreement) its interventions had to be such as to ensure that the spot value of the pound always stayed within one per cent of its parity.

The London gold market[1]

Though prior to the second world war a 'convertible' currency usually meant one convertible into gold (in the sense that the central bank concerned was prepared to sell it at a published price[2]) the adjective 'convertible' in the post-war period has meant 'convertible into US dollars'. Thus in the post-war period the link between gold (on the one hand) and the national currencies of countries other than the United States (on the other) has depended on the readiness of the US authorities to deal in gold with other countries' central banks at a price of 35 dollars an ounce.

Holders or would-be holders of gold, other than central banks and exchange equalisation accounts, have in the post-war period enjoyed no rights of conversion of national currencies into gold: at the best they have been able (legally or illegally) to buy gold (frequently at a premium on $35 an ounce) in one or other of the free gold markets which have been in operation in various parts of the world (e.g. Tangiers) throughout the post-war period, despite the IMF's initial disapproval.

The gold market in London is however in many important respects different from those in operation elsewhere. It was closed altogether in the post-war period until March 1954,[3] by which

---

[1] See the article on 'The London Gold Market' in the Bank of England's *Quarterly Bulletin*, March 1964.
[2] Above, p. 29, footnote 2.
[3] The Fund had by then abandoned all attempt to prevent the operation of free gold markets.

time the post-war demand for gold for private hoarding purposes had for the time being considerably declined,[1] and with it the premiums which had on earlier occasions obtained in other gold markets.[2] Moreover the London market has since March 1954 been open only to purchasers resident outside the Sterling Area and able to pay in dollars or in other currencies convertible into dollars.

The dealers in the re-opened London market were the Account itself, the authorised dealers in foreign exchange and the specialised bullion houses. The supply of gold to the market comprised newly mined gold from the Sterling Area and contributions from anyone outside the Sterling Area who chose to sell for sterling. In the latter case the sterling obtained by the seller would be either American Account sterling (if he lived in that area) or so-called 'registered' sterling, which could be exchanged for gold again in the London market whenever the holder so desired. The demand for gold from the market comprised purchases by the Bank of England (for the Exchange Equalisation Account), plus purchases by any holder of American Account or Registered sterling. Among the latter were operators intending to re-sell to the US authorities at the latter's official purchase price. The organisation of the market remained unchanged until the end of the 1950s except that on the introduction of non-resident convertibility in December 1958 (see below) the market was opened up to purchases by *all* holders of sterling resident outside the Sterling Area. The course of events in the gold market in the 1960s will be treated in Chapter 21.

The return to convertibility

As we shall see in the next chapter, there were until December 1958 'free' markets in foreign countries wherein Transferable Account sterling was sold against dollars at a discount which was commonly slight but sometimes considerable (e.g. immediately before the devaluation of September 1949).

Towards the end of 1954 the free market price for Transferable Account sterling declined from only slightly below the then official parity of $2.80 to a level of little more than $2.70 to the £, and

---

[1] There was however later on, in the 1960s, a strong resurgence of private demand, mainly for speculative purposes. See Chapter 21.

[2] Not only had the demand for gold on the free markets declined, but the supply of new gold to them had increased: South Africa and other gold producers had to an increasing extent permitted the sale of their output in the free markets, instead of selling the whole of their output to central banks and the British Exchange Equalisation Account.

the daily amount of Transferable Account sterling sold against dollars increased considerably. On 24 February 1955, the Chancellor of the Exchequer, concerned (for reasons which will be explained in Chapter 14) with these 'markets through which sterling is traded at a discount to the detriment both of our traders and of our reserves', announced that (among other measures) he had 'authorised the Exchange Equalisation Account authorities to use wider discretion in operating in these markets so that they may be in a better position to carry out our general exchange policy and make the most prudent use of our reserves'.[1]

After the date of this announcement, the free rate for Transferable Account sterling was hardly ever at a discount of more than 1 per cent, which may be taken to imply that the Exchange Equalisation Account was almost always prepared to buy such sterling for dollars, whenever its price would otherwise have fallen to a larger discount. In other words, Transferable Account sterling became as from February 1954 de facto convertible.

Official recognition of this de facto situation followed in December 1958, when Transferable Account sterling was assimilated to American Account and Registered sterling, all three being amalgamated under the common label of External Account sterling. Thus there were now only two varieties of sterling,[2] External Account and Resident (the latter being sterling held within the Sterling Area). The status of Resident sterling was unaffected by the changes of December 1958, and has indeed remained unchanged throughout the post-war period.

The formal resumption of non-resident convertibility in 1958 was not confined to sterling, but (as we saw in Chapter 12) also applied to twelve other European currencies.[3] Moreover the European Payments Union was at the same time superseded by the European Monetary Agreement. These changes had important implications for the foreign exchange markets. In the words of the 29th *Annual Report* of the BIS:

So far as the foreign exchange markets are concerned, the measures taken in December 1958 have brought unification and at the same time greater freedom of movement for rates. Previously each European currency was traded against the US and Canadian dollars in a separate market, while eleven different European currencies were traded against

[1] See the IMF's *Sixth Annual Report on Exchange Restrictions*, p. 3.
[2] Apart from security sterling: see below, p. 196.
[3] See p. 159, footnote 1.

one another on what was one market, under the arbitrage arrangements introduced in May 1953. At the end of December 1958 these two
kinds of market were amalgamated and all the principal European
currencies are now freely traded against one another and against the
US and Canadian dollars in one market. This has meant, of course,
the disappearance of the free, semi-official markets in which current-
account balances in European currencies were traded against the dollar,
the most important of which was the transferable sterling market.[1]

[1] op. cit., p. 186.

14

THE PATHOLOGY OF EXCHANGE CONTROL

The powers which the monetary authorities of a country are able to exercise over transactions in that country's currency are in practice severely limited, and any currency which is subject to exchange controls is almost sure to provide examples of 'leaks' and of 'black' or 'cheap' exchange rates. Sterling has been no exception to this rule, especially prior to the resumption of non-resident convertibility, for during this period the exchange controls of the Sterling Area found their task considerably complicated by the widespread use of sterling as an international currency. It is therefore instructive to consider the weaknesses which appeared in the sterling arrangements described in Chapter 13, whenever they were subject to pressure, as for example, in 1949, before the devaluation of sterling in September.

Resident sterling

One of the difficulties in the way of stopping leaks in an exchange control (even in the case of a currency which is not used inter-nationally) is that an illegal exchange of currencies is *as such* virtually undetectable. To take a case where sterling is being used no differently from any other currency subject to exchange control: the British authorities can do little or nothing to stop an Englishman offering an American sterling in London at a cheap exchange rate in return for dollars in New York. The transaction is likely to be revealed only when either party attempt to *use* the currency he has acquired. Let us consider each of the two parties in turn:

The *Englishman* may want simply to transfer his capital abroad, and be prepared to hold his dollars indefinitely or use them to buy US securities. If so, there is no reason why he should arouse the suspicions of the British authorities. Or he may want to use the dollars to have a good time in America, instead of living more austerely within his travel allocation. In this case also he may well escape detection, provided his amusements are not too ostentatious. However, if he tries to use his dollars to finance the unauthorised import of American commodities, he has to hoodwink the British customs. He could, of course, sell his dollars to another Englishman, but the buyer would have just the same difficulty in disposing of them without detection.

The *American* too can simply retain the currency he has acquired, though at a time when Englishmen are anxious to move their capital to America it is unlikely that many Americans will want to move their capital to England. Or he can use his cheap sterling to pay for a holiday in England. But if he uses it to finance (cheaply) the export of British commodities he also (or his British supplier) will have to hoodwink the British customs, either by smuggling or by undervaluing his goods.[1]

An alternative device available for transferring capital abroad is the granting of extended trade credit. It is of course normal commercial practice for exporters to sell on credit to their foreign customers, and the most that an exchange control can reasonably attempt to do is to set an upper limit (six months, or some such period) to the term of credit that an exporter may allow. If therefore a British exporter, A, likes to hold a promise of dollars from an American customer, B, in preference to holding sterling, he will grant B at least the full permitted term of credit and may then attempt to extend it further on one pretext or another; and since there are perfectly legitimate reasons why a foreign customer might need to delay payment, it is virtually impossible for the British control to take action against any but the most flagrant cases of procrastination.

Experience in the post-war years has shown that no exchange control can prevent very considerable capital movements in the form of variations in international trade credit. If for example a particular country's currency is distrusted, a transfer of capital

---

[1] If he exports British goods costing £2,000, but persuades the customs that they are worth only £1,500, he will have to undertake to sell dollars equivalent to only £1,500 to an authorised dealer. Thus the remaining £500 of the cost price can be paid in cheap sterling, acquired as the result of an illegal transaction.

out of the suspect country occurs both as the result of an extension of trade credit by the country's exporters and also because imports are paid for as promptly as possible. A considerable part of the drain of gold and dollars from Britain in the months prior to the devaluation of sterling in September 1949 was undoubtedly caused by the need to accommodate an increase in export credit granted, and a reduction in import credit accepted, by British traders.

Let us now turn to those leaks in the sterling control arrangements which arise from the use of sterling as an international currency. These leaks have been serious on occasions (e.g. mid-1949) and are difficult to prevent. Indeed Britain has been unusual in both practising exchange control and at the same time attempting to promote the international use of her currency; most countries with exchange controls have thought it desirable to prevent the international use of their currencies, for example by requiring their exporters to exact payment in foreign currencies. (British exports can of course *always* be paid for in sterling.)

The mere fact that sterling is in use throughout the Sterling Area leads inevitably to a multiplication of possible leaks, in that all the subterfuges practicable to an Englishman are no less open to an Australian or Indian, and in addition some parts of the Sterling Area have customs regulations which are considerably less strict than ours. Moreover, neither Sterling Area countries of the Middle East (e.g. Kuwait) nor Hong Kong (also a member of the Sterling Area) operate the usual Sterling Area regulations requiring the full surrender of foreign currency earnings (particularly dollars) to the appropriate exchange control authorities. Finally, some products of the outer Sterling Area (for example South African diamonds) lend themselves to being smuggled.

Non-resident sterling before 1955

The use of sterling as an international currency outside, as well as inside, the Sterling Area, led to further difficulties with the enforcement of exchange controls in the post-war period, at any rate up to the time when Transferable Account sterling was made *de facto* convertible (a step which was taken, as we shall later see,[1] as an alternative to the stricter enforcement of certain of the control procedures).

The most serious 'foreign' leak in the sterling control arrangements prior to that time (i.e. before February 1955) occurred

[1] Below, p. 196.

whenever the monetary authorities in a foreign country either refused to stabilise the price of sterling by buying and selling it freely against the local currency, or when alternatively they did stabilise the price of sterling, but at a level which gave rise to a disorderly cross rate between sterling and a hard currency, particularly the US dollar. The effect of disorderly cross rates between sterling and the dollar has already been considered in Chapter 7 in connection with the currency practices of Italy before November 1948 and of France between February 1948 and September 1949.[1] There we saw that the result of 'cheap' sterling[2] in Italy and France was to divert trade in such a way that these countries obtained dollars which would otherwise have gone into the Exchange Equalisation Account. A similar result tended to occur if any other country's monetary authorities failed to stabilise the price of sterling, in terms of the local currency, at the appropriate level. In practice most countries agreed to avoid disorderly cross rates in sterling, but there always remained a number of smaller countries (e.g. Siam, Syria, and the Lebanon) and free ports (such as Tangiers) where although there might be an official rate of exchange for certain governmental transactions, the local price of sterling bought by importers was simply allowed to find its own level in a free market, which usually meant that sterling was 'cheap' in relation to the dollar.

It will be recalled that one way in which a disorderly sterling-dollar cross rate caused a loss of dollars to the Exchange Equalisation Account is that it encouraged merchants to buy goods in the Sterling Area for export to the United States, without surrendering the dollar-proceeds to one of the authorised dealers referred to on page 170. A similar diversion of trade might arise for other reasons, of which two were from time to time (before 1955) of considerable importance in practice.

First, foreign holders of sterling might (no less than British holders) decide that it would be to their advantage to hold dollars instead—because, for instance, they expected that sterling was shortly to be devalued in relation to the dollar. In these circumstances the discontented foreign holders of sterling could achieve their object either by themselves buying Sterling Area goods with their sterling and reselling them in America for dollars, or alter-

[1] Above, p. 91.
[2] This 'cheap' sterling was not 'black' sterling, since none of the transactions which led to the purchase or sale or sterling at a cheap price in relation to dollars were in contravention of any country's laws or regulations.

natively by selling their sterling at a discount to a merchant who would undertake the same transaction. What exactly the latter alternative involved can be made clear by a hypothetical example. Mr X, a Ruritanian resident, has a holding of £100,000 of Transferable Account sterling (Ruritania being a Transferable Account country) which he wishes to convert into dollars. This holding he makes over to a merchant, Mr Y, at a cheap rate of (say) £1 = $3, the official rate at the time being £1 = $4. Y uses the £100,000 to buy Sterling Area goods which he then resells in America for something more than $300,000—let us say for $400,000. Of this amount, $300,000 is paid into an American bank deposit in X's name (in this way X is paid for his sterling) and the remaining $100,000 is available to cover expenses and as profit for Y.

Second, it can be shown that merchants importing goods into countries outside both the American Account Area and the Sterling Area might have found it to their advantage to exchange sterling for dollars at a black rate, whenever the sterling prices of commodities were higher (at the prevailing official rate of exchange) than the dollar prices of the same goods, or when certain commodities could not be bought for sterling at all. Such a state of affairs did indeed obtain from time to time: for example in the middle of 1949 the sterling prices of many primary commodities were appreciably higher than the corresponding dollar prices,[1] while many luxury goods, produced mainly in the United States, could hardly be bought for sterling at all. The kind of transactions which occurred at this time, and caused a leak in the sterling exchange control, can be illustrated by a variant of our previous story about Mr Y.

In our new version, we abandon our Mr X, the Ruritanian holder of sterling, and replace him by a Mr Z, a Ruritanian importer. Mr Z, to pay for many of the goods he imports, needs either sterling or dollars, which he can obtain at the official rates of exchange from the Ruritanian monetary authorities. Unfortunately for him, however, he is allowed only a very limited ration of dollars for the purchase of 'non-essential' goods or of goods which can be obtained (though more expensively) for sterling. If only he could obtain more dollars he could make larger profits, for he could then import from the United States more of the goods which are relatively expensive, or even unobtainable, from sterling sources. The Ruritanian authorities are however prepared to

---

[1] For examples see pp. 236–7.

make a concession. Their general rule is that if a Ruritanian obtains dollars in a 'normal' way (for example by exporting Ruritanian-produced goods to the United States) he must sell them to the authorities at the official exchange rate, but if Z, or any other Ruritanian, obtains *extra* dollars for his country he may use all or a proportion of them himself for buying extra imports. This is where Y comes in. He can obtain extra dollars by the export of Sterling Area goods to the United States, and these dollars he is prepared to sell to Z for sterling at a black rate, just as he was prepared in our previous example to sell them to X.

It may be wondered why, if merchants such as Y could obtain cheap sterling in this way, they should ever have bought sterling at the official price. The answer is that Y, in 'shunting' Sterling Area commodities to the United States (i.e. sending them there without selling the dollar proceeds to an authorised dealer), would incur expenses and run risks which could be avoided if the goods were shipped normally to the United States and the dollar proceeds exchanged for sterling at the official rate.

On the one hand, if Y shipped his goods, say Australian wool, from Sydney to the United States direct, without troubling to send them first to Blackport (a port outside the Sterling and Dollar Areas) he found it relatively difficult to conceal from the Sydney customs officers the true destination of his wool, and if his attempted deception failed he would be blacklisted (i.e. debarred from future trade with the Sterling Area). On the other hand, if he shipped the wool in the first place to Blackport, he found it easier to hoodwink the Sydney customs, but he incurred extra shipping expenses. Moreover, he would have trouble with the Blackport exchange-control authorities, who would be likely to require Y to sell to them (and not to X or Z) the dollar-proceeds of the wool he proposed to re-export to the United States. Y however might believe the customs authorities to be considerably less strict at Blackport than at Sydney—though if such was their reputation the Sydney customs would be particularly suspicious of goods consigned to that destination. Alternatively Y might know that Blackport operated a scheme of dollar retention quotas, as described already in Chapter 7 (p. 95). Such a scheme would be most useful to him if a high percentage retention was conceded, but a generous concession would be unlikely unless Y could show that his activities would in some way benefit the country where Blackport is situated. If, for instance, Blackport is itself in Ruritania, the Ruritanian authorities might be disposed to allow Y to retain a generous proportion of his dollars for sale to Z, whose extra imports from America would help to relieve shortages in the Ruritanian home market. If on the other hand Blackport was not in Ruritania, the Blackport authorities would be less likely to be generous to Y.

Moreover, if Blackport were not in Ruritania there would prior to March 1954 have been the problem of transferring the Transferable sterling owned by X or Z to a Blackport account, so as to give plausibility to the fiction that Blackport was the final destination of the Australian wool. For such a transfer of sterling would have been contrary to the British exchange control regulations.

It is thus clear that our *dramatis personae*, and particularly our merchant Y, would have been involved in considerable expense and trouble in evading the Sterling Area exchange control regulations if these were very rigorously enforced. But could they be? A completely rigorous enforcement would have imposed an impossible burden on the Sterling Area officials concerned (particularly the customs officers at Sterling Area ports), so that enforcement in practice could at best have amounted to a detailed scrutiny of only a small proportion of the relevant transactions. Moreover, undue formalities prescribed by customs officers and other officials would also have been burdensome to the Sterling Area's customers, whose goodwill would depend on tolerating a certain degree of laxity.

Imagine a customs officer at Sydney satisfying himself that a particular consignment of wool could be released for export. He would need to satisfy himself on all the following questions:

(1) In which foreign currency or in which brand of sterling is the consignment being paid for?

(2) What is the intended ultimate destination of the wool?

(3) Is the proposed method of payment appropriate to that destination?

(4) Will the purchaser of the wool be able to establish in due course the *actual* ultimate destination of the wool, and can he be relied upon to reveal whether it differs from what he now declares to be the intended destination?

Given that in the normal course of business an exporter of Australian wool would very often not know the ultimate destination of the wool[1] (which normally would pass through many hands before reaching the spinner) it is apparent that the above questions would often not admit of easy answers, and that the procedure required to establish the correct answers would often be vexatious to the traders concerned.

Very likely the liberalising of the Sterling Area exchange control regulations in March 1954 was due in part to the burden they imposed on Sterling Area officials and on the Sterling Area's customers. It would also seem that the decision taken in February 1955 to make Transferable Account sterling de facto convertible was an implicit admission that (in the face of mounting 'customer resistance') it was no longer wise to attempt to enforce the regulations required to prevent commodity shunting. Shunting could not in practice be prevented by controls: it could only be discouraged by making it unprofitable. This meant supporting (with official purchases) the dollar price of Transferable Account sterling, and though such purchases involved an expenditure of dollars by the Exchange Equalisation Account, this loss may have been less than that which would have resulted from the continuance of shunting.

Security sterling

Security sterling was introduced in 1940 and remained in existence until April 1967. During the intervening period, owners of sterling securities who were resident outside the Sterling Area were allowed to sell them for sterling only on condition that this sterling went into a 'security sterling' account from which payments could then be made only for the purpose of buying other sterling securities (other than short term ones) to be held by the same, or some other, *non-resident*. Security sterling was thus always inconvertible, irrespective of the holder's nationality, the policy of the British authorities being to allow dividends and interest to be remitted to non-resident holders of sterling securities in the same way as payments are remitted to non-residents selling goods to the Sterling Area, but prior to April 1967 not to allow the conversion of capital, except in the case of securities being redeemed.

The effect of these regulations was frequently (though not always) to lower the dollar value of these securities held by foreigners. An American, for example, who held British shares might feel that the investment was insecure by reason of political

[1] Or even the immediate destination, since (thanks to wireless) this need not be settled until after the ship has left port.

or other local influences, or he might fear a devaluation of the pound. Or again, the yield on his shares might be lower than he could get on a US security of comparable standing. Accordingly he might sell his British shares abroad at dollar prices appreciably lower than the ruling London prices multiplied by the dollar-sterling exchange rate ruling in the official market. Alternatively, he might sell his shares in London for security and then sell his security sterling abroad for dollars at a discount on the exchange rate ruling in the official market.

In the preceding paragraph, we have taken the example of an *American* seller of sterling securities or of security sterling, but we could equally well have taken any resident outside the Sterling Area selling to any other non-resident.

Though in principle the market for security sterling was open only to non-residents, an important class of purchasers was constituted by Sterling Area residents in the Middle East (e.g. Kuwait) and in Hong Kong, who (as we have seen) are free from the usual Sterling Area regulations requiring the surrender of all dollars and other foreign currencies to an authorised dealer. The dollar expenditure of such Sterling Area residents on security sterling (which thereby became resident sterling) may therefore be regarded as having been a 'gap' in the Sterling Area exchange control. This gap disappeared with the assimilation of security sterling to normal external account sterling in April 1967.

The security dollar gap

As we saw in the previous section, a market in security sterling was possible because residents outside the Sterling Area own, and trade among themselves in, sterling securities. In much the same way residents within the Sterling Area own, and trade among themselves in, dollar or other foreign currency securities. Before July 1957 such trade in foreign currency securities within the Sterling Area was unimpeded by the UK exchange control, but since then UK residents have required special permission (rarely given) to buy foreign currency securities from persons resident in other parts of the Sterling Area. Nevertheless, UK residents still trade freely among themselves in foreign currency securities, many of which are indeed quoted (usually at a premium in relation to their New York price—the *security dollar* premium) on the London stock exchange.

Prior to the restrictions imposed in July 1957 on the transfer of dollar securities within the Sterling Area, the security dollar arrangements gave rise to a 'security dollar gap' (popularly referred to at the time as 'the Kuwait gap') in addition to the 'security sterling gap' already described in the preceding section.[1] Both these 'gaps' were made possible by the fact that residents in certain parts of the Sterling Area, and in particular Kuwait, are not subject to the normal discipline of the Sterling Area exchange controls. In consequence there was prior to July 1957 no very satisfactory way by which the British authorities could prevent operations along the following lines:

(a) A UK resident transferred sterling to an operator in Kuwait,

(b) the latter used the sterling to buy dollars in the free market (at a premium) from, say, an international trader who could use the sterling to finance commodity shunting or pay for services rendered by Sterling Area residents,

(c) the operator in Kuwait used the dollars bought in the free market to buy dollar securities in New York,

(d) the dollar securities thus acquired were then sold for sterling in London. (It was this last step, involving e.g. the purchase of dollar securities by a British resident from a resident in Kuwait, which was made illegal in July 1957.)

This kind of operation through the Kuwait gap was profitable whenever the percentage premium on dollars bought in the free market was appreciably less than the premium on dollar securities in London, i.e. than the percentage excess of sterling value in London of dollar securities, converted to dollars at the dollar-sterling rate ruling in the official market, over the dollar price of such securities in New York.

[1] See the article on 'Sterling Today' in the August 1957 issue of *Barclays Bank Review* and Mr A. C. L. Day's article in the *London and Cambridge Economic Bulletin*, published in the September 1957 issue of *The Times Review of Industry*.

15

STERLING AFTER CONVERTIBILITY

Non-resident convertibility

The move to convertibility made in December 1958 by Britain and twelve other European countries,[1] followed by the transition in February 1961 by Britain and nine other countries from Article XIV status to Article VIII status,[2] had a much more direct implication for residents outside the Sterling Area than for Sterling Area residents. Henceforth, all non-SA residents' sterling was, with one minor exception, External Account sterling, which could be transferred freely with no British official restrictions and be converted freely into US dollars at a spot rate within one per cent of the official parity. External Account sterling could also be used to buy gold on the free market, and in particular on the London gold market. The one exception to this uniform pattern of non-resident convertibility was in respect of security sterling, which was however assimilated to External Account sterling in April 1967.[3]

The Sterling Area

For the residents of the Sterling Area the steps taken in December 1959 and February 1961 were not decisive turning points. Nonetheless, the Sterling Area was in rapid evolution, both before and after these two events. As we saw in Chapter 13, the pre-war Sterling Area was a loose and somewhat ill-defined group of

[1] See pp. 159 and 197.
[2] See pp. 101–2.
[3] See pp. 196–7.

countries whose common characteristic was that their monetary arrangements to a greater or lesser degree centred on London. The introduction in 1939 of drastic exchange controls led to a much clearer delimitation of the Area, which henceforth corresponded to the 'Scheduled Territories' listed in the UK exchange control regulations. Moreover the provisions of the exchange control tended to consolidate the Sterling Area into a single economy, and to cut it off (by payments restrictions and import quotas) from the rest of the world. Throughout the 1950s however there was a progressive dismantling of exchange controls and other restrictions imposed by the Sterling Area on transactions with non-SA countries. The last example I can find of the Sterling Area being used as the basis for trade discrimination was at the time of the Commonwealth Prime Ministers' Conference in January 1952, when the Sterling Area countries agreed to re-impose quotas directed against non-SA countries. The move to convertibility in December 1958 and our acceptance of Article VIII status in the IMF in February 1961 merely confirmed that the Sterling Area was no longer a device for discrimination in trade and current payments.

As regards *capital* payments, the Area has been in the post-war period characterised by the fact that up to May 1966 the UK exchange control imposed no impediments to capital movements within the Area except (as from July 1957) in the case of dollar securities.[1] However this freedom did not imply freedom for Outer Sterling Area countries to make capital issues on the London market, since there was all the time a UK capital issues control on *all* overseas issues and this has always been highly restrictive. On the other hand there was up to May 1966 no restriction on UK portfolio investment in securities issued in OSA countries nor on bank credit or trade credit to OSA countries, nor on direct investment by UK companies in OSA branches, subsidiaries, or associated companies. Measures taken by the UK in May 1966 modified these rules of the game, in that the British government:

(1) introduced a 'voluntary' programme to confine direct investment[2] in the four 'developed' OSA countries (South Africa, Australia, New Zealand, and Ireland) to projects which promised an 'early, substantial and continuing benefit to the UK balance of payments'.

(2) introduced a restraint on *institutional* portfolio investment in the same four OSA countries. The restraint on institutions was that they

[1] This restriction was imposed in connection with the Kuwait Gap. See p. 198.
[2] i.e. company investment in branches or subsidiaries overseas.

should not increase the level of their portfolios of securities denominated in the currencies of the four countries beyond that ruling at the time the programme was announced in May 1966.

In brief, then, the evolution of the UK exchange control on current transactions had by the early 1960s extended to all overseas holders of sterling the freedom from restrictions which had earlier been enjoyed only by some of them, while the modification introduced in 1966 in the UK controls on capital transactions somewhat weakened the contrast between outer-sterling-area and non-sterling-area residence from the point of view of access to additional sterling by certain kinds of capital transactions.

UK residents

The position of UK residents has not improved as the result of the evolution of the British exchange control. As regards *current* transactions, the control has (apart from travel allowances) always authorised payments outside the Sterling Area by anyone authorised to buy foreign goods or services: the significant change here has been the dismantling of import licencing, rather than a relaxation of exchange control arrangements as such. As regards *capital* transactions with the non-sterling-area, including the trade credit arrangements of British exporters and importers, an exchange control has been in operation continuously, with only mild relaxations quickly reversed. In the special case of transactions in securities denominated in dollars or other non-SA currencies, the control has since 1957 applied to transactions with the OSA as well as with the non-SA and, in confirmation of its effectiveness, the security dollar premium[1] has always been appreciable, occasionally exceeding 50 per cent. Finally, as was explained above, the measures adopted by the UK in May 1966 have extended control to additional categories of capital transactions between the UK and the four most developed countries of the OSA.

Sterling as a reserve currency

Throughout the 1960s sterling has been important as a reserve currency, though mainly within the Outer Sterling Area. At the beginning of the decade, all the OSA except South Africa held their official reserves predominantly in sterling. Total OSA reserves amounted to about £2,000 millions in sterling, compared

[1] Above, p. 197.

with about £800 millions in gold, mainly held by South Africa. In the course of the sixties the sterling holding fluctuated from time to time, but the general trend was roughly level, or only slightly declining. In contrast, the official OSA holdings both of gold and of non-sterling currencies (mainly US dollars) have been increasing steadily, which mainly accounts for the considerable annual increase in OSA holdings of these assets, as shown below in Table 14. These figures indicate a considerable retreat from the

TABLE 14

ANNUAL CHANGE IN OSA HOLDINGS OF GOLD
AND NON-STERLING CURRENCIES[1] (1958–69)

(*excluding Euro-dollars and other non-sterling currencies
held in London*)

	£ million
1958	15
1959	65
1960	− 20
1961	112
1962	131
1963	97
1964	73
1965	54
1966	335
1967	266
1968	712
1969	198

accepted Sterling Area rules of the game as understood in the 1950s, when (apart from South Africa) the countries of the OSA felt themselves bound by an understanding that any build-up of their reserves should be almost exclusively in sterling.

The motives which have led to a diversification of reserve media in the OSA are various. First, sterling has been weak throughout the 1960s because the underlying weakness of the UK economy has been such as to make very difficult the sustaining of a reserve currency role. Second, the political cohesion of the Commonwealth has steadily weakened. Third, there has been a weakening of trading links within the Sterling Area, an increasing proportion of sterling area countries' trade being with non-SA countries. Fourth, Britain has become progressively less important as a source of capital to OSA countries, especially since her adoption of exchange control measures in May 1966. Despite these sources

[1] Source: *Economic Trends*, no. 173, page xxxvi and subsequent issues.

of weakness, a series of rescue operations, described below in Chapter 21, enabled the sterling exchange rate to be maintained at its 1949 parity of $2.8 to the £ right up to 1967, but the fear of devaluation was almost continuously present, and even when it occurred in November 1967 (the parity being reduced from $2.8 to $2.4) the fear persisted for some months that further devaluation might be needed, with the result that this period saw an intensification of the OSA's tendency to diversify reserves.

The Basle Group Arrangements of 1966 and 1968

Many of the rescue operations described in Chapter 21 were known as 'Basle-type operations', in that they were arranged as between the central banks of the major powers, frequently on the occasion of the monthly meetings held at the Bank for International Settlements at Basle. Typically these Basle-type operations were short-term credits or swaps, running for a period not exceeding three months, but two of them, the so-called Basle Group Arrangements of June 1966 (renewed in March 1967 and March 1968) and of September 1968, were for longer periods, and were also unusual in being specifically intended to offset the depletion of UK reserves on account of the conversion of overseas-held sterling balances.

The Basle Group Arrangement made in June 1966 were with the central banks of Austria, Belgium, Canada, Germany, Holland, Italy, Japan, Sweden and Switzerland and with the Bank for International Settlements: in addition the Bank of France also concluded a three months' credit facility with the Bank of England, renewable by mutual consent. Together with US 'special' facilities (i.e. those other than the standing reciprocal swap: see below, page 258), the total of all these facilities amounted to $1,000 million. Their agreed purpose was to relieve pressure on the official reserves of the United Kingdom arising from fluctuations in the sterling balances of overseas countries, whether held by monetary authorities or privately, and thus to give added strength to the sterling system. They were specifically *not* intended to finance a British balance of payments deficit.[1]

The Basle Group Arrangement negotiated in 1968 is described as follows in the Bank of England's Annual Report for the year 1968–9:

[1] *Financial Times*, 14 March 1967.

From the United Kingdom's point of view, the major developments during the year were the conclusion of arrangements with the overseas sterling area countries relating to their official sterling holdings and the linked medium-term facility of $2,000 million extended by the Basle group of central banks. For some years before the devaluation of sterling a number of sterling area countries had gradually been reducing the proportion of sterling in their total foreign exchange reserves; however, the direct burden on the United Kingdom's gold and convertible currency reserves had been fairly small, mainly because only net accruals to national reserves were held in, or converted into, non-sterling currencies. After the devaluation of sterling, continued nervousness about the pound and about the stability of the international monetary system caused these countries to speed up the process of reserve diversification, and it became necessary to reduce the drain on the United Kingdom's resources. The method adopted was to negotiate first for a 'safety net' facility, which, by providing an assured means of financing unavoidable falls in the sterling balances, was designed to dispel most of the fears that had promoted the earlier decline.

Discussions in Basle between the central bank Governors who regularly meet there led to an agreement in principle in July 1968. The central banks and the BIS were willing to provide jointly a facility on which the United Kingdom could draw during a three-year period in order to offset fluctuations below an agreed base level in the sterling balances of sterling area holders, both official and private; the net amount drawn on this facility at the end of three years would be repayable in instalments spread over five years, starting five years after the arrangements were concluded. Before finally agreeing, the central banks wished to be assured that sterling area countries were also willing to make some contribution to this stabilising process: first, by refraining from making excessive calls on the United Kingdom's reserves simply for the sake of diversifying their own, so that the Basle facility would be left to finance only unavoidable falls in their holdings such as those caused by balance of payments difficulties; second, by some of them placing part of their non-sterling reserves on deposit with the BIS to help finance UK drawings on the facility.

A series of agreements was therefore negotiated between the United Kingdom and individual overseas sterling area countries: each of these countries formally undertook to hold a specified proportion of its total official external reserves in sterling, the proportion being based on the position at the middle of 1968; in return, the United Kingdom guaranteed the value, in terms of the US dollar, of the country's official holdings of sterling that exceeded 10% of its total official external reserves—provided that the minimum sterling proportion was maintained throughout the period of the agreement. Thus, taking account of their existing gold and non-sterling currency reserves, together with guaranteed sterling, 90% of each country's reserves would be safeguarded, in one way or another, against any loss that might be directly entailed by a future devaluation of sterling against the US dollar. By early September it was clear that agreement was sufficiently advanced for the necessary assurances to be given in Basle, and the conclusion of the $2,000 million facility was announced on 9th September. At the same time it was announced that the earlier, short-term, facility negotiated in June 1966 and subsequently renewed, which related to fluctuations in all overseas countries' sterling balances, would be progressively liquidated and ended by 1971.

The formal agreements with sterling area countries came into force on 25th September. Most are initially for three years, with a possible extension for two more years; some are for five years but provide for reviews in 1971; all are uniform in substance.[1]

The arrangements helped to give some stability to the international monetary system. By the time the supporting facility had been concluded at Basle, the United Kingdom was entitled to draw some $600 million to finance earlier reductions in the sterling balances. Afterwards, as already noted, sterling holdings increased and this reduced the United Kingdom's net entitlement to draw on the facility.[2]

The arrangements made for financing the 1968 Arrangement have been described in greater detail by the Bank of International Settlements, in its 39th Annual Report:

The BIS, backed by a group of twelve central banks—those of Austria, Belgium, Canada, Denmark, Germany, Italy, Japan, the Netherlands, Norway, Sweden, Switzerland and the United States—has placed at the disposal of the Bank of England credit facilities totalling $2 milliard for the purpose of protecting the UK reserves from the effects of any declines in the sterling balances, both official and privately held, of the overseas sterling area below an agreed starting level. The facilities have a ten-year life starting from 23 September 1968. Drawings may be made at any time during the first three years and the net amount ultimately drawn has to be repaid between the sixth and tenth years. The facility is administered by the BIS, which meets requests for drawings by the Bank of England by short and medium-term borrowings in the markets and out of the use of foreign currency deposits made at the BIS by sterling-area monetary authorities. To the extent that these resources might be insufficient, the BIS could have recourse to the group of twelve central banks, up to the amounts of their respective participations.[3]

[1] The texts of the agreements are set out in two White Papers (Cmnd. 3834 and Cmnd. 3835); a third White Paper (Cmnd. 3787) gives more general information about the arrangements.
[2] Bank of England *Report* for the year ended 28 February 1969, pp. 12–14.
[3] BIS, 39th *Annual Report*, p. 117.

In the same Report (p. 168) the BIS notes that, in the year ended 31 March 1969, central banks' deposits at the BIS rose by the equivalent of rather more than half a billion dollars, 'mainly due to the receipt of funds from central banks in the overseas sterling area'.[1] This presumably refers to the OSA's practice, made possible by the Second Basle Group Arrangement, of holding reserves 'of foreign currency deposits made at the BIS'. (According to the previous quotation from the BIS Report, such deposits are then available to be on-lent by the BIS to the Bank of England.) However by mid-1969 'as the result of the continued rebuilding of the sterling balances of the sterling area countries during the early months of 1969, almost the whole of what remained outstanding under the medium term facility, agreed at Basle in September 1968' had been repaid[2], and by the end of 1969 they had been completely repaid.

---

[1] There was a further increase of over two billion dollars in the year ended 31 March 1970. 'Part of the rise was accounted for by the funds received from various central banks in the overseas sterling area under the terms of the Second Group Agreement.' BIS *40th Annual Report*, p. 174.

[2] Bank of England, *Quarterly Bulletin*, September 1969, p. 280.

16

THE DOLLAR AND EURODOLLAR

1945–1957

In the first two of the three phases into which I have suggested we may divide the post-war period (the bilateral phase and the two-area phase[1]), the US dollar shared with gold the role of providing the non-communist world with a medium for hard settlement. In this arrangement, gold was the junior partner, prized by most holders only because it could be converted into dollars at a fixed rate of $35 an ounce (the price at which the Federal Reserve Bank of New York, acting as agent for the US Treasury, would deal in gold with other central banks). The international status of the dollar on the eve of the transition from my Phase Two to Phase Three (the convertibility phase) has been authoritatively explained in an essay, published in May 1957, by Mr Klopstock,[2] the then head of the balance of payments division of the Federal Reserve Bank of New York, who summarised the recent history of the dollar in the following terms:

Following the stabilisation of the dollar in terms of gold in January 1934, a heavy and rapid rebuilding of dollar assets set in. In the period 1934–1940 inclusive, foreign dollar assets rose by no less than $3.4 billion. But this increase was of an entirely different nature from that of the more recent period, since it reflected essentially 'autonomous' private transfers of 'hot money' from Europe and was accompanied,

[1] Above, pp. 80–1.
[2] The International Status of the Dollar, no. 28 of the series *Essays in International Finance*, published by the International Finance Section, Princeton University. My quotation is from page 7.

and in fact made possible, by large gold exports to this country. During the past decade on the other hand, the build-up was largely of the 'accommodating' variety . . . .

In the 'forties, the dollar fortunes of foreign monetary authorities improved and deteriorated successively, depending on whether or not their dollar earnings together with dollar aid receipts exceeded or lagged behind their purchases of munitions and foodstuffs in the war years, and of raw materials and foodstuffs in the early post-war years. In 1941 foreign monetary authorities were compelled to sell large amounts of gold to the United States Treasury, but beginning in 1942 Lend Lease aid more than sufficed to cover the dollar deficits of foreign countries, and foreign monetary authorities were able to add substantially to their dollar holdings which they then invested to a considerable extent in United States Treasury bills. With the sudden termination of Lend Lease after the war, and as a result of heavy dollar requirements of foreign countries, dollar balances of foreign monetary authorities in 1946 and 1947 had to be drawn down considerably, and heavy gold sales to the United States Treasury became necessary. The year 1947 saw foreign short-term dollar holdings reaching their post-war low of $4.8 billion; since then there has occurred an unprecedentedly large rise, carrying these assets to $8.9 billion by the end of 1952 and to more than $13 billion at the end of 1956.

Of this total, about $8 billion were officially held, predominantly in the reserves of other central banks, whose gold reserves at that time were $14.7 billion.

During that part of the post-war period about which Mr Klopstock was writing, the division of the world into separate monetary regions called for a great deal of international cooperation, but all the devices adopted to regulate settlements as between the different regions were applied to the various media for soft settlement, such as sterling and the EPU, and not to the dollar, which was not subject to any exchange control by the American authorities (and was incidentally one of the few currencies which never needed to take advantage of the transitional provisions of Article XIV of the IMF charter).

The 1960s

Mr Klopstock was not expressing just his own opinion, but the unanimous opinion of all monetary experts, when at the time of writing he thought it 'difficult to visualise a deterioration of faith in the soundness of the dollar sufficient to make foreigners wish to withdraw their dollar balances'.[1] Yet this is precisely what did

[1] See his essay, p. 21.

happen in the following decade, in the course of which the US
gold reserve was run down from nearly \$23 billion in 1957 to
about \$11 billion in 1969, and the US government felt obliged to
resort to a great variety of measures, including exchange control
on some capital transactions (see below), and various kinds of
compensatory financing (including currency swaps and Roosa
bonds[1]) in order to protect its reserve from an even bigger drain.
For the date of Mr Klopstock's essay (1957) marked the turning
point in the US balance of payments: thereafter the rest of the
world began to be concerned with what came to be called the
negative dollar gap,[2] and with the dollar glut rather than the
dollar shortage. A symptom of the concomitant decline of confidence in the dollar, in comparison with gold, is that the market
price of the latter in the London market has tended to rise above
the official price of \$35 an ounce except during the period when
it was stabilised at approximately this level by the operations of
the gold pool (see below, page 253).

The Eurodollar market[3]

The lack of confidence in the dollar in the 1960s was initially a
lack of confidence by private speculators and hoarders, but with
the passage of time a number of official holders, and in particular
the French authorities, have from time to time professed reserva-
tions as to the suitability of the dollar as a reserve medium.[4] In
all these cases, the preferred alternative to the dollar has been not
some other national currency but gold. But where gold is not a
satisfactory alternative to a national currency, as in the case of
the bulk of private trading, banking and financial transactions,
the dollar has retained a loyal clientele, and has indeed come into
wider and wider use by virtue of the development of what has
come to be known as the Eurodollar market.

Europe acquired US dollars under the Marshall Plan, and later
on, with the US balance-of-payments deficits beginning about
1958, the accumulation of dollars proceeded further. European
central banks converted some billions of their surplus dollars into
gold but they also reduced restrictions on the private holding of

---

[1] See below, p. 209 et seq.
[2] See below, p. 242.
[3] Parts of this section are quoted almost verbatim from Norris O. Johnson,
Eurodollars in the new international money market, published in 1964 by the First
National City Bank of New York.
[4] The dollar has however remained unquestioned as the intervention currency used
by central banks in their dealings in the foreign exchange markets.

dollars. Thereafter European banks, merchants and industrialists accumulated short-term dollar deposits, and it was this which opened the way for the development of the Eurodollar market.

What distinguishes a Eurodollar deposit from a 'native' dollar deposit is that it is the liability of a bank located outside the US. Thus it is the location of the debtor bank and not of the holder (who may possibly be a US resident) which makes a deposit 'Euro'. Eurodollar deposits are however readily convertible into native dollars, since they are all promises to pay dollars in New York. If we think of them as a separate currency, they sell at par; the debtor normally settles by cable transfer on New York, which serves as a clearing house for transfers of Eurodollar deposits, following instructions from foreign centres.

In the simplest kind of Eurodollar business, banks located outside the US (which may be overseas branches of US banks) take (that is, borrow) dollar deposits, lend the dollars as Euro-dollar advances, and earn a differential between average rate paid and average rate earned to cover expenses and produce a profit. In more common practice, however, foreign exchange transactions become involved: banks can obtain dollars for making Eurodollar advances by selling for dollars other currencies they have on deposit; while on the other hand banks receiving deposits of dollars can sell them for other currencies they want to use. Thus a bank's Eurodollar liabilities may be either less than or greater than its Eurodollar assets.

The risks of exchange rate fluctuations—involved in taking one currency and lending another—can be minimised by what foreign exchange traders call 'swaps'—trading one currency for another in the present (spot) and contracting to reverse the transaction at an appropriate date in the future (forward). For example, a bank in London may obtain sterling to lend to (say) UK local authorities by taking dollars as interest-bearing deposits, selling them for sterling and covering forward.

Alternatively, the currency swap may be undertaken not by the bank but by its borrowing customer. For example, a London bank may lend dollars to a firm on the Continent. The firm may get the dollars at a lower interest rate than by borrowing local currency, and it may be that it is dollars that are needed for the firm's transactions. But if the borrower needs local currency, to be acquired by selling the dollars, he takes a risk that the local currency may be devalued in terms of the dollar, so that the amount of his loan, in local currency, will be increased. Unless he is prepared to accept this risk, he will obtain forward cover—that is, he will enter into a contract to buy dollars against the local currency on the date the loan matures. If the dollar is selling at a premium in the forward market, it will cost him something to cover the risk. If the cost of forward cover, expressed as an annual rate, is added to the interest rate on the dollar loan, the total cost of borrowing may still be competitive with the rate he would have had to pay on a local currency loan.

The volume of Eurodollar deposits had by 1970 risen to over $40 billions, the bulk of which was on-lent by the banks whose liabilities the Eurodollar deposits were. The geographical distribution of this Eurodollar business is world-wide, with Canada, Japan[1] and the main centres in Continental Europe all participating on a large scale, but by far the largest Eurodollar centre has always been London, where a substantial proportion of the business is in the hands of the London offices of the large American banks, which on-lend to their US head offices (occasionally on a very large scale).

So much for the actual organisation of the Eurodollar market. Let us now consider some of the reasons for its very rapid growth after about 1957.

(1) On the demand side an important initial spur to the development of the market was the increase of the United Kingdom Bank Rate to 7 per cent in 1957 and the restriction then put on the use of acceptance credits in sterling for the financing of trade between non-sterling-area countries.[2] In consequence sterling was no longer available for part of its traditional uses, and not unnaturally London banks looked for resources to meet the needs of their customers.

(2) There are legal limitations on interest rates payable by banks located in the US. Such banks are prohibited from paying any interest on demand deposits and are officially restricted (under so-called Regulation Q) as to the maximum rate they can pay on time deposits. In 1959, when limits of $2\frac{1}{2}\%$ at 90 days and 3% at 6 months were in force, Regulation Q made American deposit rates uncompetitive with Eurodollar deposit rates and this has occurred again on various occasions. To alleviate this problem for US banks, certain *foreign*-owned deposits (namely officially held ones) at banks located in the US were exempted from Regulation Q as from October 1962, but until June 1970 Regulation Q still applied to all US-owned deposits at such banks. As from 24 June 1970, however, Regulation Q was suspended for 30 to 89 day certificates of deposits, issued by banks located in the US, in denominations of $100,000 or more.

[1] 'Euro' is a misleading label, in that it refers to deposits *anywhere* outside the US.
[2] Such credits have been banned altogether as from October 1968.

(3) On several occasions (1966 and 1968–9) when US banks have been short of cash, they have been anxious to attract dollar deposits at their foreign branches for on-lending to their US head offices as a means of improving their cash position. The reserve requirements imposed by the US authorities on US banks do not apply to Eurodollar deposits at their overseas branches, nor before August 1969 to amounts on-lent by these branches to the US head office. As from October 1969, however, liabilities of banks located in the US to their foreign branches in excess of their amount in May 1969 have been subject to a 10% reserve requirement.

Interest equalisation tax

In July 1963, after receiving a special balance-of-payments message from the President, the US Congress enacted the so-called interest equalisation tax. This was a tax of 15 per cent on purchases by Americans from foreigners of new or outstanding foreign securities of three or more years' maturity originating in any industrial nation. The principal object of the legislation was to reduce foreign securities issues in New York by increasing costs to foreigners of long-term financing in the United States by approximately 1 per cent per annum. Subsequently an understanding was reached with the Canadian government to exempt new Canadian issues needed to maintain an unimpeded flow of trade and payments between the two countries; the Canadian authorities simultaneously agreed not to increase Canada's official reserves through the proceeds of borrowings in the United States.

The interest equalisation tax, originally imposed on a temporary basis, has been renewed from time to time and under the Democratic administration was in various ways made more onerous. Thus in 1965 (as the result of evidence that bank credit was being used to avoid the tax) bank loans with maturities of one year or more were brought within its scope, and later its rate was increased. However, the Nixon administration reduced the rate: as from 1970 it has been ten per cent.

Voluntary restraint programme

In February 1965, at the same time as the inclusion of certain bank loans within the scope of the interest equalisation tax, the US government also introduced a programme of voluntary restraint on lending abroad. This programme had three facets:

(1) The US monetary authorities issued guidelines to the *commercial banks* requesting them to limit the increase in their foreign claims

during 1965 to no more than 5% of the amount outstanding at year-end 1964. Within this ceiling, banks were to give priority to the financing of United States exports and to loans to less developed countries and were to avoid placing an undue burden on the balance of payments of Canada, Japan, and the United Kingdom. In December 1965 the ceiling on foreign credits applicable in 1966 was increased from 105 to 109% of their 1964 base, but banks were asked to space out the use of the leeway under the ceiling. The 109% ceiling was then retained during 1967, except that banks were asked to limit the use of their leeway 'to a rate not exceeding 20% thereof per quarter beginning with the fourth quarter of 1966'.[1] In January 1968 the ceiling was reduced from 109 to 103% and in addition the banks were asked to reduce outstanding term loans to the developed countries of Continental Western Europe and also to cut outstanding short-term credits to these countries by 40% during the course of 1968, with each bank's general ceiling lowered by the amount of such reductions over the course of the year. On the other hand all claims on Canadian residents were shortly afterwards (March 1968) exempted from the banks' ceiling. The banks were offered a minor easement in April 1969, in that they were permitted to opt for an alternative ceiling equivalent to $1\frac{1}{2}$% of their total assets as at the end of 1968. This easement chiefly benefited the smaller banks. In December 1969 the guidelines for US banks were changed 'to give greater and more explicit recognition to the established priority for export financing .... Under the revised program, each bank is to have a ceiling exclusively for loans of one year or longer that finance US goods exported on or after December 1. This Export Term-Loan Ceiling is to be separate from a General Ceiling that will be available for loans of any type and of any maturity. Under the new program, the aggregate General Ceiling of banks currently reporting to the Federal Reserve Board will be $10.1 billion, and the Export Term-Loan Ceiling for these banks will be about $1.3 billion, for a total ceiling of $11.4 billion. Aggregate ceilings under the previous guide-lines were $10.1 billion.'[2]

(2) Guidelines were issued early in 1965 to *nonbank financial institutions* (such as insurance companies and pension funds) on broadly similar lines to those for banks. The 1965 increase in foreign credits maturing in ten years or less was to be kept within 5 per cent of the amount outstanding at year-end 1964, and short-term investments in foreign money markets were to be reduced to the year-end level of either 1963 or 1964, whichever was lower. In 1966 these guidelines were simplified: institutions were requested to limit the increase in certain types of loans and investments in selected foreign countries until the end of 1967 to no more than 5 per cent of the level on September 30,

[1] 1967 Guidelines for Bank and Nonbank Financial Institutions, Circular no. 5916 December 13, 1966.
[2] *Federal Reserve Bulletin*, January 1970, p. 11 (which gives full details).

1966. In January 1968 the guidelines became stricter, in line with the stricter ones imposed on the banks: nonbank financial institutions were requested to reduce their holdings of certain foreign assets by 5 per cent during 1968 and also to repatriate all liquid assets not essential for the conduct of their foreign business. However (as in the case of the commercial banks) the guidelines for nonbank financial institutions were amended in March 1968 to exclude Canadian claims from restriction, and in April 1969 the 5 per cent reduction in specified foreign assets imposed by the 1968 guidelines was rescinded. The principle of a separate ceiling for *export* term-loans introduced in December 1969 into the guidelines for banks was not extended to nonbank financial institutions, which continue to operate under a single ceiling. 'However, an institution may exceed its ceiling moderately if the excess reflects new export credits which could not be accommodated under its ceiling. In addition, an institution that has had either a low ceiling, or none at all, may now hold certain covered foreign assets up to a total of $500,000.'[1]

(3) The guidelines of February 1965 also covered the overseas financial business of *industrial companies*. The US Department of Commerce asked US firms with substantial business abroad to improve by 15 to 20 per cent the aggregate of selected components of their individual balance of payments. The choice of means to achieve this target was left to the cooperating companies, which could increase their exports, accelerate repatriation of income from their direct investments[2] abroad, or decrease their direct investments financed from the US by postponing or cancelling marginal direct investment in developed countries and by relying more on foreign financing. In addition, the firms concerned were requested to reduce their short-term investments held abroad to a level no higher than the amount outstanding at the end of 1963. The guidelines were in December 1965 extended to a larger number of industrial companies and reinforced by setting a specific target for cuts in direct investments for each company. Further guidelines issued for 1967 were stricter still: as part of the overall target, the total of direct investment outflows and retained earnings in selected countries, minus borrowings abroad, was limited under a formula designed to hold the net total of such flows close to the 1966 experience.

Mandatory restraint programme

In January 1968, the tightening up of the guidelines for financial intermediaries was accompanied by measures imposing *mandatory* restrictions on direct investment abroad.[3] Net transfers of capital

---

[1] *Federal Reserve Bulletin*, January 1970, p. 11.
[2] As defined in footnote 2, p. 200 above.
[3] In addition to the measures directed toward private capital outflows, the President requested a series of other programmes to improve the US surplus on *current* account. In particular, the President appealed to Americans to defer non-essential travel outside the Western hemisphere, and requested the Congress to earmark $500 million of Export-Import Bank funds to provide improved export insurance,

by US investors for direct investment in all advanced Continental European countries and South Africa were subject to a moratorium during 1968. For certain developed countries, such as Canada, Japan, the United Kingdom, and Australia, in which a high level of capital inflow is essential either for the maintenance of economic growth or for financial stability, the total of new capital transfers plus reinvested earnings might not exceed 65 per cent of the average of direct investment in these countries during 1965–6. The ceiling for the less developed countries as a group was, however, 110 per cent of the average in 1965–6. These regulations were relaxed, but only very slightly, by the Nixon administration in April 1969, and again as from the beginning of 1970.

and generally broaden the scope of government financing of US exports, as part of a more comprehensive export-promotion programme. At the same time, it was announced that negotiations would be initiated with NATO allies to offset the foreign exchange costs of US military spending in Europe—a goal that could be achieved either by increasing their defence purchases in the US or through investments in US Treasury securities.

Part III

The course of events since the war

Part III

The course of events at our money

17

1945-49

The flood of devaluations released by the devaluation of sterling in September 1949 marked a turning point in international monetary history. The period from the end of hostilities up to September 1949 was characterised by a considerable degree of historical unity, partly because the major international disequilibria of the period arose from the war and from economic problems directly attributable to the war, partly because there was no widespread attempt in the period to deal with these disequilibria by means of adjustments to exchange rates. The devaluations of September 1949 not only represented an abrupt break with the previous tradition of exchange stability, but also liquidated, at any rate partially, the disequilibria of the preceding period. It therefore seems appropriate to treat the period 1945-9 separately from the succeeding period.

Exchange rates

Though the post-war period prior to September 1949 was characterised by remarkably stable exchange rates, this stability was achieved only by the use of exchange controls, which sometimes led to disorderly cross rates and (particularly in South America) to multiple currency practices. This state of affairs, as the BIS points out in its nineteenth *Annual Report*, was in marked contrast to what happened after the war of 1914-18:

After the First World War, it took more than five years before any European currency was formally 'stabilised', which at that time meant linked to gold again at the par rate. Before stabilisation took place, the various currencies were subject to sometimes rather wild, sometimes quite moderate, fluctuations; but for each currency there was not more than one rate quoted (apart from a slight spread between buying and selling rates) and the various currencies could be bought and sold freely for all purposes at the rates thus quoted in the respective exchange markets. In order to steady quotations, central banks (and sometimes governments also) had at times to support their currencies by entering the market as purchasers or had to buy up any offer of foreign currencies which might threaten to raise the value of the national currency more than was desired. . . .

Since the Second World War, the exchange system has been of a different kind. 'Par rates' have been fixed for most currencies and at those rates current commercial and other transactions have to be settled, the settlements taking place largely through clearing and other bilateral accounts without any specific transactions in the open exchange markets. Not only capital transfers but current operations, whether commercial or financial, are, in most countries, dependent upon an 'allotment of foreign exchange' by the official Control. This being so, there are normally no fluctuations in the official rates. Any alterations (beyond such minor modifications of a fractional nature as the authorities may decide upon from time to time) are, under the new system, made on the basis of official decisions applicable from certain definite dates (as was the case in July 1946 when the Canadian dollar was appreciated by 10 per cent and the Swedish crown by 16·6 per cent). Thus, the official par rates are in no immediate way dependent upon quotations in actual exchange markets. . . .[1]

Though the general picture prior to September 1949 was one of stability, there are a number of events to record. *First*, the main ex-enemy countries, China, and several eastern European countries, entered upon the peace with their economies in a highly inflationary condition and the value of their currencies steadily falling. Apart from China, all of these countries had restored stability before September 1949. In particular, Greece, Hungary and Poland stabilised their currencies in 1946, Rumania and Italy followed suit in 1947, Germany introduced a completely new currency, the Deutsche mark, in June 1948, and Japan stabilised the yen in April 1949. *Second*, there were three cases of currencies being appreciated in relation to the US dollar— namely the Canadian dollar and the Swedish crown in July 1946 (respectively by 10 and 16·6 per cent) and the New Zealand pound in August 1948 (by 24 per cent). In all three cases the main

[1] op. cit., p. 118.

purpose was to combat excess demand in the home market.[1]
Third, there were a small number of deliberate depreciations of
wholly or partly stabilised currencies, notably by Turkey in 1946,
and by Mexico and France in 1948 and 1949.

The most important examples of disorderly cross rates in the
period we are considering were those which prevailed in Italy up
to November 1948 and in France between February 1948 and
September 1949. Both of these cases have been mentioned
already (page 91) in Chapter 7. The resort to multiple currency
practices was more widespread, as will be seen from the following
list[2] of countries engaging in such practices:

COUNTRIES WITH MULTIPLE EXCHANGE RATES IN 1949

Latin America	*Elsewhere*
Argentina	Austria
Bolivia	Spain
Brazil	Iran
Chile	Lebanon
Colombia	Syria
Costa Rica	Thailand
Ecuador	
Nicaragua	
Paraguay	
Peru	
Uruguay	
Venezuela	

The causes of disequilibria

The chief cause of the major post-war disequilibria, and particularly of the so-called dollar gap, was the devastation of Europe
and of certain other countries, including the important dollar-
earning regions of Malaya and the East Indies. Not only was
there actual destruction of material assets, but maintenance work
and the replacement of worn-out and obsolete equipment were
postponed; moreover, a great deal of manufacturing industry
became highly specialised for the production of munitions and
other requirements of war. This last factor was particularly
important in the case of the United Kingdom, whose contribution
to the war effort required her to direct her economy away from
exports and civilian requirements and to rely on Lend-Lease
imports for goods which had previously been either made at

[1] See above, pp. 73–4.
[2] Assembled from various IMF publications.

home or obtained from overseas in exchange for British exports.[1]

The return of peace brought further causes of disequilibria, which served particularly to aggravate Europe's need for dollars. The European harvests of 1946 and 1947 were very poor, owing to unfavourable weather, and the hard winter of early 1947 was partially responsible for the British coal crisis. The establishment of an Iron Curtain, through which trade passed only with great difficulty, between the complementary economies of Eastern and Western Europe, had the effect of delaying reconstruction and industrialisation in the East and of making the West more dependent than before on non-European sources of supply for foodstuffs and raw materials.[2] The division of Germany was a special case of this malady: Western Germany, whose population was increased by 10 million refugees and displaced persons, was cut off both from its former granary in Eastern Germany and from its pre-war markets behind the Iron Curtain.[3]

The fortunes of industry and agriculture in the American continent during and immediately after the war, and especially in the United States, were in marked contrast to what happened in Europe. Nowhere in the former continent was productive capacity impaired by the war, and in the USA there was a vast increase in industrial output, with little or no decline in the production of civilian goods, a great increase in agricultural acreage, and a remarkable series of good harvests. Hence the goods which Europe so urgently needed, and which she could not produce for herself, were available from across the Atlantic, and the only problem was to find means to pay for them. Had the American continent shared the misfortunes of Europe there would not have been so intractable a settlement problem, because such a problem arises only when there are goods to be bought; but on the other hand there would have been immeasurably more hardship in Europe. Rough measures of the decline in industrial and agricultural output in Western Europe which had occurred by the end of the war are provided by the indices shown in Table 15. These indices also show the extent of the subsequent recovery.

Another factor which contributed to the post-war international

[1] See *Statistical Material Presented during the Washington Negotiations,* published by HMSO, 1945, Cmnd. 6707.
[2] See 'The Problem of East-West Trade' in the ECE's *Economic Survey of Europe in 1949,* p. 91.
[3] See the article on 'Pre-war Regional Interdependence and Post-war Inter-zonal Trade in Germany', in the ECE's *Economic Bulletin for Europe,* Vol. 1, No. 3.

TABLE 15
INDICES OF INDUSTRIAL AND AGRICULTURAL PRODUCTION IN EUROPE[1]

Industrial Production:

1938	1946	1947	1948	1949	1950
100	72	82	96	109	124

Agricultural Production:

1934–38	1946–47	1947–48	1948–49	1949–50
100	81	80	91	94

disequilibria was the change in the pattern of international indebtedness brought about by the war. In the early stages of the war, before the advent of Lend-Lease, Britain and her European allies, but particularly Britain herself, were forced to realise a large amount of their overseas investments in order to finance their imports. Moreover, the rise in prices which occurred during the war greatly reduced the purchasing power of the income from the investments which remained. In Britain's case she had to realise about £1 billion of her overseas assets, and in addition she acquired about £3 billion of new indebtedness in the form of accumulations of sterling by other countries. Measured in the overseas goods which it could command, Britain's net income from overseas investments declined to about one third of its pre-war amount.

The disequilibria of the post-war years are attributable not only to the war itself but also to its economic aftermath and in particular to inflation. In the immediate post-war years, conditions of excess demand were virtually general throughout the world. A United Nations' survey comments thus:[2]

A major factor in the world-wide inflationary pressures was the existence of demand for consumption goods pent up during the war. In many instances this pent-up demand was supported by accumulated holdings of liquid assets. In the devastated countries and in some under-developed areas of the world an even more important factor was the decline in *per capita* consumer supplies, especially of food, through reductions in agricultural output, declines in industrial productivity, and in some cases increases in population.

In many countries these inflationary tendencies were reflected in 'open' inflation, with rapidly rising prices. In other cases the

[1] Calculated by the ECE.
[2] *Inflationary and Deflationary Tendencies 1946–1948*, published in June 1949, p. 3.

inflation was 'suppressed' by the use of price controls and rationing.

The open inflations which occurred after the first world war were all associated with rapid currency depreciation and the net effect on the balance of current payments of the countries concerned was therefore probably small. In the period from the second world war to September 1949, however, the countries suffering inflation maintained their exchange rates and admitted imports to the extent permitted by their available supplies of liquidity, for they had come to realise that any reduction in the availability of imports, and any diversion of goods to export markets, would have the effect of reducing the supplies of goods on which the excessive home demand could be expended, thus aggravating the inflationary pressure. In these circumstances, open inflation tended to have an adverse effect on a country's balance of current payments.

In the case of a country with suppressed inflation (a widespread condition after 1945) the excess of demand over supply is not permitted to lead to a rise in prices, which are held down by price controls.[1] Instead, the excess demand is held back by rationing and by shortages, but unless rationing is very strict (stricter than in practice it ever is) any increase in the pressure of demand tends to stimulate imports (since imported goods find a ready market) and to divert to customers at home the supplies that would normally be available for export.

Thus in the conditions prevailing after the war of 1939–45, inflation, whether open or suppressed, almost invariably had the effect of worsening a country's balance of current payments, and the countries which mastered their inflations first tended to develop external surpluses, while those where inflation remained longest had deficits. Hence the chronology of the control of inflation is important to an understanding of the international disequilibria of the post-war world. The following quotations from various official reports give an outline of what happened:

In 1948, the inflationary patterns of the preceding two years were still prevalent in a large part of the world. Nevertheless there was some tendency for the relaxation of the inflationary pressures. The pressure of pent-up demand weakened in many countries. There was also some increase in the supplies of consumption goods *per capita* and consider-

[1] Sometimes the price controls are informal: thus a government may 'advise' a manufacturers' association to restrain the increase in the prices of its members' products.

able easing of specific shortages. The supply of food generally improved towards the end of the year after the favourable harvests of 1948. The full anti-inflationary impact of this factor, however, could not be felt until 1949.

For the first time since the end of the war, there appeared in 1948 and early 1949 some deflationary tendencies, in the form of actual slackening in economic activity or appearance of factors foreshadowing such slackening. Italy, which suffers from considerable chronic unemployment, experienced in addition a recession which began in the autumn of 1947. It was followed by a recovery in the second half of 1948, and another set-back in early 1949. There was also a considerable rise in unemployment in Belgium in the course of 1948. Finally, there was some involuntary accumulation of inventories in the United States in 1948, and unemployment increased significantly at the beginning of 1949.[1]

Hence it would appear that, apart from a temporary recession in Italy in 1947, the first signs of the end of inflation appeared in 1948 in Belgium and the United States.

'In the first half of 1949, inflationary pressures continued to weaken throughout the world.'[2] By the middle of the year deflation, rather than inflation, had become a problem in the United States, and in Western Europe the same could be said of Belgium and to a lesser extent of Western Germany, Italy and Switzerland. Indeed, of the larger OEEC countries, only the United Kingdom, Scandinavia and the Netherlands could be said to be still subject to inflationary pressures.[3]

In other parts of the world the subsidence of inflation in 1949 was uneven. In Latin America, 'anti-inflationary factors were significant'[4] in four of the smaller American Account countries, namely 'Cuba and Venezuela and, to a lesser extent, in Mexico and Colombia', but outside the American Account Area inflation continued: 'inflationary elements were still active in Argentina, Brazil, Paraguay, Peru and Uruguay'. 'In Asia and the Far East [but not in China] inflationary pressures also diminished towards the end of 1948 and early in 1949, largely as a result of an increase in the food supply.'

---

[1] Both quotations are from *Inflationary and Deflationary Tendencies*, p. 4.
[2] United Nations: *Recent Developments in the World Economic Situation*, published October 1949, p. 4.
[3] For the history of the progress of deflation in Western Europe, and the causes thereof, see the OEEC's *Report on Internal Financial Stability*, published in October 1949, pp. 15–20. Also see the ECE's *Economic Survey of Europe in 1949*, Chapter 3.
[4] The quotations in this paragraph are from *Recent Developments in the World Economic Situation*, p. 10.

In the light of the preceding description of the causes of the disequilibria in the period 1945–9, we should expect a strong tendency for there to be flows of settlements in the direction of certain countries and groups of countries, namely:

(1) The whole American continent, but particularly the USA and Canada, where inflationary pressure was never so pronounced as in Latin America.

(2) The former neutral countries, or at any rate those neutrals (particularly Switzerland, Portugal and Sweden) which had efficient governments, capable of taking measures to moderate inflation.

(3) The first ex-belligerents to master inflation, namely the United States, Belgium, Italy and Western Germany.

The tendency for settlements to flow towards these countries might be expected either to show itself openly, in the form of settlements actually effected, or alternatively to be suppressed, whether by unemployment in the rest of the world or by trade and payments restrictions. To what extent did these various symptoms appear in practice?

Suppressed and open disequilibria

So far as *suppressed* disequilibria are concerned, there is little evidence in the period 1945–9 of suppression by unemployment. As we have seen, the only countries which may have suffered from inadequate demand in this period were the United States, Switzerland, Belgium, Western Germany and Italy. In the first two of these cases, the trouble coincided with an external surplus, which suggests that the inadequacy of demand was not related to any need to suppress an external deficit. Hence there remain only three possible cases of the suppression of disequilibria by means of unemployment, and even then there is no clear evidence that the emergence of unemployment was due to balance-of-payments difficulties.

Though unemployment was rare in the period 1945–9, the other symptoms of suppressed disequilibria—restrictions on trade and payments—were endemic, and it is safe to conclude that many were imposed specifically to suppress flows of settlements which would otherwise have exhausted the paying country's liquidity. Such a conclusion can be safely drawn in the case of discriminating restrictions, which were in widespread and continuous use against the United States, Canada, Switzerland and Belgium, and in occasional use against various other countries (for example Germany).

In the case of non-discriminatory restrictions the evidence is much more difficult to interpret, since such restrictions may be imposed for so many reasons other than the suppression of disequilibria. Our task is however made somewhat easier by the widespread, though admittedly far from universal, tendency in the post-war period for countries to deal with external disequilibria by means of restrictions enforced by import quotas and exchange control—other restrictions, such as tariffs, being reserved mainly for other purposes.[1] On this basis it would seem that the only countries which did not impose serious restrictions for suppressing disequilibria were the United States, Canada, some of the smaller American Account countries, Switzerland and Belgium.[2] The evidence of restrictions, for what it is worth, thus points to these countries as being those to which settlements tended to flow so strongly as to call for suppressive action by the rest of the world.

The remarkable feature of the period 1945–9 was however the size of the *open* disequilibria which persisted, despite the drastic measures which were taken to suppress them. The available balance-of-payments statistics are so unsatisfactory that the total of the open disequilibria in the period cannot be estimated very accurately, but the overall surplus of the United States alone is known to have been in the region of $30 billions, and it is doubtful whether all the other overall surpluses taken together would add more than 10 per cent to this total. On this basis the total overall surpluses in the period would be some $33 billions, a truly enormous amount, and—more remarkable still—a single country accounted for almost the whole of it.

The second largest surplus country was Canada, with an overall surplus of about $1 billion. A few members of the Sterling Area had surpluses, but the Area as a whole was in deficit with the rest of the world. A number of Latin American countries also had surpluses, among them Argentina and Venezuela. In Europe probably only Switzerland had an overall surplus, taking the period as a whole.

The main overall deficits which balanced these overall surpluses were as follows, the figures being highly approximate:

[1] There is no strong economic foundation for this distinction, since the two classes of restrictions can be made to produce almost identical results. See above, pp. 31–3.
[2] IMF's *First Annual Report on Exchange Restrictions*, pp. 22–6.

(1) The OEEC countries, other than the UK and Switzerland, together with their dependent colonial territories—about $20 billions.

(2) The United Kingdom—about $5 billions.

(3) The outer Sterling Area—about $2 billions.

(4) The United States' Pacific protégés: China, Japan and the Philippines—about $4 billions.

International settlements

If however we wish to understand the pattern of international settlements in the period 1945-9, it is not sufficient to look simply at the overall surpluses and deficits which prevailed. We also need information about bilateral relationships—preferably in the form of a table, like Table 3 on page 49, showing all the bilateral deficits of all the countries of the world, with closed circuits of deficits eliminated and the various countries ranged in order of their 'strength'. Unfortunately the compilation of such a table—Table X, let us call it—is at present quite impossible, owing to the inadequacies of available statistics: all we can do is to try to establish very roughly the order in which the various countries, or groups of countries, might be expected to appear.

Our first task is to settle whether any country was stronger than the United States—the country with the largest overall surplus. Of the countries with overall surpluses, only one—Switzerland—seems to be able to claim a bilateral surplus with the United States: this evidence therefore points to Switzerland as being the strongest country, followed by the United States. Next to the United States, in an order which we cannot satisfactorily guess, would be a group—the 'Intermediate Group', let us call it—comprising the remaining surplus countries and those deficit countries[1] whose appreciable bilateral deficits were solely with the surplus countries. This group would include Canada and most of the Latin American countries. Belgium would also be included, but otherwise it is doubtful whether any other Western European country would fall within this group, taking our period as a whole. After the Intermediate Group of countries in Table X would be countries which ran appreciable bilateral deficits not only with the surplus countries but also with other deficit countries. This 'Weak Group' of countries would be very extensive, and would range from those whose bilateral deficits were solely with Switzerland, the USA and our Intermediate Group of countries to the (unidentifiable) weakest country. The most im-

[1] The label 'surplus (or deficit) country' refers of course to a country with an *overall* surplus (or deficit).

portant members of Weak Group would be the Sterling Area and almost all the European countries except Switzerland and Belgium.

The order in which we have placed countries in our imaginary Table X throws considerable light on the hierarchy of currencies in our period. The strongest country, Switzerland, was prepared to accumulate gold and the currencies of certain other countries in strictly limited amounts, but otherwise she required settlement in her own currency, Swiss francs, of which however there were only very limited holdings outside Switzerland after the war. It soon appeared that the total means available to the rest of the world for settling with Switzerland were not sufficient to go round: the Swiss franc became a hard currency—so hard that it was reserved almost exclusively for making bilateral settlements with Switzerland.

The second strongest country in Table X, the United States, was prepared to accumulate gold without limit, but would not accept settlement in any national currencies except her own, unless they were unconditionally convertible into dollars.[1] However, the rest of the world's official holdings of gold and US dollars at the end of the war were about $20 billions, and in the course of the period 1945–9 there were further immense supplies made available as the result of the output of new gold, the operations of the IMF, and compensatory official financing by the United States government. This last occurred under various guises, including the loan granted to the United Kingdom in 1946, contributions to UNRRA and other relief organisations, credits extended by the Export-Import Bank, and Marshall Aid. Thanks to these supplies of gold and dollars, the United States' vast overall surplus was accommodated with a reduction of only about a third in the rest of the world's official reserves of these assets.

Yet this draining of the rest of the world's means of settlement with the United States, modest though it was in relation to the United States' overall surplus, caused widespread anxiety and led to the adoption of drastic policies to prevent a more rapid depletion of reserves. Countries tried not to waste their gold and dollars in making payments whenever softer currencies, such as sterling, could be substituted. In consequence, dollars went out of use as a regular means of multilateral settlement except in the Dollar Area, comprising the United States itself and certain of our Intermediate Group of countries. In the remaining Inter-

[1] American Account sterling was accepted in the United States only by virtue of the British monetary authorities' undertaking to convert it into dollars on demand.

I.M.C.—H*

mediate countries, gold and dollars had to be used for settling with the Dollar Area, but otherwise were in only occasional use for making settlements.

It will be remembered that countries in our Intermediate Group were either surplus countries with bilateral deficits with the United States and Switzerland or deficit countries whose only appreciable bilateral deficits were with the surplus countries—in practice mainly with the United States. All of the countries in this group had therefore a strong motive for preferring to receive settlements almost exclusively in US dollars. They differed however very greatly in their ability to exact dollar settlements from their customers. The ones that were members of the Dollar Area —the American Account countries in Table 12, page 180—could all exact dollar settlements[1] by virtue of being exporters predominantly of commodities which are either important United States imports (e.g. wood pulp, sugar, bananas) or which were basic necessities which their customers would otherwise have had to buy from the United States (e.g. oil). The other Intermediate Group countries were exporters either of less essential foodstuffs and raw materials in which the United States was self-sufficient (e.g. meat, cotton) or of manufactured goods. There was little possibility, for example, of Argentina, Brazil or Belgium exacting payment in dollars for all their exports without suffering a very serious contraction in their trade. Most of the Intermediate Group countries outside the Dollar Area had to accept and accumulate soft currencies from at least some of their customers for at least some of their exports but nevertheless constantly tried to exact gold or dollars wherever possible.

Within our Weak Group of countries, gold and dollars were scarcely used at all except for settling with Switzerland, the Dollar Area and, much less frequently, with the Intermediate countries outside the Dollar Area.[2] In the Weak Group, however, as within the Dollar Area, there was a widely accepted medium for multilateral settlement, which in this case was sterling. Within this group were the Sterling Area itself, most of the Transferable Account countries and many of the 'Bilateral' countries which enjoyed the most liberal facilities for 'administrative transferability'. This is not to say that sterling was the *only* means of settlement in use among the Weak Group of countries: there

[1] Settlements from the Sterling Area in the form of American Account sterling are dollar settlements at one remove, owing to the unconditional convertibility of such sterling.
[2] e.g. Belgium.

were, for example, non-sterling payments under bilateral agreements and there were the Indirect Aid provisions of the two Intra-European Payments Agreements. Nevertheless it is clear that a high proportion of settlements was made in sterling.

The advantages of sterling as an international currency have already been considered, in general terms, in Chapter 13, but two aspects of this question are perhaps worthy of emphasis here, as being specially relevant to the period 1945–9. *First*, the United Kingdom herself, and the Sterling Area as a whole, would always accept settlement in sterling, and never attempted to exact gold or dollars for passing on in settlement to the Dollar Area. The Sterling Area's dollar deficit had therefore to be met almost entirely from the reserve held by the Area at the end of the war, from the Area's current output of gold, and from loans and grants from the United States and Canada. *Second*, though there were many countries weaker than the Sterling Area, their currencies did not to any appreciable extent displace sterling as a means of settlement. This was partly because some of the countries running deficits with the Sterling Area were never seriously short of sterling, thanks to the balances they accumulated during the war, and partly because the possible rivals to sterling did not inspire enough confidence to ensure their acceptability.

The international transmission of depressions

This was not a serious question in the period 1945–9, which was characterised by an excess, rather than a deficiency, of effective demand. The only significant manifestations of inadequate demand were, as we have seen, in the United States, Switzerland, Belgium, Western Germany and Italy. In all these cases, except perhaps the last, other countries were troubled by the international impact of the depressions, but almost without exception the ground for legitimate complaint was the adverse effect on the victim-country's balance of payments, not on its domestic prosperity.

The more likely problem was the opposite one of the international transmission of inflation. Here however the countries suffering from inflation were mainly forced by their limited liquidity to apply import restrictions and thus to restrain their excess demand from spilling over into other countries.

Only two cases have to be noted of countries having enough liquidity to permit them to 'export' their excess demand. The first is that of the countries which had accumulated large sterling balances during the war, but here the blocking of part of the balances kept the problem within bounds. Britain did indeed complain of the 'unrequited exports' which were being bought with 'old sterling', but on the balance-of-payments ground that such exports ought to have gone to hard currency markets, not on the ground that they should have been sold on the home market to combat inflation. The second case is that of the recipients of Marshall Aid, whose purchases in the United States would have aggravated an inflationary condition in the American economy, had such a condition existed. However, the warnings which were issued on this score in the early days of Marshall Aid proved in the event to be largely unjustified, since despite the export surplus financed by Marshall Aid the US economy always maintained a pool (and in 1949 a rather excessive pool) of unemployment.

A country which considered that it was importing inflation from abroad would be likely to turn to remedies in the form of expedients which would (1) stimulate its imports or (2) reduce either the volume of its exports or the home-currency earnings of its export producers. Such expedients would comprise mainly the reduction of restrictions on the country's imports, the appreciation of its currency, the imposition of export quotas and the levying of export taxes. Two of these devices, currency appreciation and export taxes, were adopted by a number of countries specialising in the export of primary commodities,[1] the prices of which were often extremely high, but it is difficult to say how much of the intense demand for most of these commodities could reasonably be attributed to 'inflation', as distinct from mere 'prosperity', or alternatively to stockpiling, in the importing countries.

As for export quotas, the industrialised countries limited exports of particular commodities, but (apart from restrictions imposed for strategic reasons) the range of goods involved was narrow, being confined mainly to coal and steel. The remaining expedient, a removal of import restrictions, was used (alas) somewhat infrequently. It would thus seem that generally speaking countries did not in fact commonly adopt expedients designed to fight inflation at home caused by inflationary conditions in other countries. This does not of course prove that they did not suffer inflation at home brought about in this way, but it surely suggests that such suffering was not intense and widespread.

[1] Canada, Sweden and New Zealand appreciated their currencies. Various countries levied export taxes—e.g. Malaya's tax on rubber. In other cases a government or producers' agency was given a monopoly of exports and levied what was in effect an export tax. This applied, for example, to Argentinian beef and West African cocoa.

18

THE DEVALUATIONS OF 1949

The devaluation of sterling by about 30 per cent on 18 September 1949 was important not only in itself but because it touched off a wholesale readjustment of exchange rates throughout the Sterling Area (except Pakistan), throughout Western Europe (except Switzerland), and in a number of other countries. It was 'the most extensive realignment of exchange rates ever carried out in a short period of time'.[1] Details are given in Table 16. As might be expected, the hardest of the currencies in use for making international payments, the US dollar and the Swiss franc, were not devalued.

What were the motives which led to the devaluations, and in particular what were the motives which led the British government to take the initiative? M. Gutt, then managing director of the IMF, regarded the devaluations as an attempt to close the dollar gap by the deficit countries 'adjusting their exchange rates in order to lower the prices of their goods and increase their sales to the western hemisphere'. Sir Stafford Cripps expressed a similar view on the day of the devaluation: 'With a low rate of exchange,' he said, 'we can sell more of our goods abroad and so should be able to earn more dollars in total.' Nine days later however he was advising British exporters to 'maintain the dollar prices of our goods whenever possible', the implication being that a 30 per cent devaluation was worth while as a means of increasing dollar earnings only in the case of certain of our export products; in the case of other goods it would be better to offset the devaluation, partially or wholly, by maintaining their dollar prices.

[1] From M. Gutt's statement on behalf of the IMF.

In the event British manufacturers did not pay much heed to Sir Stafford's advice,[1] presumably because, as might have been expected, they were competing with each other too fiercely to allow dollar prices to be maintained when costs had risen only slightly in sterling (i.e. had fallen by nearly 30 per cent measured in dollars). The short-run effect of this large and almost general fall in the dollar prices of our exports was, as Sir Stafford appears

TABLE 16

DEVALUATIONS: 18 SEPTEMBER 1949 TO THE END OF 1949

	Devaluation in relation to the US dollar %
The Sterling Area except Pakistan	30
European Countries:	
Austria	53[2]
Greece	33
Denmark ⎫	
Finland ⎪	
Netherlands ⎬	30
Norway ⎪	
Sweden ⎭	
France	22[2]
Germany	20
Belgium	13
Portugal	13
Italy	8
Other Countries:	
Argentina	47[2]
Egypt	30
Canada	9

to have feared, a disappointingly small increase in our dollar earnings. Indeed, it might well have been *nil*, but for the effect on our exports of the American business recovery after mid-1949 and

[1] According to Table 7 on p. 11 of the ECE's *Economic Bulletin for Europe*, vol. 2, no. 1, British export prices, measured in dollars, fell 28 per cent between the third quarter of 1949 and the first quarter of 1950.
[2] Austria introduced multiple rates in December 1949, so that the end-1949 rate is an average. The pre-devaluation rate for the French franc is taken as the mean of the basic and free official rates. Argentina changed some, but not all, of her multiple rates in October 1949, so that the percentage shown is necessarily approximate. See the 20th *Annual Report* of the BIS, p. 154.

for the speculative factors which (as we shall shortly see) depressed our exports before devaluation and stimulated them afterwards. Moreover, our short-run gain (if any) in dollar earnings was purchased at high cost, since if one puts the reduction in our dollar prices at one quarter (and in practice it may have been rather more) an increase of one third in the volume of our exports would be taken up simply in maintaining our dollar earnings unchanged[1] —a most unwelcome burden on the already overloaded British economy.

On the side of imports, the British government had already taken such wide powers of control (by trade restrictions, bulk purchase agreements, etc.) that devaluation was hardly needed as a means of reducing imports into the United Kingdom. Moreover, devaluation had the disadvantage, as the government well knew, of raising the sterling prices of imports and consequently the British cost of living.

Was there then no short-run advantage to Britain in devaluing sterling? Did the British government take the step only with a view to the improvement in dollar earnings which could reasonably be expected to accrue over the long period?[2] No, there were a number of immediate advantages to be gained by devaluation, and it is indeed these which were probably decisive in leading the government to act as it did. In the first place, in so far as the countries of the outer Sterling Area could be counted on to follow Britain's lead in devaluing, it was reasonable to expect that their dollar expenditure would be curtailed and the strain on the Exchange Equalisation Account correspondingly reduced.[3] In theory the same economy in dollar expenditure could have been achieved by tightening up still further the import restrictions already adopted by the outer Sterling Area countries earlier in 1949, following the London meeting in July 1949 of the Commonwealth Finance Ministers. But 'whether the independent members of the

[1] If the prices of our exports changed in the ratio of $1:\frac{3}{4}$, their volume would have to change in the ratio of $\frac{3}{4}:1$ (i.e. of $1:1\frac{1}{3}$) in order to keep our total earnings unchanged.

[2] As we saw in Chapter 4, page 61 et seq., the elasticity of demand for the exports of a country in Britain's position is to be presumed to be much higher in the long run than in the short run.

[3] On the other hand, the outer Sterling Area's dollar receipts could not reasonably be expected to improve as the result of devaluation, since most of the products which the outer Sterling Area exports for dollars are primary commodities, the supply of which is inelastic. That these earnings did improve after September 1949 must be attributed to other factors, notably the business revival in the United States and elsewhere, and the increase of stockpiling by the US government.

Sterling Area could in fact make the cuts through physical import controls, while dollar goods remained so attractively priced as they were at the old exchange rate, always seemed very doubtful'.[1] In the event the rather uncertain effect of these additional restrictions was strongly reinforced by the devaluation of sterling; the whole of the outer Sterling Area except Pakistan[2] followed Britain's lead and there followed a spectacular reduction in dollar expenditure.

The other advantages to be gained from devaluation were (1) to put an end to the strong speculative position which had been built up against sterling, based on the belief that sterling would soon be devalued, and (2) to stop the serious leaks which had developed in the British exchange control.[3]

The speculative position against sterling took two forms. The first was that foreigners were holding back from buying British goods, in the belief that devaluation would occur and that as a result British prices, measured in the importing countries' currencies, would decline. The second type of speculation against sterling was itself a leak in the exchange control, and consisted of the transfer of capital to the United States, to which reference was made in Chapter 14, motivated by the expectation that sterling would shortly be devalued. The expedients adopted for making the capital transfers commonly involved the 'shunting' of Sterling Area exports destined for the United States.

The other important leaks[4] in the British exchange control also involved 'shunting': they arose partly on account of the disorderly sterling-dollar cross rates ruling in Paris (and in less important centres) and partly from the fact that many commodities could be bought more readily or more cheaply in the Dollar Area than elsewhere.

The devaluation of sterling served to stop the leaks in the British exchange control for three reasons. First, it led the French authorities to re-establish an orderly system of exchange rates.[5] Second, it served to reduce the price differentials that had grown up between the prices of certain commodities (e.g. cotton, wheat, wood-pulp, newsprint, sugar, copra, edible oils, tallow, aluminium and certain other non-ferrous metals) in the Dollar Area and

[1] From a very illuminating article by T. W. Kent on 'Devaluation One Year After', in *Lloyds Bank Review*, October 1950.
[2] Pakistan devalued in 1955.
[3] See Sir Stafford Cripps's speech in the House of Commons on 27 September 1949.
[4] Also described in Chapter 14.
[5] See above, pp. 91 and 92.

the (higher) prices prevailing elsewhere.[1] Third, it led to a reversal of the speculative capital flow. In addition, once devaluation had occurred, the orders for British exports which had previously been held up in anticipation of devaluation came forward in a rush.

Why did other countries follow Britain's lead in devaluation? The speculation which had occurred against sterling had not spread to other currencies; indeed some of the countries which followed Britain's example had actually been receiving capital as part of the flight from sterling.[2] The loss of dollars through 'shunting' is a strong ground for devaluation only in the case of a currency which is in extensive use as a means of international payment: hence this reason for devaluation cannot have been as strong for other currencies as it was for sterling, and indeed for most of the currencies which were devalued this particular consideration was largely irrelevant.

On the other hand, if the initiative in devaluation is taken by one country (Britain in this case) this may be accepted by her competitors as a reason for following suit, so as to redress the balance of competition. If Britain devalues, British exports will to some extent undercut Belgian goods in the Belgian home market and also in third markets such as the United States; hence (it may be argued) the Belgian franc must be devalued too. This line of argument was undoubtedly important in practice, and not only for Belgium.[3]

Not only Britain's competitors, but also many of her main suppliers, took Britain's devaluation as a reason for following suit, so as to prevent the deterioration in the market conditions which their export-producers would otherwise have to face. If, for example, the Australian pound had not been devalued with sterling the Australian farmer would have found it impossible to earn the same number of Australian pounds in selling his produce on the British market, and the Australian devaluation may have been intended to prevent such a reduction in Australian prosperity. If this was the purpose of the Australian government, the

[1] The examples quoted are taken from the *Economist* of 6 April 1949, p. 721, 13 August 1949, p. 370, and 20 August 1949, p. 426.
[2] e.g. Australia.
[3] For example, the French Finance Minister (quoted in *The Times* of 21 September 1949) commented, 'The pound had to be devalued, but the rate chosen is a trade-war rate, which forces other countries on the defensive in regard to their economies and their international markets. These are the circumstances which have compelled the French government to readjust the franc.' (Prior to September 1949, the French had argued that the value of sterling had been fixed unfairly high. See above, pp. 91–2.)

devaluation had nothing to do with correcting international disequilibria; moreover, since the Australian economy was at the time suffering from an excess, rather than a deficiency, of demand, it is not easy to sympathise with the case for devaluing as an anti-depression measure.[1]

---

[1] But, as *The Times* Australian correspondent commented, 'all political parties woo the farming vote'.

19

TOWARDS EQUILIBRIUM

The course of events in the eighteen months after September 1949 served to emphasise the disadvantages, rather than the advantages, of devaluation, owing to the effects of the Korean War and rearmament. The result of the 1950 rearmament and stockpiling programmes in the United States was to increase the volume of her imports and reduce the availability of goods for export. Moreover (and more importantly) the increased demand for primary commodities, not only in the United States but also in all the rearming countries, very greatly bid up their prices, and this affected the value of US imports considerably more than of US exports.[1] Thanks to these factors the dollar shortage seemed, in late 1950 and the early part of 1951, to be in the course of disappearing altogether.[2]

However, none of the devaluing countries retreated from the decisions taken in September 1949 with the exception of Canada, where in October 1950 the official par value which had been in force for twelve months was cancelled and the value of the currency left to 'be determined by conditions of supply and demand'.[3] Under these arrangements the Canadian dollar

[1] See 'The New Commodity Inflation', by Oscar R. Hobson, in *Lloyds Bank Review* of April 1951.
[2] See the IMF's *Annual Report* for 1951, Chapter I.
[3] IMF *Financial News Survey*, 6 October 1950. This survey also indicates that complete *laissez faire* was departed from at least to the extent necessary to ensure an orderly sterling-US dollar cross rate. 'In order to ensure that rates for sterling in terms of Canadian dollars reflect an orderly sterling-US dollar cross rate, the Canadian Foreign Exchange Control Board is prepared to buy and sell sterling against US dollars . . . at the official rates. . . .'

appreciated to slightly above the value which it had in terms of US dollars prior to September 1949.[1]

In the event the widespread reluctance to reverse the devaluations of September 1949 turned out to be justified, for with the subsiding of the Korean crisis the dollar gap began to reopen.

In 1951 the factors tending to reduce the deficit of the rest of the world with the United States in 1950 were reversed. A fall in United States consumption in relation to disposable income after the first quarter of the year was accompanied by an involuntary accumulation of inventories as a result of which [US] private imports of consumption goods declined. At the same time there was a fall in new governmental commitments for strategic stockpiling owing to the abnormally high prices of some of the stockpiled commodities in the previous period. [US] exports, however, rose sharply from the second half of 1950 to the first half of 1951, and still further in the second half of 1951, reflecting the rise in dollar earnings by the rest of the world during earlier periods, and notwithstanding the marked fall in the supply of dollars by the United States between the first and second halves of 1951. The gap resulting from these opposite movements in exports and imports was magnified by speculative capital movements. . . . Owing to the fact that foreign economic aid from the United States declined much more slowly after 1949 than the surplus on goods, services and private capital accounts, the rest of the world as a whole was not required to draw upon its gold and dollar reserves for the financing of dollar deficits until the second half of 1951.[2]

It was also in the second half of 1951 that the fall in the prices of primary commodities showed itself in the level of sterling liabilities and in the EPU. The sterling balances of the whole outer Sterling Area fell steadily, and Australia's in particular fell rapidly. At the same time Britain's position in the EPU quickly deteriorated, with the decline in Western European expenditure on such Sterling Area exports as wool. Drastic action had to be taken to curb these developments, and the Commonwealth Prime Ministers' Conference in January 1952 ushered in a period of tightening restrictions on imports from all sources into most Sterling Area countries.[3]

1952 and 1953 were years of movement towards equilibrium:

[1] Some ten years later the Canadian dollar began to depreciate in relation to the US dollar. In May 1962 a new par value was fixed at 1·081 Canadian dollars per US dollar.

[2] United Nations, *World Economic Report*, 1951–52, p. 89.

[3] See below, p. 243.

By the early months of 1952, the trend in the rest of the world's dollar deficit was again downwards. There was a partial recovery in United States imports of goods and services. In addition, the net outflow of United States private capital for direct investment abroad . . . rose sharply in the first half of 1952. . . . The partial recovery of imports, together with the increased outflow of private capital, more than offset the continuing decline in economic aid to foreign countries, so that the total supply of dollars by the United States in the first half of 1952 considerably exceeded the level to which it had fallen in the previous half-year and nearly regained the high level of the first half of 1951. [US] exports, on the other hand, began to decline, reflecting a fall in the rate of inventory accumulation in other countries and the re-imposition of more severe restrictions on purchases of dollar goods by countries which had encountered difficulties in their dollar balances during 1951.[1]

The effect of these restrictions was undoubtedly supplemented by the effect of the devaluations of September 1949, which were by this time beginning to have an appreciable (if not readily calculable) influence on the pattern of world trade. The reduction, and eventual disappearance, of 'the rest of the world's dollar deficit' was however not due solely to its having been suppressed by additional import restrictions or cured by devaluation, since there was also a considerable easing of the pressure of demand in the rest of the world. 1952 will be remembered as the year of the 'textiles slump' (which in fact spread to other industries producing durable consumption goods) in Britain and many other Western European countries,[2] while in the outer Sterling Area the collapse in the preceding year of the boom in primary commodities was beginning to exert a strong deflationary effect. Several countries, notably Denmark and the Netherlands, introduced generally restrictive fiscal and credit measures, and even pushed them to excess.[3] Thus while in the United States 1952 was a year of both low and declining unemployment, this was not the case in important parts of the rest of the world.

United States' prosperity continued at a high level throughout 1953, and though there was a modest revival of demand in the rest of the world the dollar gap did not reopen. It did however reopen somewhat in 1954, as the result of a further American recession, but for a variety of reasons the impact on the rest of the world was

---

[1] United Nations, op. cit., p. 89.
[2] op. cit., p. 35.
[3] op. cit., p. 37.

unusually slight,[1] and in any case full prosperity returned to the United States in the course of 1955.

The next US recession, that of 1958, also had little impact on the rest of the world: indeed that year saw the recognition of what came to be called the *negative* dollar gap—a development which from that year onwards assured a massive outflow of gold and dollars from the United States to the rest of the world and which both facilitated and justified the concerted move in 1958 by many European countries towards the greater convertibility of their currencies.

[1] See A. R. Conan's article in *The Banker* of August 1954.

20

BACK TO CONVERTIBILITY

The resumption of non-resident convertibility
After the Conservatives came to power in Britain in November
1951 they espoused the cause of convertibility. The circumstances
were prima facie not very promising. At the Commonwealth
Prime Ministers' Conference in January 1952 it was necessary to
agree a drastic increase in import restrictions in the Sterling Area
countries and in particular the UK's percentage of liberalised
imports from OEEC countries had to be reduced from 95 to 45
per cent. Thus for the time being it was necessary to mark time.

In December 1952 there was another Commonwealth Conference, which discussed convertibility in some detail, and certain
prior conditions were laid down. In particular, there had to be an
improvement in the balance-of-payments position of the Sterling
Area, and the promise of adequate financial support from the
IMF or the United States Government. In addition, there seems
to have been some discussion as to the desirability of introducing
flexible exchange rates.[1] Unfortunately nobody seems to have
given much thought to the question of how this plan for convertibility would fit in with the EPU: hence it was not surprising
that when a British mission went to Washington in March 1953
it found the Americans uncooperative, for they were strongly
adverse to any undermining of the economic cohesion achieved
in Europe through the EPU.[2]

The plan of December 1952 was also considered by the Manag-

[1] *The Banker*, September 1943, p. 133.
[2] *The Banker*, May 1953, p. 266.

ing Board of the EPU, where however the majority view was 'that any system of convertibility should be accompanied by the removal, or at least the substantial reduction, of quantitative restrictions on visible and invisible trade within Europe . . . and by the easing of quantitative restrictions on imports from the dollar area.'[1] (It was indeed surprising that the British were apparently after convertibility in the very narrow technical sense of making non-resident sterling convertible: no change was envisaged in the status of resident sterling and the move towards convertibility was not regarded as being associated with the dismantling of trade restrictions. In fact, there seems to have been a willingness to tolerate even greater restrictions on UK imports, at any rate temporarily, as a price worth paying for the narrow conception of convertibility that the British then aimed at.)

The drive to convertibility therefore for the time being lost its urgency, but technical discussions on the best means of advancing to convertibility were got under way at the OEEC. The first results of these discussions were the decision to increase, as from the middle of 1955, the proportion of gold settlement in the EPU from 50 to 75 per cent,[2] and an agreement (in August 1955) on a procedure (eventually acted upon in December 1958) for winding up the EPU and replacing it by a European Monetary Agreement, when the time came for the major European currencies to be made convertible. The discussions at the OEEC also explored the desirability of introducing fluctuating (or 'floating') exchange rates when convertibility was resumed, but the news that such a possibility was even under consideration touched off a run on sterling which was stopped only by Mr Butler's firm denial, in his speech at the IMF meeting in Istanbul in September 1955, that any change in the value of sterling was seriously contemplated.

By then, however, Britain had already (in February 1955) introduced the de facto convertibility of non-resident sterling, rather on the lines envisaged in the plan of December 1952, but this was done as a defensive measure at a time of weakness,[3] without the prior conditions previously laid down having been satisfied. The step was also taken unilaterally, not as part of an OEEC scheme, but this was presumably simply because we were acting under duress.

The concerted move to convertibility envisaged in the August

[1] *The Banker*, May 1953, p. 266.
[2] Above, p. 155.
[3] Above, p. 196.

1955 agreement did not occur until December 1958. In that month France devalued her currency by 17 per cent and she and twelve other European countries announced that their respective currencies were now freely convertible on current account for nearly all, and in some cases all, non-resident holders. As the BIS put it:

Two of them—Germany and the United Kingdom—have now put their current payments with all other countries on a basis of convertibility and they now have only one kind of current account for non-residents, freely convertible into any foreign currency and freely transferable between all non-residents. The other eleven countries—Austria, the BLEU, Denmark, Finland, France, Italy, the Netherlands, Norway, Portugal, Sweden and Switzerland—still maintain bilateral payments arrangements with certain countries. France and the Netherlands still have transferable accounts for residents in countries which are neither in the dollar area nor in the bilateral group. As, however, the uses of these transferable accounts have, since the end of December 1958, been virtually indistinguishable from those of the convertible non-resident accounts in these two countries, they can be said to exist as a third category of current non-resident account in name only, and it seems likely that they will soon be formally amalgamated with the convertible accounts. In effect, therefore, all the eleven countries which have not yet adopted overall current-account convertibility now distinguish only between countries with which transactions take place on the basis of full convertibility and those with which payments are still strictly bilateral. The number of bilateral payments agreements still maintained is different in each of the eleven countries, but in none do they comprise more than a small fraction of the foreign trade and payments of the country concerned.[1]

This move to non-resident convertibility by European countries brought in its train a similar move on the part of '15 other countries, most of which are closely related as members of a monetary area to one or another of the European countries'.[2]

The position in 1959
As the result of the events of December 1958, we may say that a large part of the world, embracing the Sterling Area, a large part of the Dollar Area and a dozen countries of Continental Europe, resumed arrangements more or less on the lines of those which came to be established in the 1920s, only to collapse in the 1930s—

[1] From the 29th *Annual Report* of the BIS, p. 188.
[2] From the IMF *Annual Report* for 1959, p. 5.

the main difference being that the foreign exchange component in official reserves was now much higher. This was the view which the BIS took in 1959 of the position:

> The remarkable growth of world trade which has taken place since the war has naturally necessitated an expansion in the supply of international means of payment. It would not appear that the present supply is inadequate, especially in view of the increase now being made in the resources of the International Monetary Fund.
>
> The expansion of international liquidity has, however, been only partly brought about by the growth in the world's stock of monetary gold; considerable recourse has also been had to the use for reserve purposes of national currencies, principally the US dollar and the pound sterling. Externally-held dollar and sterling balances now represent 26 and 16 per cent respectively of the international means of payment in the hands of countries other than the USSR.
>
> The fact that such a considerable proportion of the total volume of liquidity consists of liabilities of the United States and the United Kingdom implies that the working of the system of international payments depends at present to a large extent on the pursuit by these countries of economic and monetary policies aimed at maintaining the purchasing power of their monetary units, and so preserving confidence, both at home and abroad, in their currencies.
>
> If in the future—as is greatly to be hoped—further expansions of trade take place, the volume of international monetary reserves may have to be adjusted to the increasing need of means of payment. The problem may then arise of deciding what will be the best ways of effecting such an adjustment. This is a technical problem which the monetary authorities will have to consider in good time.[1]

A more detailed contemporary appraisal of the arrangements established at the end of 1958 is to be found in an article by Professor Robert Triffin, published in 1959.[2] In his exposition, Professor Triffin treats separately the centre and non-centre countries, the former (taken to be the UK and the USA) being those whose national currencies predominantly provide the 'exchange' component of other countries' reserves.

His information relating to the centre countries (see Table XI of his article) showed the gold backing of their external short-term liabilities to be inadequate in the case of the UK and

[1] From the 29th *Annual Report* of the BIS, pp. 243–4.
[2] 'The Return to Convertibility: 1926–1931 and 1958–?', published in the March 1959 issue of the *Quarterly Review* of the Banca Nazionale del Lavoro.

adequate but deteriorating in the case of the United States:[1] thus taken together the gold reserves of the two centre countries were in Triffin's view not over-generous even in 1958, and he foresaw (correctly, as events have since shown) a further deterioration.

As regards the non-centre countries, Triffin showed the prevailing arrangements to be a less robust structure than that of the 1920s. In 1928, for instance, the ratio of reserves to imports was somewhat higher than in 1956 and 1957, only 38 per cent was in the form of foreign exchange (as against more than half in 1956 and 1957), and these foreign exchange reserves were predominantly in one currency (sterling) instead of being (as in the post-war period) in two.[2]

Thus Professor Triffin feared that there could develop, on an international scale, the kind of instability which characterised the internal monetary system of this country between the introduction of non-metallic money and the development of the Bank of England into a reliable lender of last resort. In that unhappy interregnum the consequences of the public's freedom to choose between rival monetary media, i.e. between holding deposits at rival banks, was that the interconvertibility of the different media was never assured and frequently broke down altogether (banks being forced by a 'run' to close their doors).

The Triffin plan

An analogy between external and internal monetary arrangements suggests that a possible direction that reform might take is the establishment of an international central bank, at which all countries could deposit their existing reserves and from which they could obtain accommodation. The acquisition by such an institution of both existing national reserves and other assets, whether in the form of advances or of securities bought in the open market, would bring into existence a new international currency, like the Bancor of Keynes' Clearing Union, which might in due course become the sole medium for holding as official

[1]

	1928	1932	1938	1947	1953	1958
Ratio of sterling blances to UK reserves (%)	320	240	95	705	440	355
Ratio of dollar balances to US reserves (%)	61	17	15	31	57	85

[2] See Tables I and X of Professor Triffin's article.

reserves. A number of proposals on these general lines[1] were put forward in 1958 and 1959. Of these, much the most thorough and detailed ones were those made by Professor Triffin in a sequel to the article which I have already quoted.[2]

Professor Triffin's plan called for certain modifications to the constitution of the IMF to enable it to operate more on the lines of a central bank: indeed under his plan the IMF would become in effect a central bankers' central bank. The essential features of his proposals may be summarised as follows:

(1) Each member country's official reserves would include a deposit at the Fund, denominated in terms of a new unit of account[3], which I shall for convenience refer to as 'Bancor', though in practice it would need a new label.

(2) A minimum demand for Bancor would be created by getting all members to agree to hold at least 20 per cent of their official reserves in this form.[4]

(3) The initial supply of Bancor would be created by the IMF accepting from all members (*a*) a deposit payable out of existing reserves (and therefore comprising mainly gold, US dollars and sterling) equal to 20 per cent of each member's present reserves and (*b*) a further deposit of all sterling and US dollar balances then remaining in official reserves.

(4) Following these initial operations, the IMF's balance sheet as at the end of 1959 would have been roughly as shown opposite, all amounts being expressed as their equivalent in US dollars.

(5) A member would normally use his Bancor balance to make payments to other members,[5] but he could also withdraw his balance— either in gold or (at the Fund's option) in his own national currency (to the extent of the Fund's holding of that currency).

(6) Could the Fund ever get into the position of not being able to meet its (conditional) obligation to repay in gold? Such a contingency is most unlikely, partly because much of the stock of Bancor would

[1] See Sir Oliver Franks's annual address, in respect of the year 1958, as Chairman of Lloyds Bank. Also see the article by Maxwell Stamp, on 'The Fund and the Future', in *Lloyds Bank Review*, October 1958, and paragraphs 678 and 985 of the Radcliffe Report (Cmnd. 827, August 1959).

[2] 'Tomorrow's Convertibility: Aims and Means of International Monetary Policy', published in the June 1959 issue of the *Quarterly Review* of the Banca Nazionale del Lavoro. More recently Professor Triffin has set out his views in his book *Gold and the Dollar Crisis*, and elsewhere.

[3] There would be nothing very novel in this, in that (as we saw in Chapter 12) the EPU's liabilities were in 'units of account' which were distinct from any national currency.

[4] Members of Keynes' Clearing Union would have had to accept *all* Bancor offered.

[5] Under Keynes' Clearing Union this was the *only* way that Bancor could be used: there were no provisions for conversion.

Liabilities	$ billion	Assets	$ billion
Bancor		1. *Gold*	
Minimum balances, as under (2) above	11·1	IMF's actual holding in 1959	1·5
		To be deposited under (3) above	3·4
Other balances	10·0		
		2. *National Currencies*	
		IMF's actual holding	1·1
		To be deposited under (3) above:	
		as per (3*a*)	5·1
		as per (3*b*)	10·0
	21·1		21·1

comprise minimum holdings which could not be presented for repayment, and partly because of the Fund's option, under (5) above, to repay in the withdrawing member's own currency. But even a remote contingency has to be provided for, and Professor Triffin proposed that this could best be done by providing for the possibility of increasing to more than 20 per cent the minimum reserve requirement, in the event of such a 'gold scarcity' condition being declared by the Fund. Any member could then refuse to agree to such an increase in his deposit obligation, but such a refusal would then bring *automatically* into operation a technical 'scarcity' of the member's currency, with the consequences spelled out in Article VII of the present IMF Charter.[1]

(7) After the initial creation of Bancor, further amounts would be created by the IMF buying gold or by acquiring (through open market purchases or by granting advances[2]) further debts in member countries' currencies. The aim would be to increase the total amount of Bancor in existence at a rate sufficient to ensure that the world's stock of Bancor plus gold should grow *pari passu* with legitimate requirements for international liquidity in an expanding world economy. In order to meet the 'inflationary bias' danger raised against Keynes' proposals, Triffin suggested very simply that a presumptive ceiling on the yearly increase of the Fund's loans and investments be agreed to in advance, and that qualified majority votes be required to exceed this ceiling over any twelve months' period of operations.

(8) The national currencies appearing in the balance sheet above together with further amounts subsequently acquired, could be held by the Fund in their original form or could alternatively be

[1] Above, p. 102.
[2] Advances would however be at the Fund's discretion. Members would not have *automatic* drawing rights, as they would have had in the Keynesian Clearing Union (above, pp. 111–12).

I.M.C.—I

switched into other currencies, though only 'in a smooth and progressive manner'. One possibility would be to give 'the Fund an option to liquidate such investments at a maximum pace of, let us say, 5 per cent a year', but other (and maybe more satisfactory) arrangements might be considered.

Professor Triffin's plan admittedly called for a not inconsiderable change in institutional arrangements, but it has the attraction that at one and the same time it would serve to get rid of the instability arising from the existence of multiple (and competing) reserve media, eliminate the dependence of the present reserve arrangements on national developments in Britain and the United States, and break the link between the supply of world liquidity and the world's stock of monetary gold.

21

THE 1960s

Though Professor Triffin's diagnosis of the weakness of the post-war gold exchange standard came to be widely accepted by informed public opinion, there was until 1964 little disposition among the powers that be even to contemplate the possibility of introducing some new kind of reserve asset, either on the lines of the Triffin Plan itself or according to rival prescriptions. In 1964 however the climate of official thinking began to change and official discussions were initiated which culminated in 1969 with the adoption of the SDR scheme, as already recounted in Chapter 10.

In the intervening period the great powers, and in particular the ten participants in the General Arrangement to Borrow, displayed an unprecedented readiness to tackle problems of international settlement on a cooperative basis, leading to a remarkable succession of innovations and developments in the field of international liquidity. The measures taken prior to 1969 were however all individually much less ambitious than the SDR scheme, which itself (as we saw in Chapter 10) is less ambitious than the Triffin Plan. None the less, the various devices adopted in the course of the 1960s—for example the increases in IMF quotas (above, page 108), the establishment of the General Arrangements to Borrow page 109), the introduction of multilateral surveillance (page 128) and the recourse to various Basle-type arrangements, currency swaps etc., which will be considered in this chapter—collectively represent a very substantial development of the international monetary regime inaugurated in December 1958.

The Basle arrangements

In 1960 the UK balance of payments once again ran into difficulties: in the second half of the year there was a large deficit both
on current and on long-term capital account. This weakness was
however temporarily masked by a considerable inflow of short-
term funds, so that it was not until the following year that confidence in sterling began to ebb and the currency became vulnerable
to sudden shocks.

Unfortunately the valuations in March 1961 of both the
Deutsche mark and the guilder (each by 5 per cent) provided just
such a shock, and thereafter until the following July, when
deflationary measures were adopted by the British government and
assistance obtained from the IMF, there were widespread fears of
further changes in exchange rates, whether in the form of a further
revaluation of the German and Dutch currencies, a revaluation of
the Italian and Swiss currencies, or a devaluation of the pound.

The reaction of the major central banks to this dangerous
situation began at the BIS monthly meeting, at Basle, in the week
following the German and Dutch revaluations.

The first action that the governors took was to state formally that
the central banks represented, namely those of Belgium, France, Italy,
the Netherlands, Sweden, Switzerland, the United Kingdom and
Western Germany, were satisfied that rumours about further currency
adjustments had no foundation: and as a practical earnest of this belief
they announced that the central banks concerned were cooperating
closely in the foreign exchange markets.

Details of the various techniques to be employed were left for agreement and in practice they varied widely, but the purpose was never in
doubt. This was to ensure that, despite such pressures as might be
generated in the foreign exchange markets during the heat of the day,
no party to the so-called 'Basle Agreement' should be forced by speculative movement of funds to deviate from the declared policy.

Whilst no one could estimate for how long or in what volume these
movements would continue, it was clear in the minds of all concerned
that this was essentially an essay in short-term banking accommodation
which would be reversed in a reasonably short space of time, either by
a reflux of short-term funds or recourse in due time, if this reflux did
not occur, to one of the international sources of longer-term financial
accommodation. . . .

The pressures on sterling varied from month to month between the
beginning of March and the end of July. The largest amount outstand-

ing at any one time under the 'Basle Agreement' . . . was approximately
£325 million.[1]

On 25 July 1961 measures were taken to reduce the pressure of
home demand: *inter alia* most indirect taxes were increased by a
surcharge of 10 per cent, steps were taken to limit government
expenditure, Bank Rate was raised from 5 to 7 per cent and various
other monetary brakes were applied.

Immediately after the announcements of the 25 July, arrangements
were made for the equivalent of £536 million to be drawn in various
currencies from the International Monetary Fund and a standby credit
of £179 million was made available in case of need. This fortification
of reserves both enabled the United Kingdom to repay the Basle
credits and provided additional assurance to overseas opinion that the
exchange parity of sterling would be maintained.[2]

From the beginning of August until the end of 1961, the
pressure of home demand unmistakably abated, and at the same
time the speculative pressure on sterling rapidly subsided. The
subsequent improvement in the UK balance of payments permitted the repayment of the British drawing from the IMF to be
completed by August 1962, though a standby of $1,000 millions
was retained.

A second operation of the Basle type was undertaken by the UK
in February and March 1963, when borrowings of £89 millions[3]
were arranged to meet a drain on her reserves, attributable in
part to (unfounded) rumours that sterling was about to be devalued, and in part to the recent revision of the EMA constitution,[4] which had had the effect of reducing the scope of the
dollar guarantee previously given by Britain to her fellow members' official holdings of sterling.

Further Basle-type rescue operations were organised in 1964 for
the benefit of Italy and the UK. These will however be described
later on in this chapter.

The gold pool

The US continued in balance-of-payments deficit in the 1960s and
the consequential accumulation of dollars in the reserves of many
countries (particularly of the members of the European Economic

[1] From the Bank of England's *Quarterly Bulletin*, September 1961, p. 10.
[2] From the Bank of England's *Report* for 1961–2, p. 4.
[3] Bank of England's *Quarterly Bulletin*, June 1963, p. 83.
[4] See above, p. 16.

Community) led to a rise in their demand for gold. To this was added from time to time a speculative demand on the part of private operators fearful of a devaluation of the dollar and other currencies in relation to gold. During the third quarter of 1960,

with a more or less continuous demand for gold against dollars, mainly by continental central banks, the price rose from the equivalent of $35·09 per fine ounce to $35·26 at the end of September. The fall in US reserves attracted attention and in mid-October concern about the US dollar became more pronounced as the Presidential election in the United States drew nearer. This showed itself partly in a recurrence of interest in the possibility of a rise in the international monetary value of gold; buying orders thought to be on private account then led to a sharp rise in the London price, which at one time on the 20th October touched the equivalent of $40 per fine ounce. On the following day, after a denial by the US Treasury of any intention to change the gold parity of the dollar, the price fell to the equivalent of $37. By the end of October it had declined to $36.[1]

The dangers of a widespread scramble to convert dollars into gold were however now plain to all, and measures were concerted among the major central banks to preserve a semblance of order in the gold market.

Information about these measures is far from precise, but generally they seem to comprise undertakings among central banks not to convert accruing dollar balances into gold, and, still further to lessen pressure on United States gold reserves, by the establishment of a 'gold pool' among European central banks.[2]

As a result of these measures, the speculative demand for gold during the Berlin crisis in September 1961 and the Cuban crisis in October 1962 did not result in any appreciable rise in the price of gold in the London market. The next test occurred when, immediately after the sterling crisis at the end of 1964 to which reference is made later on in this chapter, the French government disclosed its intention to convert into gold a part of its reserves then held in dollars, but even then the gold pool was so well able to meet the resulting speculative demand for gold that the London price never rose above 35·35 dollars.

The final crisis in the history of the gold pool began with a surge of speculative gold buying in October 1967:

[1] Bank of England's *Quarterly Bulletin*, December 1960, p. 10.
[2] *Midland Bank Review*, August 1962, p. 5.

Shortly before the middle of October demand became heavier, for confidence in sterling was fast deteriorating and there were growing fears about possible changes in US gold policy. After a lull towards the end of the month, buying of gold again grew heavy early in November; and in the week after the devaluation of the pound, when speculative pressures against the dollar became intense, there was a record demand for gold. An expression of confidence by the active members of the central bank gold pool,[1] meeting in Frankfurt on 11th December, that they would be able to maintain the existing gold price and exchange parities, afforded some respite for a week or so, but heavy buying of gold was resumed in mid-December upon rumours that access to the London gold market might be restricted . . . .

January [1968] and much of February were quieter, but doubts about the US dollar were building up again, while sterling remained under suspicion. . . . Early in March buying accelerated rapidly, in the belief that the official price of gold could not be held. The run on gold quickly became very serious and a conference of the active members of the gold pool was convened in Washington for 16th and 17th March. Those taking part expressed their resolve that all gold in their hands should be used for monetary purposes only. Consequently they would no longer sell gold in the market, nor did they feel it necessary to buy it; nor would they sell to monetary authorities to replace gold sold in the market. They invited the cooperation of other monetary authorities. in making these policies effective. The conference effectively brought to an end the gold pool arrangements which had been in existence since 1961 and re-established a system of free gold markets in which central banks would not deal.

The London gold market remained closed until 1st April [1968]. . . .

Until December [1968] the price in the London market mostly ranged between $38·50 and $41 per fine ounce and turnover remained moderate. Prices in free markets were restrained by the knowledge that members of the gold pool had sold over $3,000 million of gold between November 1967 and March 1968, the greater part of it to private buyers who in many cases had been acquiring gold for speculative purposes or for hoarding.[2]

In the course of 1969 the trend of the gold price in the London market was downwards, so much so that by December it became a live issue whether the agreement reached at the Washington conference meant, or alternatively did not mean, that central banks would not buy gold in the market even if the market price should fall as low as the official price of $35 an ounce. The issue

[1] At that time Belgium, Italy, the Netherlands, Switzerland, the United Kingdom, the United States and Western Germany. It was disclosed in November that France had ceased to take an active part in the gold pool in July 1967.
[2] Bank of England *Report* for 1967–8, page 3, and for 1968–9, page 8.

was of course a serious one for South Africa, since the first of the
alternative interpretations (which had the US authorities' support)
implied that her output of newly mined gold might have to be
sold in the market at a price lower than $35, unless she was
entitled to sell at this price to the IMF—an issue which was also
in doubt (at any rate according to the US authorities). In the end,
however, the dispute between South Africa and the US was
resolved by an agreement announced at the end of 1969:

New arrangements for South African gold sales were announced by
the International Monetary Fund at the end of December. Various
circumstances have been defined in which South Africa may sell gold
to the IMF (sales will not ordinarily be made to other monetary
authorities). First, newly-mined gold may be sold to the Fund when the
market price falls to $35 or below and South Africa indicates that the
sales are necessary to meet current foreign exchange needs. Secondly,
sales may be made from South Africa's reserves, regardless of the market
price, to the extent that the country has a foreign exchange requirement, over a six-monthly period, larger than can be met from the sale
of all newly-mined gold in the market (or, if the market price is below
the agreed minimum, to the Fund). Thirdly, South Africa may also
make regular sales of up to $35 million a quarter from the stock of
gold it held on 17 March 1968—when the main central banks decided
to withdraw from the gold market—as reduced by subsequent sales to
monetary authorities (including the IMF). Finally, South Africa may
sell gold to the Fund when designated to receive Special Drawing
Rights in return for its currency, and will continue to convert into gold,
on request, rand purchased from the Fund by other member countries.
The arrangements thus put an effective floor of $35 (less the Fund's
charge of $\frac{1}{4}$%) to the price South Africa receives for its gold, but not
to the market price.[1]

Defence of the dollar

Confidence in the dollar, weakened by the continuing deficit in
the US balance of payments, was no more immune than the
pound from the speculative pressure generated by the German
and Dutch revaluations of March 1961. To combat this pressure
the US authorities departed for the first time from their previous
practice of dealing in only one international currency—gold.

In these circumstances, the United States Treasury, operating through
the New York Reserve Bank as its fiscal agent, began dealing in
foreign exchange, in close consultation with foreign monetary authorities. These consultations were aided by Federal Reserve participation,

[1] Bank of England, *Quarterly Bulletin*, March 1970, pp. 4 and 5.

on a regular basis, in the monthly meetings of central bankers at Basle. Although operations were conducted in several currencies during the course of the year, the Treasury transactions were mainly in Deutsche marks and Swiss francs and were concentrated in the comparatively 'thin' forward markets, where intervention might prove most effective. In the case of the mark operations, for example, more than one billion marks of such forward sales were outstanding at the end of June. The speculative tide had, however, already begun to recede before the Berlin crisis and, by mid-December, the entire volume of forward contracts had been liquidated at maturity. With the market again operating smoothly, only token intervention was required to counter a temporary widening in the forward dollar discount in the final weeks of the year.[1]

This intervention by the US authorities in the exchange market was not an isolated episode, but the beginning of a deeper involvement. In February 1962 the Federal Reserve System decided to follow the US Treasury's example in undertaking operations in other national currencies. In that month,

the chairman of the Federal Reserve Board stated that the System was entering into cooperative arrangements with foreign central banks to help to steady the rate for the United States dollar, and on 1 March an agreement was announced by which the Federal Reserve Bank of New York provided $50 million for the dollar account of the Bank of France, in exchange for a corresponding transfer of NF 245 million for the account of the Federal Reserve Bank with the Bank of France. It was explained that the funds were provided to facilitate official intervention in markets for foreign currency to support the dollar-franc rate. . . .

Since then, further reciprocal arrangements on similar lines between the Federal Reserve Bank of New York and central banks of other countries have been made—with the United Kingdom, the Netherlands and Belgium—the amounts involved for each currency being $50 million on the part of the United States and its equivalent in the currencies of other countries.[2]

Under these reciprocal arrangements, or 'swap lines' as they were (called, the Federal Reserve Bank of New York would offer say) the Bank of England a stand-by facility which either country could activate on demand, this being effected by the New York bank crediting the Bank of England with $50 million and the Bank of England crediting the New York bank with its sterling

---

[1] Federal Reserve Bank of New York, *Annual Report*, 1961, p. 32.
[2] *Midland Bank Review*, August 1962, p. 7.

equivalent, i.e. £18 million. Both parties would then by agreement reverse the transaction on a specified date, say three months later, at the same rate of exchange, thus affording forward cover against the possibility of one currency having in the meantime depreciated in terms of the other.

An article in the *Federal Reserve Bulletin* for March 1963, after noting that swap lines had by then been negotiated with ten central banks and the BIS to the tune of $1,100 million, went on to explain:

Actual utilisation of such swap lines takes the form of drawings, which in general are made only in response to specific short-term needs. When the Federal Reserve initiates a drawing under a swap, it acquires a convertible currency that can provide temporary resources for exchange market operations. In what has been a more typical use, it can purchase from a central bank dollars in excess of those that the bank would ordinarily hold, in effect absorbing or mopping up these dollars for the period of the swap. . . .

The first line of defence against speculation provided by this strengthened swap network has been reinforced by negotiation of a series of Treasury issues of special certificates and bonds denominated in the currencies of the European central banks and treasuries to which they have been issued. Lira bonds taken up by the Bank of Italy now amount to $200 million in US dollar equivalents. Mark bonds placed with the German Federal Bank amount to another $200 million, while Swiss franc bonds and certificates acquired by the Swiss National Bank and the Swiss Confederation amount to $129 million. The precise purpose of each issue has varied somewhat from country to country, but one common characteristic is that these issues provide the foreign countries concerned with an advantageous investment medium for past or present balance of payments surpluses.

Since the date of the above description, the swap network has been greatly increased, the total amount of facilities being on 10 March 1970 no less than $10,980 millions (made up as shown in Table 17). The amount of actual drawings outstanding at that date was $m 215 in the case of the United States and (at end-1969) $m 650 in the case of her partners. At the same time the issuance of United States bonds denominated in foreign currencies ('Roosa bonds' as they are now commonly called) has continued, the amount outstanding in March 1970 being $1,400 millions.[1]

In February 1964 the United States made its first-ever drawing

[1] The information in this paragraph and in Table 18 is from The Federal Reserve Bank of New York's *Monthly Review*, March 1970, pp. 225–300.

TABLE 17

THE DOLLAR SWAP NETWORK AS AT 10 MARCH 1970

	$ *millions*
Austria	200
Belgium	500
Canada	1,000
Denmark	200
France	1,000
Germany	1,000
Italy	1,000
Japan	1,000
Mexico	130
Netherlands	300
Norway	200
Sweden	250
Switzerland	600
United Kingdom	2,000
BIS	1,600
Total	**10,980**

from the IMF by purchasing the equivalent of $125 millions of European currencies under a stand-by credit arranged in July 1963.

During the first decade of the Fund's operations, purchases from the Fund had been made overwhelmingly in US dollars, so that the United States was the only member that had extended a large amount of credit to other members through the Fund. Following the adoption in December 1958 of external convertibility by many European countries, and the accompanying increase in strength of these members' currencies relative to the US dollar, a broader use of currencies has been made in Fund operations. In the past few years the Fund has encouraged members using the Fund's resources to purchase currencies other than the US dollar. At the same time, repurchases by members have been made primarily with US dollars, thereby gradually reducing the creditor position of the United States in the Fund.

In July 1963 the Fund entered into a standby arrangement which permitted the United States to purchase currencies from the Fund to a total equivalent to $500 million. Early in . . . 1964, the Fund's holdings of US dollars . . . reached 75 per cent of the US quota. Under Article V, Section 7(c) (iii), this precluded the Fund from accepting further US dollars in repurchase from members. On 13 February 1964, the United States purchased the equivalent of $125 million, mainly in Deutsche marks and French francs, under its standby arrangement. These currencies, which can be accepted by the Fund in repurchase, were intended for sale for US dollars at par by the United States to those members of the Fund that keep their international reserves mainly in US dollars and that have repurchase commitments to the Fund.[1]

Further drawings of this type were made by the United States on the Fund so that other dollar-holding members might be in a position to repay their earlier drawings. However, as already explained in Chapter 9, the outstanding amount was wholly repaid at the end of 1968.

In 1966 the United States and Italy conducted a novel three-cornered transaction with the IMF, which may conceivably serve as a precedent for future IMF transactions. The details of the transaction were as follows:

> The Federal Reserve made drawings of $225 million in Italian lire on the swap line of the Bank of Italy in July and early August, and this swap drawing was liquidated in August. The lire needed to repay the Bank of Italy were acquired by a United States Treasury drawing of $250 million equivalent of lire from the IMF. In order to insure that the Fund's supply of lire would be adequate to finance such a United States drawing, the IMF, whose regular lira holdings were at a low level, arranged to borrow from Italy the lire needed for the United States drawing.[2]

Rescue of the lira[3]

The Italian balance of payments deteriorated badly in the course of 1963 and by early 1964 the lira was under considerable speculative pressure. This pressure was answered in mid-March by the mobilising of international credit facilities totalling $1,225 millions. Some $550 millions of this assistance was made available through Basle-type swap arrangements with the Bank of Italy by European central banks and the American Treasury; the US Export-Import Bank arranged a standby credit for $200 millions and the US Commodity Credit Corporation a three-year loan of $250 millions; a further $225 millions was automatically available at the International Monetary Fund. This massive assistance was in addition to the extensive support already given

---

[1] IMF *Annual Report, 1964*, pp. 10–12.
[2] Federal Reserve Bank of New York's *Monthly Review*, September 1966, pp. 191–2.
[3] This section is taken mainly from *The Banker*, April 1964, p. 205.

in the market by the US Treasury and, through its $150 millions swap agreement, by the Federal Reserve Bank of New York.

News of these stabilisation credits brought a sharp subsiding of the speculative fever, which in the preceding days had pushed the discount on the one-month forward lira to the equivalent of almost 10 per cent per annum. Moreover, in the course of 1964 Italy's external balance improved steadily, so that by October the danger had completely passed.

The sterling problem 1964–8

The position of sterling deteriorated steadily as from the middle of 1964, the root cause being the continuing UK external deficit, which for the year as a whole reached the alarming total of about £750 millions. In the third quarter of the year, the weakness of the pound was aggravated by the general election, the change of government and the November budget. In consequence, the Exchange Equalisation Account had to draw heavily on its reserves to support the spot value of sterling and in addition 'between the end of November [1964] and the middle of January [1965] the authorities . . . assumed very heavy forward commitments in foreign exchange'.[1]

In these circumstances, the first line of defence mobilised by the British authorities was a third Basle-type operation. A $500 million swap arrangement with the Federal Reserve Bank of New York was already in existence, and a small drawing of $15 million was made at the end of August. Further use was made of this swap arrangement in September, when facilities totalling a further $500 million were also arranged with the central banks of Belgium, Canada, France, Italy, the Netherlands, Switzerland and Western Germany. The swift response of these banks provided invaluable help for sterling during a difficult period. At the end of September the total aid which had been taken under these various arrangements was $200 million, of which $35 million resulted from swaps with the Federal Reserve Bank. Further use of these facilities was made in October and November.[2]

The second line of defence, mobilised at the beginning of December 1964, was a drawing of $1,000 million under the UK standby facility with the IMF. This drawing, which was used *inter alia* to repay the credits obtained under the Basle-type operation described above, was made in the following eleven currencies:

[1] Bank of England's *Quarterly Bulletin*, June 1965, p. 107.
[2] See the Bank of England's *Quarterly Bulletin*, December 1964, p. 258.

Currency	Equivalent in US $ millions
Austrian schillings	28
Belgian francs	57
Canadian dollars	69
Deutsche marks	273
French francs	163
Italian lire	23
Japanese yen	54
Netherlands guilders	66
Spanish pesetas	40
Swedish kronor	27
US dollars	200
Total	1,000

This distribution was arranged chiefly in the light of the prevailing payments positions of the countries concerned. Of the total, the equivalent of $345 million was provided from the Fund's existing holdings of currencies, the equivalent of $405 million was obtained under the Fund's General Arrangements to Borrow, and the equivalent of $250 million was obtained by the Fund from the sale of gold.[1]

The third line of defence, arranged a few days prior to the IMF drawing, was an agreement between the United Kingdom and eleven countries (Austria, Belgium, Canada, France, Germany, Italy, Japan, the Netherlands, Sweden, Switzerland, and the United States), together with the Bank for International Settlements, to provide the equivalent of $3 billion to support the United Kingdom's determination to defend the pound sterling. The total included an increase of $250 million (from $500 million to $750 million) in the swap arrangement between the Federal Reserve System and the Bank of England, together with a credit of $250 million from the Export-Import Bank of Washington.[2]

Thanks to these resources, the British authorities were able to give massive support to the pound, in both the spot and the forward markets, and by the middle of January 1965 it seemed that the speculative pressure was abating.

Alas, the respite proved to be only temporary. In the first quarter of 1965 the UK had to draw $415 million against the Basle facilities arranged in the previous November, making a cumulative drawing of $940 million, and a further $157 million

[1] Bank of England, op. cit., pp. 258–9.
[2] IMF *International Financial News Survey*, 4 December 1964.

was taken in April. 'In May, this borrowing was put on a longer-term basis, as earlier assistance had been, by borrowing from the International Monetary Fund. The United Kingdom had announced in February that it intended to make a further application to the Fund, and on 25 May the equivalent of $1,400 million (£500 million) was drawn for repayment by May 1970.' To finance the drawing, the Fund used $475 million of its existing currency holdings, sold $400 million in gold, and mobilised $525 million through the GAB. 'At the same time Switzerland provided a parallel credit equivalent to $40 million. From these borrowings the whole of the outstanding short-term debt of $1,097 million was repaid, and the balance of $343 million was added to the reserves. . . . Further resort to short-term borrowing was to become necessary in subsequent months to counter renewed pressures on sterling; all of this was provided from the United States, although in July, in addition, Western Germany deposited £41 million as provision for future purchases to offset part of the cost of United Kingdom military expenditure in Germany. In June $360 million was taken from the Federal Reserve Bank of New York under the reciprocal swap arrangement of $750 million. Pressure intensified during July and August, and the balance of the swap facility was drawn. In addition, a further $140 million was made available by the Federal Reserve Bank.'[1]

Early in September 1965, the Bank of England entered into new borrowing arrangements with the central banks of Austria, Belgium, Canada, Germany, Holland, Italy, Japan, Sweden and Switzerland, and with the Bank for International Settlements. No details as to amount or period of the new facilities were disclosed. The Federal Reserve Bank also agreed to provide a $200 million credit and the United States Treasury a further substantial amount, over and above the standing reciprocal swap facility with the Federal Reserve Bank of $750 million.

Sterling enjoyed a six-month period of recovery, following the announcement of new international support for the pound in September 1965. As dollars flowed back to the Bank of England between September and February 1966, the Bank repaid in its entirety $890 million in short-term credit received from the United States and, in addition, succeeded in liquidating a substantial part of its forward exchange commitments. Beginning in late February, however, sterling began to weaken once again, and by July the pressures had reached crisis proportions. Indeed, even when the British Government reacted to the massive

[1] Quotations are from the *Midland Bank Review*, May 1966, p. 9.

attack on the pound by announcing on 20 July a profound and far-reaching austerity programme, the exchange markets were so demoralised after two years of almost continuous tension that there was no immediate recovery in sterling.[1]

During this unhappy period in 1966, which included the general election on 30 March and the seamen's strike in May and June, the British authorities had to give massive support to sterling in both the spot and the forward markets, and to this end help had once again to be sought from our Basle associates, under the arrangements concluded in the preceding September. These arrangements were due to expire in June 1966, but on the 13th of that month it was announced that the 'Basle' group 'were collaborating in new arrangements specifically designed to counter the stresses to which sterling is subject as a reserve and international trading currency.'[2] This was the 'First Basle Group Arrangement', already described in Chapter 15. Separate from this Arrangement there remained in existence the standing reciprocal swap with the Federal Reserve Bank of New York. This in September 1966 was increased from $750 millions to $1,350 millions.

Thanks to all these measures of support, and to the drastic austerity programme introduced by the British government on 20 July 1966, the speculation against sterling abated,

but no vigorous recovery developed as the market waited to see whether the British Government would succeed in carrying through so drastic a program. Indeed, sterling remained vulnerable to downward pressures throughout the month of August. . . . Nevertheless, there was evidence that the British Government's new program had begun to take hold at the same time that the measures introduced in the April 1966 budget were also taking effect.[3]

The authorities were able to acquire foreign exchange for the reserves, and in October they began to repay the drawings that they had made on central bank facilities during the summer and to reduce again their outstanding market commitments in forward exchange.[4]

The improvement in the UK payments position continued in the early part of 1967 but began to deteriorate as from May, so much

[1] Federal Reserve Bank of New York's *Monthly Review*, September 1966, p. 192.
[2] Bank of England's *Quarterly Bulletin*, September 1966, p. 209, which also gives details of official transactions in the second quarter of 1966.
[3] Taken almost verbatim from the Federal Reserve Bank of New York, op. cit.
[4] Bank of England's *Quarterly Bulletin*, December 1966, p. 311. Further details are given on p. 320 of this *Bulletin*.

so indeed that by November we were forced into our second post-war devaluation of sterling, from $2.8 to $2.4:

By the beginning of 1967 the measures taken in the previous July had markedly improved the external position. The improvement, however, depended heavily on the continuance of favourable conditions in the United Kingdom's export markets; and in the spring and summer, as the growth of world trade temporarily stopped, the underlying weakness of the balance of payments was again exposed. Exports fell, while imports remained high.

Confidence in sterling began to weaken in May. Shortly afterwards, the Middle East crisis led first to an outflow of short-term funds and then, after the Suez Canal was closed, to higher freight costs, dearer oil imports and delayed exports. From September onwards, strikes in the London and Liverpool docks placed a fresh strain on the by then precarious balance of payments position. During the summer and early autumn, moreover, pressures on sterling were increased by rising short-term interest rates in the United States and in the euro-dollar market; to reduce the incentive to withdraw funds from London, Bank rate was raised from $5\frac{1}{2}\%$ to 6% on 19 October and to $6\frac{1}{2}\%$ on 9 November.

Meanwhile, because exports had fallen away at a time when growth in most other components of demand had ceased, the margin of unused domestic resources continued to increase, and from June onwards the Government took a number of mildly reflationary measures. The rapid deterioration in the external position (with little hope of early relief) combined with the prospect of renewed growth in domestic demand, proved too much for confidence, and losses of foreign exchange became very heavy. . . .

During the first two weeks of November sterling came under very heavy pressure and there was much talk of devaluation. Early in the third week it became widely believed that a substantial support operation for sterling was being negotiated; when this was not confirmed the market became convinced that devaluation was imminent, and the pound was sold, both spot and forward, on a massive scale. . . .

On 18 November the Government announced that the par value of the pound in terms of the US dollar had been reduced by one seventh, from $2.80 to $2.40. At the same time Bank rate was raised to 8% and a number of measures were announced to divert resources from the domestic economy to improving the balance of payments.[1]

These difficulties at the end of 1967 called for a further rescue operation:

It was announced in November that a loan (equivalent to some $250 million) had been extended to the United Kingdom through the BIS

[1] Quotations from Bank of England *Report* for 1967–8, pp. 1 and 2.

to finance the final repayment to the IMF of the 1964 drawing. Follow-ing devaluation, a one-year standby facility of $1,400 million was provided by the IMF, and additional credit facilities of about $1,500 million were placed at the disposal of the Bank of England by other central banks. At the end of November and in mid-December, the Federal Reserve enlarged generally its swap arrangements with other central banks—the facility with the Bank of England being increased from $1,350 million to $1,500 million.[1]

These facilities provided resources for the Exchange Equalisation Account to support spot sterling in the exchange markets: in addition the Account supported forward sterling on a massive scale prior to 18 November by contracting to sell dollars forward against sterling at the pre-devaluation exchange rate.[2] After devaluation the Account attempted to unwind its short forward position as quickly as possible: by October 1968 it had been reduced to about one fifth of the peak reached before devaluation.[3]

The year 1968 witnessed a series of international monetary crises, which implied no respite for sterling, and hence further rescue operations. At the time of the Washington conference of 17 March, at which the gold pool arrangements were suspended (above, page 255) the US Federal Reserve System increased the UK swap facility by $500 million to $2,000 million, and the central banks of other countries participating in the conference also extended Basle-type facilities to the tune of $1.1 billions.[4] Then in September there was concluded the Second Basle Group Arrangement, as described in Chapter 15. The use made of these facilities, and of the IMF, during the year 1968 is summarised by the Bank of England as follows:

The largest single element of official financing during the year was a drawing of £583 million from the IMF in June under the standby facility of November 1967; the drawing, in various currencies, was used to reduce the United Kingdom's outstanding short-term indebtedness to central banks; on the other hand, repurchases and other transactions reduced the United Kingdom's liabilities to the Fund by £58 million.

. . . The United Kingdom drew a substantial amount during the year under central bank credit facilities, the greater part of it in the first quarter—though drawings were also quite heavy in the fourth. In June

[1] Bank of England, op. cit., p. 5.
[2] This commitment, plus other banking commitments guaranteed in terms of dollar-value, involved the UK authorities in revaluation losses of over £350 millions.
[3] Bank of England *Report* for 1968–9, p. 7.
[4] Report of the Deutsche Bundesbank for 1968, p. 41.

the whole of what was then outstanding ($1,200 million, equivalent to £500 million) under the $2,000 million swap facility with the Federal Reserve Bank of New York was repaid out of the proceeds of the IMF drawing; but in the latter part of the year it became necessary to draw again on the FRB facility, and by the end of December $1,150 million (£480 million) was outstanding. Meanwhile, the first drawing was made on the new $2,000 million medium-term facility agreed at Basle in September. However, there were net repayments by the United Kingdom in the second half of the year of other special short-term facilities.[1]

Taking the five years 1964–8 as a whole, the UK deficit which had to be financed in gold and foreign currencies amounted to no less than £3,600 millions, and was compounded of the following ingredients:

	£ millions
Current account deficit	1,300
Long-term capital outflow	800
Net withdrawal of sterling balances	1,200
Other	300
Total to be financed	3,600

This total was financed as follows,[2] taking both drawings on the IMF and 'other official borrowing' on a net basis (i.e., net of repayments made in the period 1964–8):

	£ millions
Change in account with IMF	1,100
Other official borrowing	2,000
Sale of Treasury dollar portfolio and change in reserves	500
Total financing	3,600

Other events in 1968

1968 was a year of great turbulence in foreign exchange markets, and concerted action was frequently needed to mitigate the effects of a whole series of crises.

(1) 'At the beginning of 1968 speculative money withdrawals from Canada—mainly because of exaggerated notions about the effects of

[1] Bank of England *Report*, 1968–9, pp. 11 and 12.
[2] Both sets of figures are taken from the *Financial Statement and Budget Report 1969–70*, p. 15.

the American balance-of-payments programme on the Canadian monetary situation—led to very large foreign exchange losses of the Canadian central bank. Within a few weeks it lost about one third of its monetary reserves. Thereupon the IMF, the American Export-Import Bank and some central banks jointly provided a credit facility for Canada.'[1] This monetary crisis was quickly overcome.

(2) In the early part of the year the US dollar came under pressure, which took the form of a massive switch into gold: these attacks came to an end with the Washington conference of 17 March, and the suspension of the gold pool arrangements.

(3) In May and June student riots and other political troubles brought severe pressure on the French franc. 'In July 1968 a group of central banks made available to the Bank of France a credit line of $1.3 billion to help France to overcome the crisis which developed in the wake of the disturbances in May and June 1968. Of this facility, $600 million was provided by the Federal Reserve System, a like amount by the central banks of the European Economic Community, and another $100 million by the BIS. . . . Since the Bank of France had arranged with the Federal Reserve System a swap facility of $100 million long before the outbreak of the crisis it now disposed of credit lines of altogether $1.4 billion. France used this credit line together with its own gold and foreign exchange reserves and its reserve position in the IMF to cover its huge foreign exchange losses which overwhelmingly resulted from speculative movements of various kinds.'[2]

(4) In November 1968 (as again in May 1969) there were massive speculative capital flows into Germany, based on the belief that the Deutsche mark was about to be revalued and the French franc devalued. At the height of the November crisis there was a meeting at Bonn of the Group of Ten at Ministerial level, during which the London exchange market had to be closed (November 20 to 22). At the meeting the Germans resisted pressure to revalue the mark and the French soon after decided not to devalue the franc, but various remedial measures were agreed upon, including a $2 billion credit facility made available to France by a group of central banks and the BIS. The Bundesbank provided the largest individual share amounting to $600 million. Beginning in December 1968, when substantial funds returned to France once the November crisis was surmounted and foreign exchange control had been tightened, the Bank of France repaid a large part of the loans.

1969-70

In the first three quarters of 1969, as in the latter part of 1968, the exchange markets were constantly under the threat of specu-

---

[1] Report of the Deutsche Bundesbank for 1968, p. 41.
[2] op. cit., p. 41.

lative flights of capital to Germany, based on the expectation of possible exchange rate adjustments. Speculative pressure on the French franc and the pound had however subsided somewhat by the end of 1968, following the crisis in November, and the relative calm persisted through the first quarter of 1969 and into April. In May however speculation was re-ignited by an open dispute between German cabinet ministers as to whether the mark should be revalued forthwith, and during the first nine days of May an estimated total of $4,000 millions of speculative funds were used to buy German currency.[1] The dispute was temporarily resolved by an announcement on 9 May that the German exchange rate would remain unchanged, but with a general election impending in October a considerable element of doubt remained as to the validity of the decision except in the very short term. This doubt became more acute as the day of the election approached, and likewise the scale of speculation: on Wednesday 24 September the German government decided to close the German foreign exchange market, and when it was re-opened, on the following Monday, the mark was allowed to float upwards, without official intervention to maintain the old parity. On 25 October, after the general election and a change of government, the mark was re-pegged at a higher parity of 3·66 per US dollar (as compared with the previous parity of 4·00 per US dollar).

The period beginning May 1969 was one of great strain on the French franc, and on 8 August (M. Pompidou having succeeded General de Gaulle after the presidential elections in June) the currency was devalued from 4·937 to 5·554 per US dollar. In the same month France requested a $985 million standby from the IMF. In addition, it was reported[2] at the end of August that 'four of France's Common Market partners—Belgium, Germany, Holland and Italy—have offered it a short-term credit line of $400m., and another similar arrangement for $200m. has been made available by the Bank for International Settlements. Finally, the Federal Reserve Bank of New York has agreed to renew the unused $1,000m. swap line opened up following the international monetary crisis last November as part of the $2,000m. short-term credits which France obtained at the Group of Ten meeting in Bonn.'

Sterling, like the franc, 'came under sharp pressure early in May, as speculation developed on a revaluation of the Deutsche

[1] *Financial Times*, 13 May 1969.
[2] *Financial Times*, 30 August 1969.

mark; but, after the West German Government had announced their determination not to revalue, markets calmed down and sterling strengthened'.[1] The May disturbances caused some fall in UK reserves during the month, despite some recourse to central bank assistance. 'The facilities used at that time included a recycling arrangement between the Bundesbank and the Bank of England designed to neutralise part of the movement of speculative funds from the United Kingdom into Western Germany.'[2] Thereafter, sufficient foreign exchange was taken into UK reserves in June and July

to make good the losses of early May and to continue repaying short and medium-term borrowing—a substantial amount of which had been repaid before May. On 18 July, the Chancellor of the Exchequer told the House of Commons that net repayments of external debt since the beginning of the calendar year had amounted to very nearly $1,000 million. In addition, there was some conversion from short to longer-term debt, because $500 million drawn in June on a new stand-by credit from the International Monetary Fund was used to repay debt of shorter term.

Early in August, the devaluation of the French franc caused inevitable uncertainties in the exchange markets, and there was some substantial selling of sterling for a few days. This selling did not persist, but markets remained nervous and subdued

and remained so up to the time of the appreciation of the mark in September. Thereafter, with a convincing improvement in the trend of our balance of payments, sterling at long last appeared to be moving out of a period of alarming weakness, in the course of which a succession of rescue operations had saddled the UK with repayment obligations to the IMF, to the BIS and to other central banks to the tune of $8 billion at the end of 1968, of which $4 billion were still outstanding at the end of March 1970 and (according to *The Times*) $3½ billion as at mid-1970.[4]

---

[1] Bank of England *Quarterly Bulletin*, September 1969, p. 275.
[2] op. cit., p. 280. The recycling arrangements referred to in this passage are described in an article by Mr Aschinger, in the Swiss Bank Corporation's *Bulletin*, No. 4, 1969.
[3] Bank of England, op. cit., p. 275.
[4] See the *Financial Times* of 22 May 1970, quoting Mr. Roy Jenkins; the Bank of England's *Quarterly Bulletin*, June 1970, p. 121; and *The Times*, 8 July 1970.

READING LIST

For an elementary exposition of that section of economic theory which deals with the factors affecting a country's balance of current payments, see Part Three of my *Wealth and Income* (Melbourne University Press, 1967) or R. F. Harrod's *International Economics* (Nisbet and CUP). More advanced students are strongly recommended to consult J. E. Meade's *The Balance of Payments* (Oxford, 1951).

The charters or agreements which established the IMF, the GATT, the IEPA and the EPU are all available from HMSO; details have already been given in footnotes. Other official literature about the work of these institutions include:

The IMF's own *Annual Reports,* and its *Annual Reports on Exchange Restrictions*

Finance and Development, published quarterly by the IMF and the International Bank for Reconstruction and Development

The BIS's *Annual Reports*

The *Annual Reports* of the EPU and EMA

The GATT's annual reports on *International Trade*

The Bank of England's annual *Report* and *Quarterly Bulletin.*

The best continuous non-official commentary on monetary developments published in the UK is provided by the *Midland Bank Review* and *The Banker.* Other literature includes:

Triffin, R., *Europe and the Money Muddle* (Yale University Press, 1957)

Triffin, R., *Gold and the Dollar Crisis* (Yale, 1961)

Diebold, W., *Trade and Payments in Western Europe* (Council on Foreign Relations and Harper and Brothers, New York, 1952)

Hansen, A. H., *The Dollar and the International Monetary System* (McGraw-Hill, 1965)

Gardner, R. N., *Sterling-Dollar Diplomacy* (Oxford, 1969)

Fleming, J. M., *The International Monetary Fund, Its Form and Functions* (IMF, 1964)

Price, H. B., *The Marshall Plan and its Meaning* (Cornell University Press, 1955)

Mikesell, R. F., *Foreign Exchange in the Post-War World* (The Twentieth Century Fund, New York, 1954)

Brown, W. A., *The United States and the Restoration of World Trade* (Brookings Institution, 1950)

J. Keith Horsefield and others, *The International Monetary Fund 1945–1965* (IMF, 1969)

The Princeton University's International Finance Section's *Essays in International Finance, Studies in International Finance*, and the annual *Survey of United States International Finance* (Princeton University Press)

Williams, J. H., *Post-War Monetary Plans* (Blackwell, 1949)

Harrod, R. F., *The Life of John Maynard Keynes* (Macmillan, 1951)

The Radcliffe Report, Cmnd. 827, August 1959.

There is an enormous flow of official literature, mainly periodical, commenting on the course of events in the field of international monetary affairs. Here is a short selection:

The IMF's *Staff Papers*, its weekly *Financial News Survey* and its monthly *International Financial Statistics*, as well as the Reports already mentioned.

The BIS's *Annual Reports*

The OEEC's two reports on *Internal Financial Stability*

The *Annual Reports* of the OEEC and OECD

The ECE's annual *Economic Survey for Europe* and its quarterly *Economic Bulletin*

The United Nations' *World Economic Reports*

The US Department of Commerce's *Survey of Current Business* (monthly)

The US *Federal Reserve Bulletin* (monthly)

The *Annual Reports* and monthly *Review* of the Federal Reserve Bank of New York

The *Reports* of the National Advisory Council to the President of the United States,

INDEX

ACCUMULATION facilities, 40–1, 50–1, 139, 150
and their 'swings', 41, 50
Adjustment process, 53 *et seq.*, 78, 128
Agreement on Multilateral Monetary Compensation, 140
Aid, 148, 162
see also Indirect Aid, Marshall Aid, Conditional Aid
American Accounts, 175 *et seq.*, 227, 229 n., 230 n.
Anglo-American Loan, 40, 229
Loan Agreement, 173 *et seq.*
Appreciation (of a currency), 73, 220, 232, 252
Arbitrage operations, 28, 33, 35, 184, 188
Argentina, 175, 179, 180, 181 n., 221, 232 n., 234
Australia, 33, 41, 54, 156, 177, 237–8, 240
Authorised dealers (in sterling), 36, 170 *et seq.*, 184

BALANCE of current payments, defined, 41
Bancor, 111, 126, 150, 248

Bank for International Settlements (BIS), 79, 80, 203 *et seq.*, 252, 258–9, 206, 262
calculation of deficits and surpluses, 143, 145, 146 n., 149 n., 155
Bank of England, 29 n., 30, 39, 139, 170, 171 n., 186, 257, 262
Bank Rate, 54, 65–8, 253
Basle arrangements, 40, 203, 252–3, 260 *et seq.*
Basle Group Arrangements (1966 and 1968), 203–6, 264
Beggar-my-neighbour remedies for unemployment, 23, 70 *et seq.*
Belgium, 139, 145, 181 n., 225 *et seq.*, 237
'Bilateral' countries, 178, 180–1, 183, 230
Bilateral payments agreements, *see* Payments agreements
and their 'swings', 139, 152, 173, 181 n.
Bretton Woods, 84

CANADA, 89, 104, 162, 171 n., 172, 180, 184, 220, 226–31, 232 n., 239, 240 n., 267

TEW. International monetary co-operation. Copy F ✳